HEINRICH BÖLL

STORIES, POLITICAL WRITINGS, AND AUTOBIOGRAPHICAL WORKS

The German Library: Volume 85

Volkmar Sander, General Editor

HEINRICH BÖLL

STORIES, POLITICAL WRITINGS, AND AUTOBIOGRAPHICAL WORKS

Edited by Martin Black
Foreword by Volkmar Sander

continuum

NEW YORK · LONDON

2006

The Continuum International Publishing Group Inc
80 Maiden Lane, New York, NY 10038

The Continuum International Publishing Group Ltd
The Tower Building, 11 York Road, London SE1 7NX

The German Library is published in cooperation with Deutsches Haus,
New York University.

This volume has been supported by Inter Nationes,
and the Erich Maria Remarque
Chair of New York University

Printed in the United States of America

Library of Congress Cataloging-in-Publication Data

Böll, Heinrich, 1917–
  [Selections. English. 2006]
  Stories, political writings, and autobiographical works / Heinrich Böll ; edited
by Martin Black.
     p. cm.—(German library ; v. 85)
  ISBN-13: 978-0-8264-1798-5 (hardcover : alk. paper)
  ISBN-10: 0-8264-1798-1 (hardcover : alk. paper)
  ISBN-13: 978-0-8264-1799-2 (pbk. : alk. paper)
  ISBN-10: 0-8264-1799-X (pbk. : alk. paper)
  1. Böll, Heinrich, 1917—Translations into English.   I. Black, Martin D.
(Martin David), 1958– II. Title.   II. Series.
PT2603.O394A2   2006
833'.914—dc22
                                                                      2006016011

Acknowledgments will be found on page 307,
which constitutes an extension of the copyright page.

Contents

Foreword

by Volkmar Sander

A volume of this nature, devoted as it is to the entire life-work of one man, is necessarily marked by brevity. I, too, will be brief. While anything connected with Böll inevitably takes on political overtones, I would like to go on record here not only for this reason, not only because I knew him and taught him in class, but because he helped shape the political awareness of my generation, a generation which had more difficulty in finding and articulating itself than most. That made him irritating—and so the German variety of the "love-it-or-leave-it" pseudo patriot had early on urged him to emigrate. He didn't, of course, and so remained controversial all his life. He was a political writer, a rare species in Germany or any other country, but one which Germany always needed, seldom had, and never appreciated. Like Heinrich Heine and Heinrich Mann before him, this Heinrich did not lack enemies, small wonder for a man who said that he considered writing "a democratic activity."

Born in 1917, "as old as the Russian Revolution" as he was fond of saying, he quickly became a symbol of contrast to Konrad Adenauer, that other cantankerous Catholic from Cologne, and his post-war policies. Because in their new-found prosperity his countrymen were so eager to start anew, and because forgetting diminishes old suffering, one's own as well as that one has meted out, he constantly pleaded for remembrance. He simply lacked indifference—he had a built-in Geiger counter which reacted violently to injustice—and for reasons of national hygiene forced him to speak out. Out of this sense of justice grew his authority, and so, in the end, with his disarming humanity, his unpretentious honesty, and his international reputation, this great humorist became what he least wanted—a moral institution.

Wilhelm Raabe (1831–1910), a sort of German Trollope, once said: *"Ruhm ist, mitgedacht zu werden, wenn an ein Volk gedacht wird"*; (fame means that one's name comes to mind, when thinking of a whole nation"). Quaint and old-fashioned as it is, it is still true. Böll's passing in 1985 was one more indication that the post-war era in German history was beginning to draw to a close. Twenty years and more on, the actual end of the chapter is still not in sight. While large events have reshaped the landscape: the end of the Cold War and emergence of the Berlin Republic, on-going democratization across Eastern Europe, the rise in the Middle East of a new challenge to Western-style globalization, never-the-less Böll's Bonn Republic proves to have far more staying power than we possibly could have imagined on that fateful day in October 1989 when the Wall came down. Because of this, because of the endurance of Bonn, because of the many accomplishments that were his in the national project of mourning and remembrance, the maintenance of a public sphere marked by critical debate, conducted by an "uncomfortable" citizenry, we are grateful that his name and what he stood for can not be excluded from his time.

In Heinrich Böll the American reader will find the voice of humanity and reason; sober, yet insisting; anything but strident, yet precise and ultimately penetrating and unforgettable. Critical as he was of state authority, it was of course fitting that despite his Nobel laurels, his many accolades, his service to the nation, he did not have a state funeral. The only music played at his grave was by a band of gypsies, that other oft-forgotten minority which Hitler almost succeeded in eliminating altogether and for whom Böll had always fought as for so many others. He wanted it that way. It was a fitting symbol.

Introduction

H einrich Böll, 1917–85: writer, soldier, citizen, critic; no other
writer of the postwar German landscape better defines and expresses the tumultuous forty-year history of the West German Bonn
Republic. Winner of the Georg Büchner Prize, the Nobel Prize for
Literature, elected president of Germany's PEN-Center and later of
PEN International, he was an international cause celèbre, yet often
found himself denounced and vilified in his own country. Like that
country, he improved with age; rarely the case with writers and almost never with countries. The Federal Republic's transition from
amnesia to memory has been a slow and painful one. Whether understood as a function of psychology or politics; of a national psychosis marked by an inability to mourn, or domestic pressures to
paper over the war and the Holocaust, the long transition is still on-
going. Many Germans of remarkable courage have helped their nation down this path, and the top of the list would certainly include
Willy Brandt, Richard von Weizsäcker, and Günter Grass. Heinrich
Böll, the everyman who turned that path to his own literary calling,
belongs there too. Though others have occupied higher promonto-
ries, it was just as much the gathering storm of his moral outrage,
and other German democrats like him, that have helped bring Germany to the forefront of democratic nations today.

In November of 2002, only months before he chose for Germany
a historic path of non-alignment with its American transatlantic
partner over the Iraq War, German Chancellor Gerhard Schroeder
served as the keynote speaker at the presentation of the first volume
of Heinrich Böll's Complete Works. He used the occasion to say
this about the author:

> Whether or not his [antiwar] views of past years have come to be
> historically disproved, what most impresses me about him is his fix,

that quiet yet irrepressible self-possession, the kind that comes from great restraint and yet expresses what Heinrich Böll always possessed: the supreme authority of his own true self.

Although the author at the time of these words had died some seventeen years earlier, a Heinrich Böll invocation was hardly a harmless and politically neutral public act.

In his almost forty years of marking and demarking in his writings the formation and life of Germany's Bonn Republic, from 1947 until his death in 1985, Heinrich Böll was probably best known, both to his friends and his enemies, as a gadfly: the tireless "conscience of the nation," the writing, speaking reminder of Germany's war past, and a constant critic of the moral hypocrisy of both the denazification process, and the *Wirtschaftswunder*, Germany's remarkable economic recovery following the war in the 1950s. An infantryman in the German army from 1939 to 1945, wounded four times on the Eastern and Western fronts, Böll took his lessons from his own history and, following the war, became an increasingly outspoken champion of democratic rights, and a steadfast critic of state authority. Whether famous or infamous, his public persona in the Federal Republic is arguably best remembered for an article he wrote for the news weekly *Der Spiegel* in 1972 defending the constitutional rights to due process of the recently apprehended Baader-Meinhof terrorist group. It was here that he sounded his clarion call, "an emergency of public consciousness," here too that he leveled both a barb directly at the shoddy reporting of the *Bild* newspaper and a breathtakingly personal attack on one of the most powerful men in Germany—owner and publisher of the same newspaper, Axel Springer himself. It was a great risk: calls came from the highest levels for his resignation as president of Germany's PEN-Club, for the revocation of his Nobel Prize; both his and his family's own constitutional rights were threatened, his home and that of his son searched by police; charges of treason were leveled at him both by prominent conservative politicians as well as virtually every media outlet of the Springer conglomerate. To Böll, however, it was no risk—it was the only way he could respond. As Gerhard Schroeder might say, it was simply the expression of "the supreme authority of his own true self." And in the early 21st century with Western democracies and their allies again under the threat of terrorism well into the foreseeable future, similar intimidation and smear tactics are very much in evidence, and exemplars similar to Böll few and far between.

Heinrich Theodor Böll was born in Cologne on December 21, 1917, the youngest of six children, to Viktor and Maria Böll. His father was a carpenter and wood sculptor and, by moving from Essen to Cologne while himself still a young man, was seeking to improve his condition. In 1923, Heinrich moved with his family from an apartment in Cologne to their own house in the Cologne-Raderberg district. But with the onset of the depression in 1930, his father lost his business and the family was forced to return to apartment living. In his autobiographical prose, Böll recounts the difficulty of this loss—the missed freedoms and games permitted by the wider spaces of the suburbs, and the cares this move and their new economic plight visited upon the family. The change ushers in a new focus that would stay with him for the rest of his life; identification with the "little guy" kept down by larger-than-life forces, and an enjoyment of simple pleasures: tobacco, coffee, newspapers.

In 1928, Böll began attending the Kaiser Wilhelm Gymnasium and remained there until completing his exams in 1937. Though he loved to read, academic success held little interest for him, and he was forced to repeat a year. The rise of Hitler in the early 1930s, and the rapid spread of Nazism throughout the ensuing years, though openly discussed and opposed by his family and their Catholic sensibilities, did not directly touch him—he managed to stay out of the Hitler Youth, which uniquely brought him little trouble, and his family held illegal Catholic Youth Association meetings, and later on even harbored Jews—but his resistance, as such, was a quiet one, an inner emigration. As late as 1953, he refers to the spread of the Nazi Terror in these years as a *lautloser* (silent) terror. Although this lends it a frightening quality, the tightening of a hand on a throat, it is the description of acquiescence, any thought of opposition brought to bay under threat of slaughter.

Following graduation Böll worked for a time, first as an apprentice to an antiquarian book dealer, but broke this off in early 1938. Uncertain of his direction, Böll attempted first to work as an assistant in his father's business, next to pursue a career as a librarian. In the fall of that year he traveled to Hesse to perform the compulsory labor required as a prerequisite to university study. Back in Cologne in spring of 1939, he enrolled at the university to study classical philology and German literature, but his studies were interrupted shortly after by a mandatory military training course. In September of 1939 after a tense summer in limbo, he was activated for military service in the infantry and for the next six years served in France, Poland, the Crimea and Rumania during which time he was wounded in the hand, leg, head, and back. The last of these, received in Rumania, was serious and forced him to convalesce in Hungary for almost a year. In August 1944 he was reactivated, deserted in late February of 1945, but rejoined the army in time to be taken prisoner of war by the Americans in early April and held in France and Belgium until his release in September of 1945. Having married Annemarie Cech in March 1943 while home in Cologne on leave, he then sought and found her in the Bergischen Land region east of Cologne only to experience the death of their first child, Christoph, born in the summer of that year. The two returned to Cologne the following month.

"Als wir Köln wiedersahen, weinten wir" ("We cried when we saw Cologne"), Böll recounts years later, referring to their return to a city over 70 percent completely destroyed. Numbers only tell a partial tale, and whether the report states that only 300 undamaged buildings remained of the former metropolis, or that Böll was one of 400,000 surviving Cologne residents from a prewar population almost twice that, the photographs from those months provide the affect statistics cannot: the ruined city, the piled corpses, the shattered churches, the massive bridges sagging into the Rhine, and the Cologne Cathedral leaning over the decimation and decay. With survival more on their minds than writing, Böll and his wife moved into a half-destroyed building, and found work as soon as they could, she as a middle-school teacher, he helping his brother Alois in the family carpentry shop. Böll also reenrolled at the university, not to study but to secure a food-rations card. Within that first year, he began to write in a disciplined fashion.

Böll's first works remained unpublished for most of his life, appearing long after his fame was established, but they may be a purer reflection of his literary gestation than the works the publisher actually accepted from this early time. An excellent point of departure is an early novel, *Der Engel schwieg (The Silent Angel)*, written in 1950 but unpublished until 1992 (St. Martin's Press, 1994). It describes the return to a ruined city of a German soldier bearing a legacy—a fallen comrade's coat concealing a will, a document that will soon drag the soldier into an intrigue. Bowing to a still-traumatized reading public of the early 1950s, Böll's publisher wanted little to do with narratives treating the war, and the early disheartening days of the return. The novel is a still-fresh witness to the immediate aftermath of war, the chaos and anarchy of the first days, and Böll's own experiences, or near-experiences, are peppered throughout. Years later, this landscape is still wrenching for its depictions of the tenuous balance between life and death, the bitterness and cynicism of its characters, and the momentary glimmers of a former way of being, a measure of human dignity lost. A second novel from this period, *Das Vermächtnis (A Soldier's Legacy)* was also published much later, in 1982, and manages to capture the treachery and deceit found in the contracting German army, by 1943 withdrawing into defeat. It is a sobering commentary on petty war profiteering, and the cheapness of human life in those times. Yet another window into the early Böll, a collection of previously unpublished short stories, is *Der blasse Hund (The Mad Dog)*, which appeared in Germany in 1995 and in this country two years later (St. Martin's Press, 1997). The collection is remarkable for containing Böll's earliest story, *"Die Brennenden"* ("Youth on Fire"), a product of 1937 prior to his graduation from high school. Though marked by sentimentalism and rather sudden character shifts, the story demonstrates vivid story-telling ability, and a preoccupation with integrating religious, intellectual, and sexual tensions. The story even contains a brief, thinly disguised criticism of Adolf Hitler. Other stories in the collection are more traditional to early Böll—soldier-survival stories like *"Gefangen in Paris"* ("Trapped in Paris"), those narrating the pointlessness of war as in *"Die Geschichte der Brücke von Berkowo"* ("The Tale of Berkovo Bridge"), or the impossibility of social reintegration (the title story). Written with a compressed tension wrought by a vain search for a refuge of meaning in a world turned upside down, at our current distance from the horror of those times it is hard to believe that these stories would not sell. One last early text, presumably his first novel, remained unpublished until 2003. *Kreuz ohne Liebe*, as yet untranslated, is a story of two brothers growing into manhood as first Nazism and then six years of war break over them. The symbol of the cross suggests the contrast of their own Christian faith with the "unloving," pagan Iron Cross of Nazism. Surviving, sustained by their faith and hope, the brothers' thoughts and words are a reckoning, a self-study, a testimony to the insanity of the war, the ideology of the war. Submitted to a competition in 1947, the novel was returned by the panel of judges for not taking sufficient issue with Nazism.

One series of previously unpublished stories which has received far less attention than it deserves is a collection entitled *Die Verwundung und andere frühe Erzählungen* which appeared in 1983 by the Lamuv Verlag. The collection was issued as *The Casualty* in 1987 by Farrar, Straus & Giroux. In 1993, the German collection reappeared under the Deutsche Taschenbuch Verlag imprint, before being incorporated into a much larger volume in 1994, edited by Viktor Böll (*Erzählungen*, Fischer). It too contains some of Böll's most trenchant stories from those early years, most of them war stories from the Eastern front, explicitly nonheroic, full of the treachery and oppression of a slowly retreating army smelling defeat. The title story, very nearly biographical, is about a German foot soldier on the Rumanian front who receives a "marvelous wound, made to order," one likely to take several months to heal by which time he believes the war will be over. The sheer joy of the soldier at this realization, and the beautiful pastoral scenes he observes as he slowly makes his way back away from the fighting, are in striking contrast to the screams and chaos of fellow soldiers, still caught between the guns of the Russians and those of the German military police, forcing the soldiers back into battle. Another story, *"Todesursache: Hakennase"* ("Cause of Death: Hooked Nose"), directly addresses the Holocaust not of the concentration and extermination camps, but of the Eastern mobile forces—the police "killing units" that traveled from town to town, rounding up Jews of all ages, positioning them before trenches, and summarily machine-gunning them. Böll glosses over very little here, takes his narrative time, walks past the sentries, engages the drunken executioners, gives voice to their baseness, and details how babies too young to stand are summarily kicked into the trench before the blasting process buries them alive. It is a grisly bit of narration. It casts little doubt that common infantry soldier though he was, Böll and his compatriots, while stationed in the East, directly experienced this more secretive and brutal practice for annihilating Eastern European Jewry. The date of authorship is thought to be 1947. While it is hardly flattering that the story remained in his desk for over thirty-five years, its publication, like so many other of Böll's public acts, serves to end a silence.

Böll's first published works of the early years were the novella *Der Zug war pünktlich* (1949; *The Train Was on Time*, 1956), a collection of stories "*Wanderer, kommst du nach Spa. . . .*" (1950; "*Stranger, Bear Word to the Spartans We. . . . ,*" 1956); and his first novel, *Wo warst du, Adam* (1951; *And Where Were You, Adam?*, 1970), brought out by Friedrich Middelhauve. They were interspersed with joint-translation work with his wife Annemarie and the arrival of three sons: Raimund, Rene, and Vincent. The translations, from Irish, English, and American literature, include Synge, Shaw, Behan, Malamud, and Salinger, some of them not appearing in print until the early 1960s. Like the unpublished pieces, these early works focus on the war years, the immediate postwar return, and life in the rubble of those years. Narrated often in the third person when featuring the war, or in the first person by the "little guy" left out in the cold, they too are marked by sentimentalism, the despair of loss, the despondency and melancholy of postwar disorientation, but possess enough wit, contemporary social commentary, or human interest to distract the public from their otherwise-depressing themes. These early writings do not yet demonstrate objective distance to Böll's material or the deft formal complexity that were to come later. Relying almost exclusively on an unshaded, realistic-narrative style, they faced stiff competition: as Peter Demetz has pointed out, one of the contributing factors to this was the sudden accessibility of writers long censored—Kafka, Thomas Mann, Hemingway. It was not until mid-1951, when Böll was invited to a meeting of the exclusive literary Gruppe 47 and awarded their annual prize—for his savvy satire of the German work ethic, "*Die schwarzen Schafe*"— that he was able to free himself from other forms of employment and support the family entirely with his pen. While those first five years were exceptionally trying, the awards now began to pile in and by 1953 Böll had been inducted into the German Academy for Language and Letters. He was on his way.

Throughout the next thirty-two years, Böll would unleash an impressive output of works—at first mainly novels and short-story collections later followed by a steady flow of political writings, many of them originating as speeches or interviews. Because of his penchant for speaking out on the issues of the day, he was roughly twice as prolific as an essayist in the latter half of his writing career as he was in the first, his opinion increasingly sought after as his reputation grew.

In fiction, Böll spent the early and middle 1950s producing works treating the more intimate spheres of love, marriage, and family. These are texts still largely focused on the lower-middle class and very much engaged with the grinding poverty, hunger, privation, and aimlessness of the aftermath—families faced with unbearable circumstances, relationships stressed to the breaking point, and the little pleasures of alcohol, gambling, smoking; the little solaces of movie-watching, coupling, even church depicted as comfortless, empty habits of dead-end lives. But from *Und sagte kein einziges Wort* (1953) to *Haus ohne Hüter* (1954) to *Brot der frühen Jahre* (1955), Böll increasingly confronts his characters with hard choices of a moral nature; as immediate demands for survival slacken, individuals reevaluate their choices. Surrounded by increasing prosperity, his characters must decide what degree of moral rectitude they can afford (or ill afford). As might be expected, this provides fertile ground for satire, and the mid-to-late 1950s saw Böll attaining a mastery of nuance in his satires far surpassing the quality of his earlier work. The best of these is *"Doktor Murkes gesammeltes Schweigen,"* (1955, "Murke's Collected Silences," 1963), a piece that is astonishingly hopeful compared to all that has gone before, and, though short, helps maintain Böll's reputation as a serious writer. In it, he pits a young editor at a broadcasting company against an established figure in the culture industry. Although both characters are flawed and very human, the editor Murke, fresh from university with a doctoral degree in psychology, uses technology, wit, guile, and his antipathy for the hypocrisy of the older generation to turn the tables on the establishment culture critic Bur-Malottke. Murke's triumph over Bur-Malottke is virtually an object lesson for Germany's first postwar generation. Though written in 1955, the signs of spring—the explosion of youth culture in the later 1950s and early 1960s and the subsequent student demonstrations—are in the air, and Böll's grasp of the *Zeitgeist* aptly demonstrated.

In 1959, Böll published the first of his six most important works of fiction. Whereas *Billard um halb zehn* (*Billiards at Half-past Nine*, 1962) would not meet with immediate critical acclaim, it would be a popular success, employing much more complex narrative techniques than Böll had used in the past. Akin to the *nouveau roman* of the same period, the novel employs interior monologue, flashback, leitmotif, and an epic structure to tell a story spanning three generations of architects within the daylight hours of a single day. *Billard* is succeeded by *Ansichten eines Clowns* (1963, *The Clown*, 1965), Böll's novel in the tradition of James Joyce's *A Portrait of the Artist as a Young Man*, but marked now by the grotesque distortions of the antihero, the outsider surrounded by a world of hypocrisy, cynicism and naked ambition. Here too, Böll employs flashbacks and interior monologue to compress a story of several years into the space of a four-hour time period. Both of these novels, at their core, still concern the war, Nazism, or both, but they both show Böll treating a far more economically stable (*Billard*) or wealthy (*Clown*) milieu. Although Nazism may have arisen out of criminal and proto-fascist elements, Böll is seeking to cast his gaze on the accommodations to fascism made by the bourgeois classes, the established political and religious elite, particularly those who did not "partake of the host of the beast," but managed to maintain their wealth and privileged status straight through the war and into the boom economy of the recovery.

With his next two novels, Böll returns to a lower economic milieu and employs a completely different narrative technique, one that was popular at the time of their publication and was frequently employed to successful effect in the documentary prose fiction of such writers as Hans Magnus Enzensberger, Peter Weiss, F. C. Delius, and Günther Walraff. The two texts are paired here for their use of a narrator, or compiler—a device that provides them both with an epic structure and a greater feeling of objectivity—and for their title characters. Both novels revolve entirely around two female anomalies—Leni Pfeiffer née Gruyten in *Gruppenbild mit Dame* (1971, *Group Portrait with Lady*, 1973) and Katharina Blum in *Die verlorene Ehre der Katharina Blum* (1974, *The Lost Honor of Katharina Blum*, 1975). These women refuse to behave as society would have them behave, both possess a charismatic self-comfort, and derive their power from a sensual confidence in who they are rather than what they have. As such, they have an emancipatory effect on the men and women they draw into their orbit. But these characters are also politically exceptionally naive and give freely and frequently of themselves to the men who stumble in, and out, of their lives. Were their lives to remain essentially unchanged by these encounters, the plots might certainly suffer; because they are changed, these saintly martyr figures must be saved from themselves or suffer the harshest punishments of society—scorn and eviction, in the case of Leni, at the hands of her own family; slander, lost honor, and criminal conviction, by Katharina, at the hands of the tabloid press and the state. As much as the institutions surrounding them do not understand Leni and Katharina, they are propositioned day and night by the men they encounter. Böll clearly locates utopian, or at least alternativist, social potential in these female outsiders. In an interview with Dieter Wellershoff, Böll says of Leni, "I attempted to describe or write the fate of a German woman in her late forties who had taken upon herself the entire burden of our history from 1922 to 1970." A tall order, and yet this is easily his largest novel and most likely the single biggest reason for his being awarded the Nobel Prize. In the case of Katharina, Böll's objective is to take a "simple girl," whose pride, loyalty, financial independence and love for a suspected terrorist make her an easy target for defamation, disgrace, and ruin at the hands of "The News." The novels were not only successful in the eyes of literary-judging panels; both books were runaway publishing successes and both came out subsequently as films (*Gruppenbild* by Alekander Petrovićs in 1976–77 with Romy Schneider in the title role, *Verlorene Ehre* by Volker Schlondorff and Margarethe von Trotta with Angela Winkler as lead). As shallowly constructed and as self-effacing as they may be, they are indomitable, their characters lent considerable additional nuance by the film adaptations, and Böll is able to construct an alternative social circle (Leni) and a virtual call for a politically conscious civil society (Katharina) upon their backs. Although not exactly ideal role-models or even fully formed, Böll's reliance on the emancipatory potential of these Rhenish women characters would continue to evolve as would his own sensitivity to gender dynamics.

The final two major works that deserve mention are *Fürsorgliche Belagerung* (1979, *The Safety Net*, 1981) and *Frauen vor Flußlandschaft* (1985, *Women in a River Landscape*, 1988). In the first of these, through a narrative made considerably more current to the American reader by the terrorist attacks of September 11, Böll confronts the duel challenge presented by terrorism on the one hand, and the need for state security on the other. Clearly related by subject to *Verlorene Ehre*, the outlook is not a comforting one: Böll demonstrates that placing complex human relationships under the scrutiny of state security creates pressures that render the state less safe than it was in the first place. For whether human relationships are instrumentalized or abstracted, the state will not and cannot comprehend them, cannot reduce them to a reliable algorithm. The latter work as well exhibits a complex network of cross-generational relationships: the older generation marred by years of wartime sacrifice and postwar hunger and compromise, the younger generation by a resulting ambivalence, a moral quandary over the artifice of success achieved by their parents' generation. Both works also employ a quasi-dramatic form, an unusual amount of expository information, and a broad number of viewpoints (one each for the twenty-one chapters of *Fürsorgliche Belagerung,* and a complex array of unique character matchings in the twelve-chapter "discussions and soliloquies" of *Frauen vor Flußlandschaft*). Three final observations about *Frauen* are key to an appreciation of this text. Firstly, while not without its flaws, this novel does more to illuminate the enduring malaise of the Bonn Republic than any other of his major works. Böll achieves this by using dramatic strategies to cast Bonn politics as the theater that they are, spoken, not narrated, by "actors" who are far more sympathetic on the whole, far more gray than his traditional choice of black or white. Böll's gray characters are the better democrats—far closer to real people who must make real moral choices: political action or emigration, suicide or aesthetic resistance. Secondly, Böll wraps these twelve scenes in a metonymic connecting device that more simply and directly captures an expression of late-20th century German *Heimat* ("homeland") than anywhere else in his writings. It is the continuing flow, the bewitching stream of the Rhine River, at moments steeped in fog, later shimmering silver in the sun, but flowing always, an unceasing melding of past and present, a current possessing German secrets, German memories, but a flow that washes other shores as well, that speaks of and leads to a wider world. Thirdly, in this last novel, published posthumously, Böll achieves a far less cardboard, two-dimensional female character than in the past. Throughout his career Böll had sought to make his women the standard-bearers of an alternative value system. In *Frauen* he creates a broader spectrum of women characters, and invests his lead, Erika Wubler, with keen perception. He is most interested in those women characters who have seen and overheard enough of the machinations of their politically ambitious husbands to see through their power rituals, to understand how their partners seek, knowingly or unknowingly, to destroy them. Just as the personal is political, the personal lives of Böll's Bonn elite are intensely political. By constantly interchanging his character pairings like so many chess pieces, Böll manages, among other things, to create multiple perspectives on the politician-husbands' shared web of domination and deceit, with which they silence and sideline their wives.

The selection of short fiction and prose presented in this volume has involved a challenging process or winnowing, but it might have been much more difficult were it not for Böll's visibility in the English-speaking world. This owes its thanks to a number of factors, foremost among them the activism of Böll's wife Annemarie, his sons Rene and Vincent, and especially his nephew Viktor, along with Heinrich Vormweg, to maintain the vision and mandate Böll set for himself with his writings. This also extends to Böll's Cologne publisher Kiepenheuer und Witsch, but his work is given further institutional visibility, political relevance, and support from the Heinrich Böll Foundation. The HBF Web site is a better resource than most online commercial enterprises for providing an overview of his written works. Finally, the early work of McGraw Hill, carried on in later years by Northwestern University Press, and Leila Vennewitz's four decades of skillfully rendering hundreds of Böll's texts into English have been essential to his reception in the United States. For all of the above reasons, the current selection is able to enjoy relative freedom from the "tyranny" of the longer novels, permitting a more trans-historical approach.

Although all of the short stories are available in English elsewhere, they rarely appear in a chronology that allows one to enjoy

Böll's development as a writer. This is not a little confounding, as it is precisely this slow and steady development that is so central to an appreciation of his work. Thus, the short stories here begin with the immediacy of the war and postwar period, and progress into the satires, political themes, and growing objectivity and sophistication of the later years. The one novel included, *The Lost Honor of Katharina Blum,* subtitled "How Violence Develops and Where It Can Lead," was selected out of the conviction that the Böll least known to the American audience is the political artist—the engaged writer who only truly found his niche, his public persona, in the mid-1960s with the rising tide of the German student movement. This also underlies the decision to include a number of newly translated essays. For what the short story is to the young Böll, the political essay, interview, speech, and newspaper editorial are to the mature man of letters. It is when he channels this engagement into his fiction, as in *Lost Honor* and *Women in a River Landscape,* that Böll is truly at the top of his form. Ultimately, it is his use of his Nobel laureate prominence to bring about progressive change at home, and international understanding abroad, which lands him on the podium at the October 10, 1981, Peace Demonstration in Bonn before an audience of 300,000 souls, and leads in 1987 to the formation of the Heinrich Böll Foundation, an activist voice to this day in environmental issues, gender discourse, democracy initiatives, nonviolence, and cross-cultural understanding.

The last essay included here, *"Den Kameras untertan"* ("Subordinated by the Cameras"), was written in the last months of Böll's life as a footnote to President von Weizsäcker's famous speech to the German Parliament of May 8, 1985, forty years to the day after the German capitulation on VE Day. Perhaps anticipating the shortness of his own remaining time, Böll manages to distill the truly essential from the swirling controversies of that time—Helmut Kohl's exclusion from the Normandy anniversary, his infamous *"Gnade des späten Geburts"* ("grace of late birth") line, Reagan's visit to Bitburg, and finally von Weizsäcker's "no reconciliation without remembrance" speech. In consummate form, Böll reminds his country with this essay that war is a raging hell that indiscriminately shreds bodies, lives, and patriotic rhetoric. We lionize it at our peril. Further, he admonishes us not to waste our time on the SS men of the past already interred—after all, he reminds us, the right to burial, to return to the earth, is a *human* right—there are criminals buried everywhere around us. Far more important are the war criminals still living among us.

The autobiographical writings, situated as they are between fiction and prose, are intended to offer a reflective quality to Böll's voice, and will serve, it is hoped, to bring the reader closer to this generous, passionate, sentimental, and profoundly human man.

M.B.

Editor's Acknowledgments

I owe a great debt of gratitude to Volkmar Sander, general editor of the German Library, for his patience, generosity, and guidance. It is in him, more than in any other, that I have witnessed firsthand the daily call, and the rewards accruing, to a life given to a struggle he shared with many of his generation, and which he personally no doubt would disavow: the German postwar democracy project. Margret Herzfeld-Sander, my teacher and mentor for many years, is due similar thanks, both for what she imparted to me, and for (somehow) sustaining him. Thanks, too, go to Matthew Griffin, Christoph Hauptmann and Jen Black for support from afar. I also owe more than I can say to Evander Lomke, senior editor at Continuum International, who has gracefully steered (and prodded) this project to completion, ably supported by Gabriella Page-Fort. But my deepest gratitude is reserved for Marylou Gramm. Her support, and the idea of her support, was crucial, her own daily example of critical inquiry my compass. This volume is dedicated to her, and to our sons Toby and Thanny: may the two of you grow to be as boisterously democratic as Heinrich Böll.

M.B.

PART ONE

STORIES

Cause of Death: Hooked Nose

When Lieutenant Hegemüller returned to his billet, his thin face was trembling with a nervous pallor; his eyes seemed to have gone dead, his face under the flaxen hair was a blank, quivering surface. All day long he had been sitting in the communications room, relaying radio messages to the incessant accompaniment of the chatter of machine pistols as they spewed out their bullets over at the outskirts of the town into the wan afternoon light: over and over again that cackling screech of a new salvo, and knowing that every single link in that rattling chain of sound meant a destroyed or mutilated human life, a body writhing in the dust and tumbling down a slope! And every half hour, with hellish regularity, the thud of a muffled explosion, and knowing that that sound, fading like a retreating thunderstorm, replaced the work of gravediggers, gravedigging in the interests of sanitation; knowing that yet another section of the quarry was at that very moment collapsing over the harvest of the last half hour and burying the living with the dead. . . .

For the thousandth time the lieutenant wiped his pale, sweat-soaked face; then with a curse he kicked open the door to his quarters and stumbled into his room, where with a groan he sat down on his chair. On and on and on rushed the venomous machinery of death—almost as if that ripping, crackling sound were the screech of a monstrous saw splitting the sky so it would collapse when the day's work was done. Often it seemed as though the traces of this destruction must be visible and, his face twitching, he would lean for a moment out of the window to see with his own eyes whether the vast grey vault of the sky were not already tilting like the prow of a foundering ship. He thought he could even hear the gurgling of the black water lying in wait to wash over the wreckage of the world and swallow it up in deadly calm.

Quaking in every limb, he smoked with trembling fingers, knowing that he must do something to fight this madness. For he felt that he was not without guilt, that he had been forced into the stony heart of guilt, a heart that must lie at the centre of this ceaselessly grinding atrocity. Neither the pain he suffered nor the nameless horror and mortal fear could wipe out the consciousness that he was shooting and he was being shot. Never before had he been so intensely aware of the great cosmic home that embraces all men, the reality of God.

On and on went that biting, grinding, spitting, demented sawing of the machine pistols. There followed a few minutes of a ghastly silence that must make the birds tremble in their hiding-places, and then a detonation: a charge of explosives, drilled into the wall of the quarry, replaced the grim labours of the gravediggers. And again shots, shots, one after the other in an endless chain, each one of them struck Lieutenant Hegemüller in his very heart.

But suddenly he heard a different sound, a subdued sound, the sobbing of a woman. He listened intently, rose to his feet and stepped out into the corridor, listened again for a moment, then flung open the kitchen door and stopped in his tracks: the Russian woman was on her knees, her fists covering her ears, and sobbing, sobbing so that the tears dripped from her blouse onto the floor. For a moment the lieutenant was gripped by a strange, cold curiosity: tears, he thought, tears, never would I have believed a person could have so many tears. The pain was dripping in great, clear beads out of the elderly woman, collecting in a veritable puddle on the floor between her knees. Before he had a chance to ask, the woman jumped up and screamed: "They've taken him away, my Piotr, Piotr Stepanovich . . . oh sir, sir!"

"But he's not . . ." the lieutenant shouted back.

"No, sir, he's not a Jew, no. Oh sir, sir!"

The tears gushed from between the fingers that she was pressing against her face as if to staunch a bleeding wound . . .

Driven by some overpowering inner force, the lieutenant turned on his heel and, calling out something to the woman, dashed out into the street.

The streets were completely deserted. An eerie tension hung in the air: what hovered over the little town was not only the terror of those crouching in their hiding-places, not only the whip of death.

The silence, which filled the streets like pale, grey dust, held a kind of mockery as if one devil were grinning at another.

The lieutenant raced along, sweat dripping from every pore, the terrible sweat that was no release but more like a death sweat poisoned by a bestiality that had been saturated with the killers' vicious lust. A strange burning cold flowed over him from the dead façades of the houses. And yet he was filled with something like joy—no, it actually was joy—what a glorious feeling to run for the life of a human being! In those minutes, racing through the streets at breakneck speed, almost beside himself, his subconscious came to understand many things; a thousand things were revealed to him from out of that nebulous haze he had called his ideology, rising like stars to pierce him with their brilliance and then die away like comets, but their reflection remained within him, as an accumulated source of subdued light.

Panting, covered with dust, he reached the outskirts of the town where the doomed had been herded together at the edge of the steppe. They formed a square surrounded by vehicles mounted with machine guns; in the vehicles, guards lounged behind the slim barrels, smoking their cigarettes.

At first Hegemüller ignored the sentry who tried to stop him, did not react when the man grabbed him by the sleeve. For a second he stared into the man's face, amazed at how close and clear it was. In fact, the faces of the sentry cordon seemed all equally dull-witted and brutish whereas the faces of those inside the cordon seemed in some exquisite manner to have been lifted high above the mass and placed on the pinnacle of humanity. A sombre silence hung over the crowd, something strangely vibrating, fluttering, like the flapping of heavy banners, something solemn, and—Hegemüller felt, as his heart missed a beat—inexplicably comforting, joyful; he felt this joy surge through him, and at that instant he envied the doomed people and was shocked to realize that he was wearing the same uniform as the murderers. Blushing with shame he turned towards the sentry and croaked: "The man whose house I'm billeted in is here. He's not a Jew . . ." and since the sentry stood there in apathetic silence he added: "Grimschenko, Piotr . . ."

An officer approached the group and raised his eyebrows at the sight of the dusty, sweat-soaked lieutenant, who was wearing neither belt nor cap. Hegemüller now realized that the executioners and their minions were all drunk. With their bloodshot eyes they looked like bulls, and their breath was like steam from a manure heap. Once again Hegemüller stammered out the name of his host, and the lieutenant in command of the minions scratched his head in a display of gruesome good nature and asked lamely: "Innocent, you mean?"

"Innocent, that too," Hegemüller replied curtly.

The lieutenant seemed taken aback as this little word fell into the pool of his heart. But the word had sunk without trace, without raising ripples, as the lieutenant stepped in front of the doomed figures and shouted: "Grimschenko, Piotr, step forward!" Since nobody moved, and that strangely fluttering silence persisted, he called out the name again, adding: "Can go home!" And when there was still no response he stepped back and said awkwardly: "Gone, maybe already done for, maybe still over there—come with me!"

Hegemüller's eyes followed the finger pointing towards the place of execution.

What he saw was the edge of an enormous quarry that sloped towards the assembly point, and a row of close-ranked soldiers armed with machine pistols. From the assembly point, a procession of the doomed led up to the rim of the quarry, where it flattened out: from this rim the regular, whiplike cracking of the machine pistols sounded through the afternoon air.

And once again, as he followed the drunken lieutenant, it seemed to Hegemüller that the crowd, the doomed crowd, had dissolved into a procession of noble personalities, while the few murderers seemed like brutish clods. Each one of those faces he so anxiously scanned in search of Grimschenko seemed to him calmer, revealing an inexpressibly human gravity. The women with babies in their arms, old people and children, men, girls smeared with faeces who had apparently been pulled out of latrines for the purpose of being murdered; rich and poor, ragged and well-dressed, all were endowed with a sublimity that left Hegemüller speechless. The lieutenant tried to make conversation by throwing out oddly apologetic fragments, not as an excuse for the killings but to gloss over his drunken condition while on duty: "Tough job, this, you know. Couldn't stand it without booze . . . hope you understand . . ."

But Hegemüller, in whom horror had aroused a strange and sober calm, was nagged by a single question: What do they do with the babies, the tiny ones who can't stand or walk—how is it technically possible? Meanwhile his eyes never left the procession of the doomed, never rose to the rim of the quarry where the pallid afternoon was punctured by the thwacking and spitting of the machine pistols. But on reaching the point where the slope flattened out and he was forced to lift his gaze, he saw the answer to that nagging question. He saw a black boot kicking the bloodied corpse of an infant into the abyss and, averting his eyes in horror and looking along the rim of the quarry, he suddenly saw Grimschenko at the head of the line, saw him collapse under a bullet. With a wild and terrible cry he shouted "Stop, stop!" so loud that the executioners held their fire in alarm. He seized the lieutenant by the arm and dragged him over to where Grimschenko, drenched in blood, was hanging half over the edge. He had not tipped forward into the quarry but, facing away from his killer, had fallen over backwards. Hegemüller grabbed him and lifted him up, and just then an official voice shouted from somewhere: "Everyone get back—blasting!" Hegemüller did not see the killers running back fifty yards in their panic, or the astonished, bewildered face of the lieutenant in charge of his drunken minions. Hegemüller had grasped Grimschenko's body and hoisted him onto his shoulders; he could feel the flowing blood congealing between his fingers. Behind him the detonation exploded in a cloud of leaden sound into the sky; scarcely a foot or two behind Hegemüller, the rim of the quarry collapsed, and the earth buried both the dead and the hall-dead, the infants and the old men who for ninety-four years had borne the burden of life . . .

It was no surprise to Hegemüller that the row of killers, waiting with smoking barrels and dull eyes for the next batch, made way for him without resistance. He felt he had the power to force them all onto their knees with a single glance, a single word, those butchers of men in their brand-new uniforms, for in the midst of the red fog of confusion, fear and noise, of stench and anguish, he had felt something that filled him with happiness Grimschenko's gentle breath that brushed his shoulder like a caress from another world, that tiny breath of the gravely wounded, whose blood had caked his fingers.

Unhindered he passed through the row of murderers, hearing behind him the upsurge of renewed firing. He found a waiting vehicle and shouted at the dozing driver: "Getgoing—the nearest field hospital!" as he jerked open the door, let Grimschenko slide from his shoulders, and laid him on the back seat.

Suddenly he was dreaming he was running, running, with a number of others in a mad, gruelling race to a lake in whose waters they wanted to cool off. The heat burned over them, and all round them. The whole world was one pitiless furnace, and they ran and ran, while the sweat flowed from their pores like streams of sour blood. It was an indescribable torture, this race along a dusty road to the lake which they knew lay beyond a curve in the road, yet it was a sensual pleasure, this sweating, a kind of swimming in torture, a dreadful yet in some mysterious way pleasurable torture, while the sweat flowed, flowed, flowed. And then came that curve in the road beyond which must be the lake; with a wild cry he raced round the curve, saw the glittering silver surface of the water, plunged into it with a jubilant shout, knelt down and joyfully dipped his face in the water. Then, just as he was marvelling at how miraculously cool the water was despite the scorching heat, he woke up and opened his eyes.

He was looking into the impassive face of an orderly who was holding an empty jug, and he instantly grasped that he had fainted and been revived with a dash of cold water. He could smell some kind of disinfectant, could hear a typewriter tapping. "Grish, Grimschenko?" he whispered, but the orderly, instead of replying, turned away. "So the Russian's name is Grimschenko—now you can complete the medical report, Sister."

The orderly stepped aside, and Hegemüller felt the cool professional hand of a doctor on his forehead and heard a complacent voice say: "Been overdoing it a bit, eh?" Then the hand slid down his sleeve to his pulse and, while Hegemüller was feeling his own pulse beating irregularly against the doctor's gentle fingers, the complacent voice spoke again:

"All right, Sister—got it? Then write down: Cause of death—let's say, hooked nose," and then the complacent voice laughed while the hands belonging to that complacent voice: were feeling Hegemüller's pulse almost tenderly. But Hegemüller sat up, took in the white room with a strangely detached expression, then laughed too, and his laughter was as strange as his expression. His eyeballs rolled back as his laughter grew louder and louder; they dimmed and seemed to turn ever further inward, like the closing shutters of a searchlight, taking the whole world inside with them and leaving nothing but a clouded emptiness; Hegemüller laughed, and from then on the only words he ever spoke were: "Cause of death: hooked nose."

Translated by Leila Vennewitz

In the Darkness

"Light the candle," said a voice.

There was no sound, only that exasperating, aimless rustle of someone trying to get to sleep.

"Light the candle, I say," came the voice again, on a sharper note this time.

The sounds at last became distinguishable as someone moving, throwing aside the blanket, and sitting up; this was apparent from the breathing, which now came from above. The straw rustled too.

"Well?" said the voice.

"The lieutenant said we weren't to light the candle except on orders, in an emergency," said a younger, diffident voice.

"Light the candle, I say, you little pipsqueak," the older voice shouted back.

He sat up now too, their heads were on the same level in the dark, their breathing was parallel.

The one who had first spoken irritably followed the movements of the other, who had tucked the candle away somewhere in his pack. His breathing relaxed when he eventually heard the sound of the matchbox.

The match flared up and there. Has light: a sparse yellow light.

Their eyes met. Invariably, as soon as there was enough light, their eyes met. Yet they knew one another so well, much too well. They almost hated each other, so familiar was each to each; they knew one another's very smell, the smell of every pore, so to speak, but still their eyes met, those of the older man and the younger. The younger one was pale and slight with a nondescript face, and the older one was pale and slight and unshaven with a nondescript face.

"Now, listen," said the older man, calmer now, "when are you ever going to learn that you don't do everything the lieutenants tell you?"

"He'll . . ." the younger one tried to begin.

"He won't do a thing," said the older one, in a sharper tone again and lighting a cigarette from the candle. "He'll keep his trap shut, and if he doesn't, and I don't happen to be around, then tell him to wait till I get back, it was me who lit the candle, understand? Do you understand?"

"Yessir."

"To hell with that Yessir crap, just Yes when you're talking to me. And undo your belt," he was shouting again now, "take that damn crappy belt off when you go to sleep."

The younger man looked at him nervously and took off his belt, placing it beside him in the straw.

"Roll your coat up into a pillow. That's right. OK . . . and now go to sleep, I'll wake you when it's time for you to die. . . ."

The younger man rolled onto his side and tried to sleep. All that was visible was the young brown hair, matted and untidy, a very thin neck, and the empty shoulders of his uniform tunic. The candle flickered gently, letting its meager light swing back and forth in the dark dugout like a great yellow butterfly uncertain where to settle.

The older man stayed as he was, knees drawn up, puffing out cigarette smoke at the ground in front of him. The ground was dark brown, here and there white blade marks showed where the spade had cut through a root or, a little closer to the surface, a tuber. The roof consisted of a few planks with a groundsheet thrown over them, and in the spaces between the planks the groundsheet sagged a little because the earth lying on top of it was heavy, heavy and wet. Outside, it was raining. The soft swish of steadily falling water sounded indescribably persistent, and the older man, still staring fixedly at the ground, now noticed a thin trickle of water oozing into the dugout under the roof. The tiny stream backed up slightly on encountering some loose earth, then flowed on past the obstacle until it reached the next one, which was the man's feet, and the ever-growing tide flowed all around the man's feet until his black boots lay in the water just like a peninsula. The man spat his cigarette butt into the puddle and lit another from the candle. In doing so he took the candle down from the edge of the dugout and placed it beside him on an ammunition case. The half where the younger man was lying was almost in darkness, reached now by the swaying light in brief spasms only, and these gradually subsided.

"Go to sleep, damn you," said the older man. "D'you hear? Go to sleep!"

"Yessir . . . yes," came the faint voice, obviously wider awake than before, when it had been dark.

"Hold on," said the older man, less harshly again. "A couple more cigarettes and then I'll put it out, and at least we'll drown in the dark."

He went on smoking, sometimes turning his head to the left, where the boy was lying, but he spat the second butt into the steadily growing puddle, lit the third, and still he could tell from the breathing beside him that the kid couldn't sleep.

He then took the spade, thrust it into the soft earth, and made a little mud wall behind the blanket forming the entrance. Behind this wall he heaped up a second layer of earth. With a spadeful of earth he covered the puddle at his feet. Outside, there was no sound save the gentle swish of the rain; little by little, the earth lying on top of the groundsheet had evidently become saturated, for water was now beginning to drip from above too.

"Oh shit," muttered the older man. "Are you asleep?"

"No."

The man spat the third cigarette butt over the mud wall and blew out the candle. He pulled up his blanket again, worked his feet into a comfortable position, and lay back with a sigh. It was quite silent and quite dark, and again the only sound was that aimless rustle of someone trying to get to sleep, and the swish of the rain, very gentle.

"Willi's been wounded," the boy's voice said suddenly, after a few minutes' silence. The voice was more awake than ever, in fact not even sleepy.

"What d'you mean?" asked the man in reply.

"Just that—wounded," came the younger voice, with something like triumph in it, pleased that it knew some important piece of news which the older voice obviously knew nothing about. "Wounded while he was shitting."

"You're nuts," said the man; then he gave another sigh and went on, "That's what I call a real break; I never heard of such luck. One day you come back from leave and the next day you get wounded while you're shitting. Is it serious?"

"No," said the boy with a laugh, "though actually it's not minor either. A bullet fracture, but in the arm."

"A bullet fracture in the arm! You come back from leave and while you're shitting you get wounded, a bullet fracture in the arm! What a break. . . . How did it happen?"

"When they went for water last evening," came the younger voice, quite animated now. "When they went for water, they were going down the hill at the back, carrying their water cans, and Willi told Sergeant Schubert, 'I've got to shit, Sergeant!' 'Nothing doing,' said the sergeant. But Willi couldn't hold on any longer so he just ran off, pulled down his pants, and bang! A grenade. And they actually had to pull up his pants for him. His left arm was wounded, and his right arm was holding it, so he ran off like that to get it bandaged, with his pants around his ankles.

They all laughed, everyone laughed, even Sergeant Schubert laughed." He added the last few words almost apologetically, as if to excuse his own laughter, because he was laughing now. . . .

But the older man wasn't laughing.

"Light!" he said with an oath. "Here, give me the matches, let's have some light!" He struck a match, cursing as it flared up. "At least I want some light, even if I don't get wounded. At least let's have some light, the least they can do is give us enough candles if they want to play war. Light! Light!" He was shouting again as he lit another cigarette.

The younger voice had sat up again and was poking around with a spoon in a greasy can held on his knees.

And there they sat, crouching side by side, without a word, in the yellow light.

The man smoked aggressively, and the boy was already looking somewhat greasy: his childish face smeared, bread crumbs sticking to his matted hair around most of his hairline.

The boy then proceeded to scrape out the grease can with a piece of bread.

All of a sudden there was silence: the rain had stopped. Neither of them moved, they looked at each other, the man with the cigarette in his hand, the boy holding the bread in his trembling fingers. It was uncannily quiet, they took a few breaths, and then heard rain still dripping somewhere from the groundsheet.

"Hell," said the older man. "D'you suppose the sentry's still there? I can't hear a thing."

The boy put the bread into his mouth and threw the can into the straw beside him.

"I don't know," said the boy. "They're going to let us know when it's our turn to relieve."

The older man got up quickly. He blew out the light, jammed on his steel helmet, and thrust aside the blanket. What came through the opening was not light. Just cool damp darkness. The man pinched out his cigarette and stuck his head outside.

"Hell," he muttered outside, "not a thing. Hey!" he called softly. Then his dark head reappeared inside, and he asked, "Where's the next dugout?"

The boy groped his way to his feet and stood next to the other man in the opening.

"Quiet!" said the man suddenly, in a sharp, low tone. "Something's crawling around out there."

They peered ahead. It was true: in the silent darkness there was a sound of someone crawling, and all of a sudden an unearthly snapping sound that made them both jump. It sounded as if someone had flung a live cat against the wall: the sound of breaking bones.

"Hell," muttered the older man, "there's something funny going on. Where's the sentry?"

"Over there," said the boy, groping in the dark for the other man's hand and lifting it toward the right. "Over there," he repeated. "That's where the dugout is too."

"Wait here," said the older man, "and better get your rifle, just in case." Once again they heard that sickening snapping sound, then silence, and someone crawling.

The older man crept forward through the mud, occasionally halting and quietly listening, until after a few yards he finally heard a muffled voice; then he saw a faint gleam of light from the ground, felt around till he found the entrance, and called, "Hey, chum!"

The voice stopped, the light went out, a blanket was pushed aside, and a man's dark head came up out of the ground.

"What s up?"

"Where's the sentry?"

"Over there—right here."

"Where?"

"Hey there, Neuer! . . . Hey there!"

No answer: the crawling sound had stopped, all sound had stopped, there was only darkness out there, silent darkness. "God damn it, that's queer," said the voice of the man who had come up out of the ground. "Hey there! . . . That's funny, he was standing right here by the dugout, only a few feet away." He pulled himself up over the edge and stood beside the man who had called him.

"There was someone crawling around out there," said the man who had come across from the other dugout. "I know there was. The bastard's quiet now."

"Better have a look," said the man who had come up out of the ground. "Shall we take a look?"

"Hm, there certainly ought to be a sentry here."

"You fellows are next."

"I know, but . . ."

"Ssh!"

Once again they could hear someone crawling out there, perhaps twenty feet away.

"God damn it," said the man who had come up out of the ground, "you're right."

"Maybe someone still alive from last night, trying to crawl away."

"Or new ones."

"But what about the sentry, for God's sake?"

"Shall we go?"

"OK."

Both men instantly dropped to the ground and started to move forward, crawling through the mud. From down there, from a worm's-eye view, everything looked different. Every minutest elevation in the soil became a mountain range behind which, far off, something strange was visible: a slightly lighter darkness, the sky. Pistol in hand, they crawled on, yard by yard through the mud.

"God damn it," whispered the man who had come up out of the ground, "a Russki from last night."

His companion also soon bumped into a corpse, a mute, leaden bundle. Suddenly they were silent, holding their breath: there was that cracking sound again, quite close, as if someone had been given a terrific wallop on the jaw. Then they heard someone panting.

"Hey," called the man who had come up out of the ground, "who's there?"

The call silenced all sound, the very air seemed to hold its breath, until a quavering voice spoke, "It's me . . ."

"God damn it, what the hell are you doing out there, you old asshole, driving us all nuts?" shouted the man who had come up out of the ground.

"I'm looking for something," came the voice again. The two men had got to their feet and now walked over to the spot where the voice was coming from the ground.

"I'm looking for a pair of shoes," said the voice, but now they were standing next to him. Their eyes had become accustomed to the dark, and they could see corpses lying all around, ten or a dozen, lying there like logs, black and motionless, and the sentry was squatting beside one of these logs, fumbling around its feet.

"Your job's to stick to your post," said the man who had come up out of the ground.

The other man, the one who had summoned him out of the ground, dropped like a stone and bent over the dead man's face. The man who had been squatting suddenly covered his face with his hands and began whimpering like a cowed animal.

"Oh no," said the man who had summoned the other out of the ground, adding in an undertone, "I guess you need teeth too, eh? Gold teeth, eh?"

"What's that?" asked the man who had come up out of the ground, while at his feet the cringing figure whimpered louder than ever.

"Oh no," said the first man again, and the weight of the world seemed to be lying on his breast.

"Teeth?" asked the man who had come up out of the ground, whereupon he threw himself down beside the cringing figure and ripped a cloth bag from his hand.

"Oh no!" the cringing figure cried too, and every extremity of human terror was expressed in this cry.

The man who had summoned the other out of the ground turned away, for the man who had come up out of the ground had placed his pistol against the cringing figure's head, and he pressed the trigger.

"Teeth," he muttered, as the sound of the shot died away. "Gold teeth:"

They walked slowly back, stepping very carefully as long as they were in the area where the dead lay.

"You fellows are on now," said the man who had come up out of the ground, before vanishing into the ground again.

"Right," was all the other man said, and he too crawled slowly back through the mud before vanishing into the ground again.

He could tell at once that the boy was still awake; there was that aimless rustle of someone trying to get to sleep.

"Light the candle," he said quietly.

The yellow flame leaped up again, feebly illumining the little hole. "What happened?" asked the boy in alarm, catching sight of the older man's face.

"The sentry's gone; you'll have to replace him."

"Yes," said the youngster. "Give me the watch, will you, so I can wake the others."

"Here."

The older man squatted down on his straw and lit a cigarette, watching thoughtfully as the boy buckled on his belt, pulled on his coat, defused a hand grenade, and then wearily checked his machine pistol for ammunition.

"Right," said the boy finally. "So long, now."

"So long," said the man, and he blew out the candle and lay in total darkness all alone in the ground. . . .

Translated by Leila Vennewitz

My Uncle Fred

My uncle Fred is the only person who makes my memories of the years after 1945 bearable. He came home from the war one summer afternoon, in nondescript clothes, wearing his sole possession, a tin can, on a string around his neck, and supporting the trifling weight of a few cigarette butts which he had carefully saved in a little box. He embraced my mother, kissed my sister and me, mumbled something about "Bread, sleep, tobacco," and curled himself up on our family sofa, so that I remember him as being a man who was considerably longer than our sofa, a fact which obliged him either to keep his legs drawn up or to let them simply hang over the end. Both alternatives moved him to rail bitterly against our grandparents' generation, to which we owed the acquisition of this valuable piece of furniture. He called these worthy people stuffy, constipated owls, despised their taste for the bilious pink of the upholstery, but let none of this stop him from indulging in frequent and prolonged sleep.

I for my part was performing a thankless task in our blameless family: I was fourteen at the time, and the sole contact with that memorable institution which we called the black market. My father had been killed in the war, my mother received a tiny pension, with the result that I had the almost daily job of peddling scraps of salvaged belongings or swapping them for bread, coal, and tobacco. In those days coal was the cause of considerable violation of property rights, which today we would have to bluntly call stealing. So most days saw me going out to steal or peddle, and my mother, though she realized the need for these disreputable doings, always had tears in her eyes as she watched me go off about my complicated affairs. It was my responsibility, for instance, to turn a pillow into bread, a Dresden cup into a semolina, or three volumes of Gustav Freytag into two ounces of coffee, tasks to which I devoted myself with a certain amount of sporting enthusiasm but not entirely without a sense of humiliation and fear. For values—which is what grown-ups called them at the time—had shifted substantially, and now and then I was exposed to the unfounded suspicion of dishonesty because the value of a peddled article did not correspond in the least to the one my mother thought appropriate. It was, I must say, no pleasant task to act as broker between two different worlds of values, worlds which since then seem to have converged.

Uncle Fred's arrival led us all to expect some stalwart masculine aid. But he began by disappointing us. From the very first day I was seriously worried about his appetite, and when I made no bones about telling my mother this, she suggested I let him "find his feet." It took almost eight weeks for him to find his feet. Despite his abuse of the unsatisfactory sofa, he slept there without much trouble and spent the day dozing or describing to us in a martyred voice what position he preferred to sleep in.

I think his favorite position was that of a sprinter just before the start. He loved to lie on his back after lunch, his legs drawn up, voluptuously crumbling a large piece of bread into his mouth, and then roll himself a cigarette and sleep away the day till suppertime. He was a very tall, pale man, and there was a circular scar on his chin which gave his face somewhat the look of a damaged marble statue. Although his appetite for food and sleep continued to worry me, I liked him very much. He was the only one with whom I could at least theorize about the black market without getting into an argument. He obviously knew all about the conflict between the two worlds of values.

Although we urged him to talk to us about the war, he never did; he said it wasn't worth discussing. The only thing he would do sometimes was tell us about his induction, which seemed to have consisted chiefly of a person in uniform ordering Uncle Fred in a loud voice to urinate into a test tube, an order with which Uncle Fred was not immediately able to comply, the result being that his military career was doomed from the start. He maintained that the German Reich's keen interest in his urine had filled him with considerable distrust, a distrust which he found ominously confirmed during six years of war.

He had been a bookkeeper before the war, and when the first four weeks on our sofa had gone by, my mother suggested in her gentle sisterly way that he make inquiries about his old firm. He warily passed this suggestion on to me, but all I could discover was a pile of rubble about twenty feet high, which I located in a ruined part of the city after an hour's laborious pilgrimage. Uncle Fred was much reassured by my news.

He leaned back in his chair, rolled himself a cigarette, nodded triumphantly toward my mother, and asked her to get out his old things. In one corner of our bedroom there was a carefully nailed-down crate, which we opened with hammer and pliers amid much speculation. Out of it came: twenty novels of medium size and mediocre quality, a gold pocket watch, dusty but undamaged, two pairs of suspenders, some notebooks, his Chamber of Commerce diploma, and a savings book showing a balance of twelve hundred marks. The savings book was given to me to collect the money, as well as the rest of the stuff to be peddled, including the Chamber of Commerce diploma—although this found no takers, Uncle Fred's name being inscribed on it in black India ink.

This meant that for the next four weeks we were free from worry about bread, tobacco, and coal, which was a great relief to me, especially as all the schools opened wide their doors again and I was required to complete my education.

To this day, long after my education has been completed, I have fond memories of the soups we used to get, mainly because we obtained these supplementary meals almost without a struggle, and they therefore lent a happy and contemporary note to the whole educational system.

But the outstanding event during this period was the fact that Uncle Fred finally took the initiative a good eight weeks after his safe return. One morning in late summer he rose from his sofa, shaved so meticulously that we became apprehensive, asked for some clean underwear, borrowed my bicycle, and disappeared.

His return late that night was accompanied by a great deal of noise and a penetrating smell of wine; the smell of wine emanated from my uncle's mouth, the noise was traceable to half a dozen galvanized buckets which he had tied together with some stout rope. Our confusion did not subside till we discovered he had decided to revive the flower trade in our ravaged town. My mother, full of suspicion toward the new world of values, scorned the idea, claiming that no one would want to buy flowers. But she was wrong.

It was a memorable morning when we helped Uncle Fred take the freshly filled buckets to the streetcar stop where he set himself up in business. And I still vividly remember the sight of those red and yellow tulips, the moist carnations; nor shall I ever forget how impressive he looked as he stood there in the midst of the gray figures and piles of rubble and started calling out, "Flowers, fresh flowers—no coupons required!" I don't have to describe how his business flourished: it was a meteoric success. In a matter of four weeks he owned three dozen galvanized buckets, was the proprietor of two branches, and a month later he was paying taxes. The whole town wore a different air to me: flower stalls appeared at one street corner after another, it was impossible to keep pace with the demand; more and more buckets were procured, booths were set up, and handcarts hastily thrown together.

At any rate, we were kept supplied not only with fresh flowers but with bread and coal, and I was able to retire from the brokerage business, a fact which helped greatly to improve my moral standards. For many years now, Uncle Fred has been a man of substance: his branches are still thriving, he owns a car, he looks on me as his heir, and I have been told to study commerce so I can look after the tax end of the business even before I enter on my inheritance.

When I look at him today, a solid figure behind the wheel of his red automobile, I find it strange to recall that there was really a time in my life when his appetite caused me sleepless nights.

Translated by Leila Vennewitz

The Post Card

None of my friends can understand the care with which I preserve a scrap of paper that has no value whatever. It merely keeps alive the memory of a certain day in my life, and to it I owe a reputation for sentimentality which is considered unworthy of my social position: I the assistant manager of a textile firm. But I protest the accusation of sentimentality and am continually trying to invest this scrap of paper with some documentary value. It is a tiny, rectangular piece of ordinary paper, the size, but not the shape, of a stamp—it is narrower and longer than a stamp—and although it originated in the post office it has not the slightest collector's value. It has a bright red border and is divided by another red line into two rectangles of different sizes; in the smaller of these rectangles there is a big black R, in the larger one, in black print, "Diisseldorf" and a number—the number 634. That is all, and the bit of paper is yellow and thin with age, and now that I have described it minutely I have decided to throw it away: an ordinary registration sticker, such as every post office slaps on every day by the dozen.

And yet this scrap of paper reminds me of a day in my life which is truly unforgettable, although many attempts have been made to erase it from my memory. But my memory functions too well.

First of all, when I think of that day, I smell vanilla custard, a warm sweet cloud creeping under my bedroom door and reminding me of my mother's goodness: I had asked her to make some vanilla ice cream for my first day of vacation, and when I woke up I could smell it.

It was half past ten. I lit a cigarette, pushed up my pillow, and considered how I would spend the afternoon. I decided to go swimming: after lunch I would take the streetcar to the beach, have a bit of a swim, read, smoke, and wait for one of the girls at the office, who had promised to come down to the beach after five.

In the kitchen my mother was pounding meat, and when she stopped for a moment I could hear her humming a tune. It was a hymn. I felt very happy. The previous day I had passed my test, I had a good job in a textile factory, a job with opportunities for advancement—but now I was on vacation, two weeks' vacation, and it was summertime. It was hot outside, but in those days I still loved hot weather: through the slits in the shutters I could see the heat haze, I could see the green of the trees in front of our house, I could hear the streetcar. And I was looking forward to breakfast. Then I heard my mother coming to listen at my door; she crossed the hall and stopped by my door; it was silent for a moment in our apartment, and I was just about to call "Mother" when the bell rang downstairs. My mother went to our front door, and I heard the funny high-pitched purring of the buzzer down below; it buzzed four, five, six times, while my mother was talking on the landing to Frau Kurz, who lived in the next apartment. Then I heard a man's voice, and I knew at once it was the mailman, although I had only seen him a few times. The mailman came into our entrance hall, Mother said, "What?" and he said, "Here—sign here, please." It was very quiet for a moment, the mailman said "Thanks," my mother closed the door after him, and I heard her go back into the kitchen.

Shortly after that I got up and went into the bathroom. I shaved, had a leisurely wash, and when I turned off the faucet I could hear my mother grinding the coffee. It was like Sunday, except that I had not been to church.

Nobody will believe it, but my heart suddenly felt heavy. I don't know why, but it was heavy. I could no longer hear the coffee mill. I dried myself off, put on my shirt and trousers, socks and shoes, combed my hair, and went into the living room. There were flowers on the table, pale pink carnations, it all looked fresh and neat, and on my plate lay a red pack of cigarettes.

Then Mother came in from the kitchen carrying the coffeepot and I saw at once she had been crying. In one hand she was holding the coffeepot, in the other a little pile of mail, and her eyes were red. I went over to her, took the pot from her, kissed her cheek, and said, "Good morning." She looked at me, said, "Good morning, did you sleep well?" and tried to smile, but did not succeed.

We sat down, my mother poured the coffee, and I opened the red pack lying on my plate and lit a cigarette. I had suddenly lost my appetite. I stirred milk and sugar into my coffee, tried to look at Mother, but each time I quickly lowered my eyes. "Was there any mail?" I asked, a senseless question, since Mother's small red hand was resting on the little pile on top of which lay the newspaper.

"Yes," she said, pushing the pile toward me. I opened the newspaper while my mother began to butter some bread for me. The front page bore the headline "Outrages Continue Against Germans in the Polish Corridor! "There had been headlines like that for weeks on the front pages of the papers. Reports of "rifle fire along the Polish border and refugees escaping from the sphere of Polish harassment and fleeing to the Reich." I put the paper aside. Next I read the brochure of a wine merchant who used to supply us sometimes when Father was still alive. Various types of Riesling were being offered at exceptionally low prices. I put the brochure aside too.

Meanwhile my mother had finished buttering the slice of bread for me. She put it on my plate, saying, "Please eat something!" She burst into violent sobs. I could not bring myself to look at her. I can't look at anyone who is really suffering—but now for the first time I realized it must have something to do with the mail. It must be the mail. I stubbed out my cigarette, took a bite of the bread and butter, and picked up the next letter, and as I did so I saw there was a post card lying underneath. But I had not noticed the registration sticker, that tiny scrap of paper I still possess and to which I owe a reputation for sentimentality. So I read the letter first. The letter was from Uncle Eddy. Uncle Eddy wrote that at last, after many years as an assistant instructor, he was now a full-fledged teacher, but it had meant being transferred to a little one-horse town; financially speaking, he was hardly any better off than before, since he was now being paid at the local scale. And his kids had had whooping cough, and the way things were going made him feel sick to his stomach, he didn't have to tell us why. No, he didn't, and it made us feel sick too. It made a lot of people feel sick.

When I reached for the post card, I saw it had gone. My mother had picked it up, she was holding it up and looking at it, and I kept my eyes on my half-eaten slice of bread, stirred my coffee, and waited.

I shall never forget it. Only once had my mother ever cried so terribly, when my father died; and then I had not dared to look at her either. A nameless diffidence had prevented me from comforting her.

I tried to bite into the bread, but my throat closed up, for I suddenly realized that what was upsetting Mother so much could only be something to do with me. Mother said something I didn't catch and handed me the post card, and it was then I saw the registration sticker: that red-bordered rectangle, divided by a red line into two other rectangles, of which the smaller one contained a big black R and the bigger one the word "Diisseldorf" and the number 634. Otherwise the post card was quite normal. It was addressed to me and on the back were the words "Mr. Bruno Schneider: You are required to report to the Schlieffen Barracks in Adenobrück on August 5, 1939, for an eight-week period of military training." "Bruno Schneider," the date, and "Adenbrück" were typed, everything else was printed, and at the bottom was a vague scrawl and the printed word "Major."

Today I know that the scrawl was superfluous. A machine for printing majors' signatures would do the job just as well. The only thing that mattered was the little sticker on the front for which my mother had had to sign a receipt.

I put my hand on her arm and said, "Now, look, Mother, it's only eight weeks." And my mother said, "I know."

"Only eight weeks," I said, and I knew I was lying, and my mother dried her tears, said, "Yes, of course"; we were both lying, without knowing why we were lying, but we were and we knew we were.

I was just picking up my bread and butter again when it struck me that today was the fourth and that on the following day at ten o'clock I had to be over two hundred miles away to the east. I felt myself going pale, put down the bread and got up, ignoring my mother. I went to my room. I stood at my desk, opened the drawer, closed it again. I looked round, felt something had happened and didn't know what. The room was no longer mine. That was all. Today I know, but that day I did meaningless things to reassure myself that the room still belonged to me. It was useless to rummage around in the box containing my letters, or to straighten my books. Before I knew what I was doing, I had begun to pack my briefcase: shirt, pants, towel, and socks, and I went into the bathroom to get my shaving things. My mother was still sitting at the breakfast table. She had stopped crying. My half-eaten slice of bread was still on my plate, there was still some coffee in my cup, and I said to my mother, "I'm going over to the Giesselbachs' to phone about my train."

When I came back from the Giesselbachs' it was just striking twelve noon. Our entrance hall smelled of roast pork and cauliflower, and my mother had begun to break up ice in a bag to put into our little ice-cream machine.

My train was leaving at eight that evening, and I would be in Adenbrück next morning about six. It was only fifteen minutes' walk to the station, but I left the house at three o'clock. I lied to my mother, who did not know how long it took to get to Adenbrück.

Those last three hours I spent in the house seem, on looking back, worse and longer than the whole time I spent away, and that was a long time. I don't know what we did. We had no appetite for dinner. My mother soon took back the roast, the cauliflower, the potatoes, and the vanilla ice cream to the kitchen. Then we drank the breakfast coffee which had been kept warm under a yellow cozy, and I smoked cigarettes, and now and again we exchanged a few words. "Eight weeks," I said, and my mother said, "Yes-yes, of course," and she didn't cry any more. For three hours we lied to each other, till I couldn't stand it any longer. My mother blessed me, kissed me on both cheeks, and as I closed the front door behind me, I knew she was crying.

I walked to the station. The station was bustling with activity. It was vacation time: happy suntanned people were milling around. I had a beer in the waiting room, and about half past three decided to call up the girl from the office whom I had arranged to meet at the beach.

While I was dialing the number, and the perforated nickel dial kept clicking back into place—five times—I almost regretted it, but I dialed the sixth figure, and when her voice asked, "Who is it?" I was silent for a moment, then said slowly, "Bruno" and "Can you come? I have to go off—I've been drafted."

"Right now?" she asked.

"Yes."

She thought it over for a moment, and through the phone I could hear the voices of the others, who were apparently collecting money to buy some ice cream.

"All right," she said, "I'll come. Are you at the station?"

"Yes," I said.

She arrived at the station very quickly, and to this day I don't know, although she has been my wife now for ten years, to this day I don't know whether I ought to regret that phone call. After all, she kept my job open for me with the firm, she revived my defunct ambition when I came home, and she is actually the one I have to thank for the fact that those opportunities for advancement have now become reality.

But I didn't stay as long as I could have with her either. We went to the movies, and in the cinema, which was empty, dark, and very hot, I kissed her, though I didn't feel much like it.

I kept on kissing her, and I went to the station at six o'clock, although I need not have gone till eight. On the platform I kissed her again and boarded the first eastbound train. Ever since then I have not been able to look at a beach without a pang: the sun, the water, the cheerfulness of the people seem all wrong, and I prefer to stroll alone through the town on a rainy day and go to a movie where I don't have to kiss anybody. My opportunities for advancement with the firm are not yet exhausted. I might become a director, and I probably will, according to the law of paradoxical inertia. For people are convinced I am loyal to the firm and will do a great deal for it. But I am not loyal to it and I haven't the slightest intention of doing anything for it. . . .

Lost in thought I have often contemplated that registration sticker, which gave such a sudden twist to my life. And when the tests are held in summer and our young employees come to me afterward with beaming faces to be congratulated, it is my job to make a little speech in which the words "opportunities for advancement" play a traditional role.

Translated by Leila Vennewitz

Murke's Collected Silences

Every morning, after entering Broadcasting House, Murke performed an existential exercise. Here in this building the elevator was the kind known as a paternoster—open cages carried on a conveyor belt, like beads on a rosary, moving slowly and continuously from bottom to top, across the top of the elevator shaft, down to the bottom again, so that passengers could step on and off at any floor. Murke would jump onto the paternoster but, instead of getting off at the second floor, where his office was, he would let himself be carried on up, past the third, fourth, fifth floors; he was seized with panic every time the cage rose above the level of the fifth floor and ground its way up into the empty space where oily chains, greasy rods, and groaning machinery pulled and pushed the elevator from an upward into a downward direction; Murke would stare in terror at the bare brick walls, and sigh with relief as the elevator passed through the lock, dropped into place, and began its slow descent, past the fifth, fourth, third floors. Murke knew his fears were unfounded: obviously nothing would ever happen, nothing could ever happen, and even if it did, it could be nothing worse than finding himself up there at the top when the elevator stopped moving and being shut in for an hour or two at the most. He was never without a book in his pocket, and cigarettes; yet as long as the building had been standing, for three years, the elevator had never once failed. On certain days it was inspected, days when Murke had to forgo those four and a half seconds of panic, and on these days he was irritable and restless, like people who had gone without breakfast. He needed this panic, the way other people need their coffee, their oatmeal, or their fruit Juice.

So when he stepped off the elevator at the second floor, the home of the Cultural Department, he felt lighthearted and relaxed, as lighthearted and relaxed as anyone who loves and understands his work. He would unlock the door to his office, walk slowly over to his armchair, sit down, and light a cigarette. He was always first on the job. He was young, intelligent, and had a pleasant manner, and even his arrogance, which occasionally flashed out for a moment—even that was forgiven him, since it was known he had majored in psychology and graduated cum laude.

For two days now, Murke had been obliged to go without his panic. Breakfast: unusual circumstances had required him to get to Broadcasting House at 8:00 a.m., dash off to a studio, and begin work right away, for he had been told by the director of broadcasting to go over the two talks on "The Nature of Art" which the great Bur-Malottke had taped and to cut them according to Bur-Malottke's instructions. Bur-Malottke, who had converted to Catholicism during the religious fervor of 1945, had suddenly, "overnight," as he put it, "felt religious qualms," he had "suddenly felt he might be blamed for contributing to the religious overtones in radio," and he had decided to omit God, who occurred frequently in both his half-hour talks on "The Nature of Art," and replace Him with a formula more in keeping with the mental outlook he had professed before 1945. Bur-Malottke had suggested to the producer that the word "God" be replaced by the formula "that higher Being Whom we revere," but he had refused to retape the talks, requesting instead that God be cut out of the tapes and replaced by "that higher Being Whom we revere." Bur-Malottke was a friend of the director, but this friendship was not the reason for the director's willingness to oblige him: Bur-Malottke was a man one simply did not contradict. He was the author of numerous books of a belletristic-philosophical-religious and art-historical nature, he was on the editorial staff of three periodicals and two newspapers, and closely connected with the largest publishing house. He had agreed to come to Broadcasting House for fifteen minutes on Wednesday and tape the words "that higher Being Whom we revere" as often as "God" was mentioned in his talks: the rest was up to the technical experts.

It had not been easy for the director to find someone whom he could ask to do the job; he thought of Murke, but the suddenness with which he thought of Murke made him suspicious—he was a dynamic, robust individual—so he spent five minutes going over the problem in his mind, considered Schwendling, Humkoke, Fräulein Broldin, but he ended up with Murke. The director did not like Murke; he had, of course, taken him on as soon as his name had been put forward, the way a zoo director, whose real love is the rabbits and the deer, naturally accepts wild animals too for the simple reason that a zoo must contain wild animals—but what the director really loved was rabbits and deer, and for him Murke was an intellectual wild animal. In the end his dynamic personality triumphed, and he instructed Murke to cut Bur-Malottke's talks. The talks were to be given on Thursday and Friday, and Bur-Malottke's misgivings had come to him on Sunday night—one might just as well commit suicide as contradict Bur-Malottke, and the director was much too dynamic to think of suicide.

So Murke spent Monday afternoon and Tuesday morning listening three times to the two half-hour talks on "The Nature of Art"; he had cut out "God," and in the short breaks which he took, during which he silently smoked a cigarette with the technician, reflected on the dynamic personality of the director and the inferior Being Whom Bur-Malottke revered. He had never read a line of Bur-Malottke, never heard one of his talks before. Monday night he had dreamed of a staircase as tall and steep as the Eilfel Tower; he had climbed it but soon noticed that the stairs were slippery with soap, and the director stood down below and called out, "Go on, Murke, go on . . . show us what you can do—go on!" Tuesday night the dream had been similar: he had been at a fairground, strolled casually over to the roller coaster, paid his thirty pfennigs to a man whose face seemed familiar, and as he got on the roller coaster he saw that it was at least ten miles long, he knew there was no going back, and realized that the man who had taken his thirty pfennigs had been the director. Both mornings, after these dreams, he had not needed the harmless panic breakfast up there in the empty space above the paternoster.

Now it was Wednesday. He was smiling as he entered the building, got into the paternoster, let himself be carried up as far as the sixth floor—four and a half seconds of panic, the grinding of the chains, the bare brick walls—he rode down as far as the fourth floor, got out, and walked toward the studio where he had an appointment with Bur-Malottke. It was two minutes to ten as he sat down in his green chair, waved to the technician, and lit his cigarette. His breathing was quiet, he took a piece of paper out of his breast pocket and glanced at the clock. Bur-Malottke was always on time, at least he had a reputation for being punctual; and as the second hand completed the sixtieth minute of the tenth hour, the minute hand slipped onto the twelve, the hour hand onto the ten, the door opened and in walked Bur-Malottke. Murke got up, and with a pleasant smile walked over to Bur-Malottke and introduced himself. Bur-Malottke shook hands, smiled, and said, "Well, let's get started!" Murke picked up the sheet of paper from the table, put his cigarette between his lips, and, reading from the list, said to Bur-Malottke:

"In the two talks, God occurs precisely twenty-seven times—so I must ask you to repeat twenty-seven times the words we are to splice. We would appreciate it if we might ask you to repeat them thirty-five times, so as to have a certain reserve when it comes to splicing."

"Granted," said Bur-Malottke with a smile, and sat down.

"There is one difficulty, however," said Murke: "where God occurs in the genitive, such as 'God's will,' 'God's love,' 'God's purpose,' He must be replaced by the noun in question followed by the words 'of that higher Being Whom we revere.' I must ask you, therefore, to repeat the words 'the will' twice, 'the love' twice, and 'the purpose' three times, followed each time by 'of that higher Being Whom we revere,' giving us a total of seven genitives. Then there is one spot where you use the vocative and say 'O God'—here I suggest you substitute 'O Thou higher Being Whom we revere.' Everywhere else only the nominative case applies."

It was clear that Bur-Malottke had not thought of these complications; he began to sweat, the grammatical transposition bothered him. Murke went on. "In all," he said, in his pleasant, friendly manner, "the twenty-seven sentences will require one minute and twenty seconds of radio time, whereas the twenty-seven times 'God' occurs require only twenty seconds. In other words, in order to take care of your alterations we shall have to cut half a minute from each talk."

Bur-Malottke sweated more heavily than ever; inwardly he cursed his sudden misgivings and asked, "I suppose you've already done the cutting, have you?"

"Yes, I have," said Murke, pulling a flat metal box out of his pocket; he opened it and held it out to Bur-Malottke. It contained some darkish sound-tape scraps, and Murke said softly, "'God' twenty-seven times, spoken by you. Would you care to have them?"

"No, I would not," said Bur-Malottke, furious. "I'll speak to the director about the two half minutes. What comes after my talks in the program?"

"Tomorrow," said Murke, "your talk is followed by the regular program 'Neighborly News,' edited by Grehm."

"Damn," said Bur-Malottke, "it's no use asking Grehm for a favor."

"And the day after tomorrow," said Murke, "your talk is followed by 'Let's Go Dancing.'"

"Oh God, that's Huglieme," groaned Bur-Malottke. "Never yet has Light Entertainment given way to Culture by as much as a fifth of a minute."

"No," said Murke, "it never has, at least"—and his youthful face took on an expression of irreproachable modesty—"at least not since I've been working here."

"Very well," said Bur-Malottke and glanced at the clock, "we'll be through here in ten minutes, I take it, and then I'll have a word with the director about that minute. Let's go. Can you leave me your list?"

"Of course," said Murke. "I know the figures by heart."

The technician put down his newspaper as Murke entered the little glass booth. The technician was smiling. On Monday and Tuesday, during the six hours they listened to Bur-Malottke's talks and did their cutting, Murke and the technician had not exchanged a single personal word; now and again they exchanged glances, and when they stopped for a breather, the technician had passed his cigarettes to Murke and the next day Murke passed his to the technician. Now, when Murke saw the technician smiling, he thought: If there is such a thing as friendship in this world, then this man is my friend. He laid the metal box with the snippets from Bur-Malottke's talk on the table and said quietly, "Here we go." He plugged into the studio and said into the microphone, "I'm sure we can dispense with the run-through, Professor. We might as well start right away—would you please begin with the nominatives?"

Bur-Malottke nodded, Murke switched off his own microphone, pressed the button which turned on the green light in the studio, and heard Bur-Malottke's solemn, carefully articulated voice intoning, "That higher Being whom we revere—that higher Being . . ."

Bur-Malottke pursed his lips toward the muzzle of the mike as if he wanted to kiss it, sweat ran down his face, and through the glass Murke observed with cold detachment the agony that Bur-Malottke was enduring; then he suddenly switched Bur-Malottke off, stopped the moving tape that was recording Bur-Malottke's words, and feasted his eyes on the spectacle of Bur-Malottke behind the glass, soundless, like a fat, handsome fish. He switched on his microphone and his voice came quietly into the studio, "I'm sorry, but our tape was defective, and I must ask you to begin again at the beginning, with the nominatives." Bur-Malottke swore, but his curses were silent ones which only he could hear, for Murke had disconnected him and did not switch him on again until he had begun to say, "That higher Being . . ." Murke was too young, considered himself too civilized, to approve of the word "hate." But here, behind the glass pane, while Bur-Malottke repeated his genitives, he suddenly knew the meaning of hatred: he hated this great fat, handsome creature, whose books—two million three hundred and fifty thousand copies of them—lay around in libraries, bookstores, bookshelves, and bookcases, and not for one second did he dream of suppressing this hatred. When Bur-Malottke had repeated two genitives, Murke switched on his own mike and said quietly, "Excuse me for interrupting you: the nominatives were excellent, so was the first genitive, but would you mind doing the second genitive again? Rather gentler in tone, rather more relaxed—I'll play it back to you." And although Bur-Malottke shook his head violently, he signaled to the technician to play back the tape in the studio. They saw Bur-Malottke give a start, sweat more profusely than ever, then hold his hands over his ears until the tape came to an end. He said something, swore, but Murke and the technician could not hear him; they had disconnected him. Coldly Murke waited until he could read from Bur-Malottke's lips that he had begun again with the higher Being, he turned on the mike and the tape, and Bur-Malottke continued with the genitives.

When he was through, he screwed up Murke's list into a ball, rose from his chair, drenched in sweat and fuming, and made for the door; but Murke's quiet, pleasant young voice called him back. Murke said, "But, Professor, you've forgotten the vocative." Bur-Malottke looked at him, his eyes blazing with hate, and said into the mike, "O Thou higher Being Whom we revere!"

As he turned to leave, Murke's voice called him back once more. Murke said, "I'm sorry, Professor, but, spoken like that, the words are useless."

"For God's sake," whispered the technician, "watch it!" Bur-Malottke was standing stock-still by the door, his back to the glass booth, as if transfixed by Murke's voice.

Something had happened to him that had never happened to him before: he was helpless, and this young voice, so pleasant, so remarkably intelligent, tortured him as nothing had ever tortured him before. Murke went on, "I can, of course, paste it into the talk the way it is, but I must point out to you, Professor, that it will have the wrong effect."

Bur-Malottke turned, walked back to the microphone, and said in low and solemn tones, "O Thou higher Being whom we revere."

Without turning to look at Murke, he left the studio. It was exactly quarter past ten, and in the doorway he collided with a young, pretty woman carrying some sheet music. The girl, a vivacious redhead, walked briskly to the microphone, adjusted it, and moved the table to one side so she could stand directly in front of the mike.

In the booth Murke chatted for half a minute with Huglieme, who was in charge of Light Entertainment. Pointing to the metal container, Huglieme said, "Do you still need that?" And Murke said, "Yes, I do." In the studio the redhead was singing, "Take my lips, just as they are, they're so lovely." Huglieme switched on his microphone and said quietly, "D'you mind keeping your trap shut for another twenty seconds, I'm not quite ready." The girl laughed, made a face, and said, "OK, pansy dear." Murke said to the technician, "I'll be back at eleven; we can cut it up then and splice it all together."

"Will we have to hear it through again after that?" asked the technician. "No," said Murke, "I wouldn't listen to it again for a million marks."

The technician nodded, inserted the tape for the red-haired singer, and Murke left.

He put a cigarette between his lips, did not light it, and walked along the rear corridor toward the second paternoster, the one on the south side leading down to the coffeeshop. The rugs, the corridors, the furniture, and the pictures, everything irritated him. The rugs were impressive, the corridors were impressive, the furniture was impressive, and the pictures were in excellent taste, but he suddenly felt a desire to take the sentimental picture of the Sacred Heart which his mother had sent him and see it somewhere here on the wall. He stopped, looked round, listened, took the picture from his pocket, and stuck it between the wallpaper and the frame of the door to the assistant drama producer's office. The tawdry little print was highly colored, and beneath the picture of the Sacred Heart were the words: "I prayed for you at St. James's Church."

Murke continued along the corridor, got into the paternoster, and was carried down. On this side of the building the Schrumsnot ashtrays, which had won a Good Design Award, had already been installed. They hung next to the illuminated red figures indicating the floor: a red four, a Schrumsnot ashtray, a red three, a Schrurmsnot ashtray, a red two, a Schrumsnot ashtray. They were handsome ashtrays, scallop-shaped, made of beaten copper, the copper base an exotic marine plant, nodular seaweed—and each ashtray had cost two hundred and fifty-eight marks and seventy-seven pfennigs. They were so handsome that Murke could never bring himself to soil them with cigarette ash, let alone anything as sordid as a butt. Other smokers all seemed to have had the same feeling—empty packs, butts, and ash littered the floor under the handsome ashtrays. Apparently no one had the courage to use them as ashtrays; they were copper, burnished, forever empty.

Murke saw the fifth ashtray next to the illuminated red zero rising toward him; the air was getting warmer, there was a smell of food. Murke jumped off and stumbled into the coffeeshop. Three free-lance colleagues were sitting at a table in the corner. The table was covered with used plates, cups, and saucers.

The three men were the joint authors of a radio series, "The Lung, A Human Organ"; they had collected their fee together, breakfasted together, were having a drink together, and were now throwing dice for the expense voucher. One of them, Wendrich, Murke knew well, but just then Wendrich shouted "Art!"—"Art" he shouted again, "art, art!" and Murke felt a spasm, like the frog when Galvani discovered electricity. The last two days Murke had heard the word "art" too often, from Bur-Malottke's lips; it occurred exactly one hundred and thirty-four times in the two talks, and he had heard the talks three times, which meant he had heard the word "art" four hundred and two times, too often to feel any desire to discuss it. He squeezed past the counter toward a booth in the far corner and was relieved to find it empty. He sat down, lit his cigarette, and when Wulla, the waitress, came, he said, "Apple juice, please," and was glad when Wulla went off again at once. He closed his eyes tight, but found himself listening willy-nilly to the conversation of the free-lance writers over in the corner, who seemed to be having a heated argument about art; each time one of them shouted "Art," Murke winced. It's like being whipped, he thought.

When she brought him the apple juice, Wulla looked at him in concern. She was tall and strongly built, but not fat; she had a healthy, cheerful face. As she poured the apple juice from the jug into the glass, she said, "You ought to take a vacation, sir, and quit smoking."

She used to call herself Wilfriede-Ulla, but later, for the sake of simplicity, she combined the names into Wulla. She especially admired the people from the Cultural Department.

"Layoff, will you?" said Murke. "Please!"

"And you ought to take some nice ordinary girl to the movies one night," said Wulla.

"I'll do that this evening," said Murke, "I promise you."

"It doesn't have to be one of those dolls," said Wulla, "just some nice, quiet, ordinary girl, with a kind heart. There are still some of those around.

"Yes," said Murke, "I know they're still around, as a matter of fact I know one." Well, that's fine then, thought Wulla, and went over to the freelancers, one of whom had ordered three drinks and three coffees. Poor fellows, thought Wulla, art will be the death of them yet. She had a soft spot for the freelancers and was always trying to persuade them to economize. The minute they have any money, she thought, they blow it; she went up to the counter and, shaking her head, passed on the order for the three drinks and the three coffees.

Murke drank some of the apple juice, stubbed out his cigarette in the ashtray, and thought with apprehension of the hours from eleven to one when he had to cut up Bur-Malottke's sentences and paste them into the right places in the talks. At two o'clock the director wanted both talks played back to him in his studio. Murke thought about soap, about staircases, steep stairs, and roller coasters, he thought about the dynamic personality of the director, he thought about Bur-Malottke, and was startled by the sight of Schwendling coming into the coffeeshop.

Schwendling had on a shirt of large red and black checks and made a beeline for the booth where Murke was hiding. Schwendling was humming the tune which was very popular just then: "Take my lips, just as they are, they're so lovely. . . ." He stopped short when he saw Murke, and said, "Hello, you here? I thought you were busy carving up that crap of Bur-Malottke's."

"I'm going back at eleven," said Murke.

"Wulla, let's have some beer," shouted Schwendling over to the counter, "a pint. Well," he said to Murke, "you deserve extra time off for that, it must be a filthy job. The old man told me all about it."

Murke said nothing, and Schwendling went on, "Have you heard the latest about Muckwitz?"

Murke, not interested, first shook his head, then for politeness's sake asked, "What's he been up to?"

Wulla brought the beer. Schwendling swallowed some, paused for effect, and announced, "Muckwitz is doing a feature about the Steppes."

Murke laughed and said, "What's Fenn doing?"

"Fenn," said Schwendling, "Fenn's doing a feature about the Tundra."

"And Weggucht?"

"Weggucht is doing a feature about me, and after that I'm going to do a feature about him, you know the old saying: 'you feature me, I'll feature you. . . .'"

Just then one of the freelancers jumped up and shouted across the room, "Art—art—that's the only thing that matters!"

Murke ducked, like a soldier when he hears the mortars being fired from the enemy trenches. He swallowed another mouthful of apple juice and winced again when a voice over the loudspeaker said, "Herr Murke is wanted in Studio 13—Herr Murke is wanted in Studio 13." He looked at his watch; it was only half-past ten, but the voice went on relentlessly, "Herr Murke is wanted in Studio 13—Herr Murke is wanted in Studio 13." The loudspeaker hung above the counter, immediately below the motto the director had had painted on the wall: "Discipline Above All."

"Well," said Schwendling, "that's it, you'd better go."

"Yes." Said Murke, "that's it."

He got up, put money for the apple juice on the table, pressed past the freelancers' table, got into the paternoster outside, and was carried up once more past the five Schrumsnot ashtrays. He saw his Sacred Heart picture still sticking in the assistant producer's door-frame and thought: Thank God, now there's at least one corny picture in this place.

He opened the door of the studio booth, saw the technician sitting alone and relaxed in front of three cardboard boxes, and asked wearily, "What's up?"

"They were ready sooner than expected, and we've got an extra half hour in hand," said the technician. "I thought you'd be glad of the extra time."

"I certainly am," said Murke. "I've got an appointment at one. Let's get on with it, then. What's the idea of the boxes?"

"Well," said the technician, "for each grammatical case I've got one box—the nominatives in the first, the genitives in the second, and in that one"—he pointed to the little box on the right with the words "Pure Chocolate" on it—"in that one I have the two vocatives, the good one in the right-hand corner, the bad one in the left."

"That's terrific," said Murke. "So you've already cut up the crap."

"That's right," said the technician, "and if you've made a note of the order in which the cases have to be spliced, it won't take us more than an hour. Did you write it down?"

"Yes, I did," said Murke. He pulled a piece of paper from his pocket with the numbers one to twenty-seven; each number was followed by a grammatical case.

Murke sat down, held out his cigarette pack to the technician; they both smoked while the technician laid the cut tapes with Bur-Malottke's talks on the roll.

"In the first cut," said Murke, "we have to stick in a nominative."

The technician put his hand into the first box, picked up one of the snippets, and stuck it into the space.

"Next comes a genitive," said Murke.

They worked swiftly, and Murke was relieved that it all went so fast.

"Now," he said, "comes the vocative; we'll take the bad one, of course."

The technician laughed and stuck Bur-Malottke's bad vocative into the tape.

"Next," he said, "next!"

"Genitive," said Murke.

The Director conscientiously read every letter from a listener. The one he was reading at this particular moment went as follows:

Dear Radio,

I am sure you can have no more faithful listener than myself. I am an old woman, a little old lady of seventy-seven, and I have been listening to you every day for thirty years. I have never been sparing with my praise. Perhaps you remember my letter about the program "The Seven Souls of Kaweida the Cow." It was a lovely program— but now I have to be angry with you! The way the canine soul is being neglected in radio is gradually becoming a disgrace. And you call that humanism. I am sure Hitler had his bad points: if one is to believe all one hears, he was a dreadful man, but one thing he did have: a real affection for dogs, and he did a lot for them. When are dogs going to come into their own again in German radio? The way you tried to do it in the program "Like Cat and Dog" is certainly not the right one: it was an insult to every canine soul. If my little Lohengrin could only talk, he'd tell you! And the way he barked, poor darling, all through your terrible program, it almost made me die of shame. I pay my two marks a month like any other listener and stand on my rights and demand to know: When are dogs going to come into their own again in German radio?

With kind regards—in spite of my being so cross with you,
Sincerely yours,
Jadwiga Herchen (retired)

P.S. In case none of those cynics of yours who run your programs should be capable of doing justice to the canine soul, I suggest you make use of my modest attempts, which are enclosed herewith. I do not wish to accept any fee. You may send it direct to the SPCA. Enclosed: 35 manuscripts.

Yours,
J.H.

The director sighed. He looked for the scripts, but his secretary had evidently filed them away. The director filled his pipe, lit it, ran his tongue over his dynamic lips, lifted the receiver, and asked to be put through to Krochy. Krochy had a tiny office with a tiny desk, although in the best of taste, upstairs in Culture and was in charge of a section as narrow as his desk: Animals in the World of Culture.

"Krochy speaking," he said diffidently into the telephone.

"Say, Krochy," said the director, "when was the last time we had a program about dogs?"

"Dogs, sir?" said Krochy. "I don't believe we ever have, at least not since I've been here."

"And how long have you been here, Krochy?" And upstairs in his office Krochy trembled, because the director's voice was so gentle; he knew it boded no good when that voice became gentle.

"I've been here ten years now, sir," said Krochy.

"It's a disgrace," said the director, "that you've never had a program about dogs; after all, that's your department. What was the title of your last program?"

"The title of my last program was—" stammered Krochy.

"You don't have to repeat every sentence," said the director, "we're not in the army."

"'Owls in the Ruins,'" said Krochy timidly.

"Within the next three weeks," said the director, gentle again now, "I would like to hear a program about the canine soul."

"Certainly, sir," said Krochy. He heard the click as the director put down the receiver, sighed deeply, and said, "Oh God!"

The director picked up the next letter.

At this moment Bur-Malottke entered the room. He was always at liberty to enter unannounced, and he made frequent use of this liberty. He was still sweating as he sank wearily into a chair opposite the director and said, "Well, good morning."

"Good morning," said the director, pushing the letter aside. "What can I do for you?"

"Could you give me one minute?"

"Bur-Malottke," said the director, with a generous, dynamic gesture, "does not have to ask me for one minute; hours, days, ate at your disposal." "No," said Bur-Malottke, "I don't mean an ordinary minute, I mean one minute of radio time. Due to the changes, my talk has become one minute longer."

The director grew serious, like a satrap distributing provinces. "I hope," he said sourly, "it's not a political minute."

"No," said Bur-Malottke, "it's half a minute of 'Neighborly News' and half a minute of Light Entertainment."

"Thank God for that," said the director. "I've got a credit of seventy-nine seconds with Light Entertainment and eighty-three seconds with 'Neighborly News.' I'll be glad to let someone like Bur-Malottke have one minute."

"I am overcome," said Bur-Malottke.

"Is there anything else I can do for you?" asked the director.

"I would appreciate it," said Bur-Malottke, "if we could gradually start correcting all the tapes I have made since 1945. One day," he said—he passed his hand over his forehead and gazed wistfully at the genuine Kokoschka above the director's desk—"one day I shall"—he faltered, for the news he was about to break to the director was too painful for posterity—"one day I shall . . . die," and he paused again, giving the director a chance to look gravely shocked and raise his hand in protest, "and I cannot bear the thought that after my death, tapes may be run off on which I say things I no longer believe in. Particularly in some of my political utterances, during the fervor of 1945, I let myself be persuaded to make statements which today fill me with serious misgivings and which I can only account for on the basis of that spirit of youthfulness that has always distinguished my work. My written works are already in process of being corrected, and I would like to ask you to give me the opportunity of correcting my spoken works as well."

The director was silent; he cleared his throat slightly, and little shining beads of sweat appeared on his forehead. It occurred to him that Bur-Malottke had spoken for at least an hour every month since 1945, and he made a swift calculation while Bur-Malottke went on talking: twelve times ten hours meant one hundred and twenty hours of spoken Bur-Malottke.

"Pedantry," Bur-Malottke was saying, "is something that only impure spirits regard as unworthy of genius; we know, of course"—and the director felt flattered to be ranked by the We among the pure spirits—"that the true geniuses, the great geniuses, were pedants. Himmelsheim once had a whole printed edition of his Seelon rebound at his own expense because he felt that three or four sentences in the central portion of the work were no longer appropriate. The idea that some of my talks might be broadcast which no longer correspond to my convictions when I depart this earthly life—I find such an idea intolerable. How do you propose we go about it?"

The beads of sweat on the director's forehead had become larger. "First of all," he said in a subdued voice, "an exact list would have to be made of all your broadcast talks, and then we would have to check in the archives to see if all the tapes were still there."

"I should hope," said Bur-Malottke, "that none of the tapes has been erased without notifying me. I have not been notified, therefore no tapes have been erased."

"I will see to everything," said the director.

"Please do," said Bur-Malottke curtly, and rose from his chair. "Good-bye."

"Good-bye," said the director as he accompanied Bur-Malottke to the door.

The Freelancers in the coffeeshop had decided to order lunch. They had had some more drinks, they were still talking about art, their conversation was quieter now but no less intense. They all jumped to their feet when Wanderburn suddenly came in. Wanderburn was a tall, despondent-looking writer with dark hair, an attractive face somewhat etched by the stigma of fame. On this particular morning he had not shaved, which made him look even more attractive. He walked over to the table where the three men were sitting, sank exhausted into a chair, and said, "For God's sake, give me a drink. I always have the feeling in this building that I'm dying of thirst."

They passed him a drink, a glass that was still standing on the table, and the remains of a bottle of soda water. Wanderburn swallowed the drink, put down his glass, looked at each of the three men in turn, and said, "I must warn you about the radio business, about this pile of junk—this immaculate, shiny, slippery pile of junk. I'm warning you. It'll destroy us all." His warning was sincere and impressed the three young men very much; but the three young men did not know that Wanderbum had just come from the accounting department, where he had picked up a nice fat fee for a quick job of editing the Book of Job.

"They cut us," said Wanderburn, "they consume our substance, splice us together again, and it'll be more than any of us can stand."

He finished the soda water, put the glass down on the table, and, his coat flapping despondently about him, strode to the door.

On the dot of noon Murke finished the splicing. They had just stuck in the last snippet, a genitive, when Murke got up. He already had his hand on the doorknob when the technician said, "I wish I could afford a sensitive and expensive conscience like that. What'll we do with the box?" He pointed to the flat tin lying on the shelf next to the cardboard boxes containing the new tapes.

"Just leave it there," said Murke.

"What for?" "We might need it again."

"D'you think he might get pangs of conscience allover again?"

"He might," said Murke. "We'd better wait and see. So long."
He walked to the front paternoster, rode down to the second floor, and for the first time that day entered his office. His secretary had gone to lunch; Murke's boss, Humkoke, was sitting by the phone reading a book. He smiled at Murke, got up, and said, "Well, I see you survived. Is this your book? Did you put it on the desk?" He held it out for Murke to read the title, and Murke said, "Yes, that's mine." The book had a jacket of green, gray, and orange and was called Batley's Lyrics of the Gutter; it was about a young English writer a hundred years ago who had drawn up a catalogue of London slang.

"It's a marvelous book," said Murke.

"Yes," said Humkoke, "it is marvelous, but you never learn."

Murke eyed him questioningly.

"You never learn that one doesn't leave marvelous books lying around when Wanderburn is liable to turn up, and Wanderburn is always liable to turn up. He saw it at once, of course, opened it, read it for five minutes, and what's the result?"

Murke said nothing.

"The result," said Humkoke, "is two hour-long broadcasts by Wanderburn on 'Lyrics of the Gutter.' One day this fellow will do a feature about his own grandmother, and the worst of it is that one of his grandmothers was one of mine too. Please, Murke, try to remember: never leave marvelous books around when Wanderburn is liable to turn up, and, I repeat, he's always liable to turn up. That's all, you can go now, you've got the afternoon off, and I'm sure you've earned it. Is the stuff ready? Did you hear it through again?"

"It's all done," said Murke, "but I can't hear the talks through again, I simply can't."

"'I simply can't' is a very childish thing to say," said Humkoke.

"If I have to hear the word 'art' one more time today, I'll become hysterical," said Murke.

"You already are," said Humkoke, "and I must say you've every reason to be. Three hours of Bur-Malottke—that's too much for anybody, even the toughest of us, and you're not even tough." He threw the book on the table, took a step toward Murke, and said, "When I was your age I once had to cut three minutes out of a four-hour speech of Hitler's, and I had to listen to the speech three times before I was considered worthy of suggesting which three minutes should be cut. When I began listening to the tape for the first time I was still a Nazi, but by the time I had heard the speech for the third time I wasn't a Nazi any more. It was a drastic cure—a terrible one, but very effective."

"You forget," said Murke quietly, "that I had already been cured of Bur-Malottke before I had to listen to his tapes."

"You really are a vicious beast!" said Humkoke with a laugh. "That'll do for now. The director is going to hear it through again at two. Just see that you're available in case anything goes wrong."

"I'll be home from two to three," said Murke.

"One more thing," said Humkoke, pulling out a yellow biscuit tin from a shelf next to Murke's desk. "What's this scrap you've got here?"

Murke colored. "It's . . ." he stammered, "I collect a certain kind of leftovers."

"What kind of leftovers?" asked Humkoke.

"Silences, said Murke. I collect silences."

Humkoke raised his eyebrows, and Murke went on, "When I have to cut tapes, in the places where the speakers sometimes pause for a moment—or sigh, or take a breath, or there is absolute silence—I don't throw that away, I collect it. Incidentally, there wasn't a single second of silence in Bur-Malottke's tapes."

Humkoke laughed. "Of course not, he would never be silent. And what do you do with the scrap?"

"I splice it together and play back the tape when I'm at home in the evening. There's not much yet, I only have three minutes so far—but then people aren't silent very often."

"You know, don't you, that it's against regulations to take home sections of tape?"

"Even silences?" asked Murke.

Humkoke laughed and said, "For God's sake, get out!" And Murke left.

When the director entered his studio a few minutes after two, the Bur-Malottke tape had just been turned on:

... and wherever, however, why ever, and whenever we begin to discuss the Nature of Art, we must first look to that higher Being Whom we revere, we must bow in awe before that higher Being Whom we revere, and we must accept Art as a gift from that higher Being Whom we revere. Art ...

No, thought the director, I really can't ask anyone to listen to Bur-Malottke for a hundred and twenty hours. No, he thought, there are some things one simply cannot do, things I wouldn't want to wish even on Murke. He returned to his office and switched on the loudspeaker just in time to hear Bur-Malottke say, "O Thou higher Being Whom we revere. . . ." No, thought the director, no, no.

Murke lay on his chesterfield at home smoking. Next to him on a chair was a cup of tea, and Murke was gazing at the white ceiling of the room. Sitting at his desk was a very pretty blonde who was staring out of the window at the street. Between Murke and the girl, on a low coffee table, stood a tape recorder, recording. Not a word was spoken, not a sound was made. The girl was pretty and silent enough for a photographer's model.

"I can't stand it," said the girl suddenly. "I can't stand it, it's in-human, what you want me to do. There are some men who expect a girl to do immoral things, but it seems to me that what you are asking me to do is even more immoral than the things other men expect a girl to do."

Murke sighed. "Oh hell," he said, "Rina dear, now I've got to cut all that out; do be sensible, be a good girl, and put just five more minutes' silence on the tape."

"Put silence," said the girl, with what thirty years ago would have been called a pout. "Put silence, that's another of your inventions. I wouldn't mind putting words onto a tape—but putting silence. . . ."

Murke had got up and switched off the tape recorder. "Oh, Rina," he said, "if you only knew how precious your silence is to me. In the evening, when I'm tired, when I'm sitting here alone, I play back your silence. Do be a dear and put just three more minutes' silence on the tape for me and save me the cutting; you know how I feel about cutting."

"Oh, all right," said the girl, "but give me a cigarette at least."

Murke smiled, gave her a cigarette, and said, "This way I have your silence in the original and on tape, that's terrific." He switched the tape on again, and they sat facing one another in silence till the telephone rang. Murke got up, shrugged helplessly, and lifted the receiver.

"Well," said Humkoke, "the tapes ran off smoothly, the boss couldn't find a thing wrong with them. . . . You can go to the movies now. And think about snow."

"What snow?" asked Murke, looking out onto the street, which lay basking in brilliant summer sunshine.

"Come on, now," said Humkoke, "you know we have to start thinking about the winter programs. I need songs about snow, stories about snow—we can't fool around for the rest of our lives with Schubert and Stifter. No one seems to have any idea how badly we need snow songs and snow stories. Just imagine if we have a long hard winter with lots of snow and freezing temperatures: where are we going to get our snow programs from? Try to think of something snowy."

"All right," said Murke, "I'll try to think of something." Humkokc had hung up.

"Come along," he said to the girl, "we can go to the movies."

"May I speak again now?" said the girl.

"Yes," said Murke, "Speak!"

It was just at this time that the assistant drama producer had finished listening again to the one-act play scheduled for that evening.

He liked it, only the ending did not satisfy him. He was sitting in the glass booth in Studio 13 next to the technician, chewing a match and studying the script.

(Sound effects of a large empty church)

Atheist (in a loud clear voice): who will remember me when I have become the prey of worms?

(Silence)

Atheist (his voice a shade louder): Who will wait for me when I have turned into dust?

(Silence)

Atheist (louder still): And who will remember me when I have turned into leaves?

(Silence)

There were twelve such questions called out by the atheist into the church, and each question was followed by—? Silence.

The assistant producer removed the chewed match from his lips, replaced it with a fresh one, and looked at the technician, a question in his eyes.

"Yes," said the technician, "if you ask me, I think there's a bit too much silence in it."

"That's what I thought," said the assistant producer; "the author thinks so too and he's given me leave to change it. There should just be a voice saying 'God'—but it ought to be a voice without church sound effects, it would have to be spoken somehow in a different acoustical environment. Have you any idea where I can get hold of a voice like that at this hour?"

The technician smiled, picked up the metal container which was still lying on the shelf "Here you are," he said, "here's a voice saying 'God' without any sound effects."

The assistant producer was so surprised he almost swallowed the match, choked a little, and got it up into the front of his mouth again. "It's quite all right," the technician said with a smile. "We had to cut it out of a talk, twenty-seven times."

"I don't need it that often, just twelve times," said the assistant producer.

"It's a simple matter, of course," said the technician, "to cut out the silence and stick in 'God' twelve times—if you'll take the responsibility."

"You're a godsend," said the assistant producer, "and I'll be responsible. Come on, let's get started." He gazed happily at the tiny, lusterless tape snippets in Murke's tin box. "you really are a godsend," he said. "Come on, let's go!"

The technician smiled, for he was looking forward to being able to present Murke with the snippets of silence: it was a lot of silence, all together nearly a minute; it was more silence than he had ever been able to give Murke, and he liked the young man.

"OK," he said with a smile, "here we go."

The assistant producer put his hand in his jacket pocket, took out a pack of cigarettes; in doing so he touched a crumpled piece of paper. He smoothed it out and passed it to the technician. "Funny, isn't it, the corny stuff you can come across in this place? I found this stuck in my door."

The technician took the picture, looked at it, and said, "Yes, it's funny," and he read out the words under the picture:

"I prayed for you at St. James's Church."

Translated by Leila Vennewitz

Action Will Be Taken: An Action-Packed Story

Probably one of the strangest interludes in my life was the time I spent as an employee in Alfred Wunsiedel's factory. By nature I am inclined more to pensiveness and inactivity than to work, but now and again prolonged financial difficulties compel me—for pensiveness is no more profitable than inactivity—to take on a so-called job. Finding myself once again at a low ebb of this kind, I put myself in the hands of the employment office and was sent with seven other fellow-sufferers to Wunsiedel's factory, where we were to undergo an aptitude test.

The exterior of the factory was enough to arouse my suspicions: the factory was built entirely of glass brick, and my aversion to well-lit buildings and well-lit rooms is as strong as my aversion to work. I became even more suspicious when we were immediately served breakfast in the well-lit, cheerful coffee shop: pretty waitresses brought us eggs, coffee and toast, orange juice was served in tastefully designed jugs, goldfish pressed their bored faces against the sides of pale-green aquariums. The waitresses were so cheerful that they appeared to be bursting with good cheer. Only a strong effort of will—so it seemed to me—restrained them from singing away all day long. They were as crammed with unsung songs as chickens with unlaid eggs.

Right away I realized something that my fellow-sufferers evidently failed to realize: that this breakfast was already part of the test; so I chewed away reverently, with the full appreciation of a person who knows he is supplying his body with valuable elements. I did something which normally no power on earth can make me do: I drank orange juice on an empty stomach, left the coffee and egg untouched, as well as most of the toast, got up, and paced up and down in the coffee shop, pregnant with action.

As a result I was the first to be ushered into the room where the questionnaires were spread out on attractive tables. The walls were done in a shade of green that would have summoned the word "delightful" to the lips of interior decoration enthusiasts. The room appeared to be empty, and yet I was so sure of being observed that I behaved as someone pregnant with action behaves when he believes himself unobserved: I ripped my pen impatiently from my pocket, unscrewed the top, sat down at the nearest table and pulled the questionnaire toward me, the way irritable customers snatch at the bill in a restaurant.

Question No. 1: Do you consider it right for a human being to possess only two arms, two legs, eyes, and ears?

Here for the first time I reaped the harvest of my pensive nature and wrote without hesitation: "Even four arms, legs and ears would not be adequate for my driving energy. Human beings are very poorly equipped."

Question No. 2: How many telephones can you handle at one time?

Here again the answer was as easy as simple arithmetic: "When there are only seven telephones," I wrote, "I get impatient; there have to be nine before I feel I am working to capacity."

Question No. 3: How do you spend your free time?

My answer: "I no longer acknowledge the term free time—on my fifteenth birthday I eliminated it from my vocabulary, for in the beginning was the act."

I got the job. Even with nine telephones I really didn't feel I was working to capacity. I shouted into the mouth-pieces: "Take immediate action!" or: "Do something!—We must have some action— Action will be taken—Action has been taken—Action should be taken." But as a rule—for I felt this was in keeping with the tone of the place—I used the imperative.

Of considerable interest were the noon-hour breaks, when we consumed nutritious foods in an atmosphere of silent good cheer. Wunsiedel's factory was swarming with people who were obsessed with telling you the story of their lives, as indeed vigorous personalities are fond of doing. The story of their lives is more important to them than their lives, you have only to press a button, and immediately it is covered with spewed-out exploits.

Wunsiedel had a right-hand man called Broschek, who had in turn made a name for himself by supporting seven children and a paralyzed wife by working night-shifts in his student days, and successfully carrying on four business agencies, besides which he had passed two examinations with honors in two years. When asked by reporters: "When do you sleep, Mr. Broscheck?" he had replied: "It's a crime to sleep!"

Wunsiedel's secretary had supported a paralyzed husband and four children by knitting, at the same time graduating in psychology and German history as well as breeding shepherd dogs, and she had become famous as a night-club singer where she was known as Vamp Number Seven.

Wunsiedel himself was one of those people who every morning, as they open their eyes, make up their minds to act. "I must act," they think as they briskly tie their bathrobe belts around them. "I must act," they think as they shave, triumphantly watching their beard hairs being washed away with the lather: these hirsute vestiges are the first daily sacrifices to their driving energy. The more intimate functions also give these people a sense of satisfaction: water swishes, paper is used. Action has been taken. Bread gets eaten, eggs are decapitated.

With Wunsiedel, the most trivial activity looked like action: the way he put on his hat, the way—quivering with energy—he buttoned up his overcoat, the kiss he gave his wife, everything was action.

When he arrived at his office he greeted his secretary with a cry of "Let's have some action!" And in ringing tones she would call back: "Action will be taken!" Wunsiedel then went from department to department, calling out his cheerful: "Let's have some action!" Everyone would answer: "Action will be taken!" And I would call back to him too, with a radiant smile, when he looked into my office: "Action will be taken!"

Within a week I had increased the number of telephones on my desk to eleven, within two weeks to thirteen, and every morning on the streetcar I enjoyed thinking up new imperatives, or chasing the words take action through various tenses and modulations: for two whole days I kept saying the same sentence over and over again because I thought it sounded so marvelous: "Action ought to have been taken;" for another two days it was: "Such action ought not to have been taken."

So I was really beginning to feel I was working to capacity when there actually was some action. One Tuesday morning—I had hardly settled down at my desk—Wunsiedel rushed into my office crying his "Let's have some action!" But an inexplicable something in his face made me hesitate to reply, in a cheerful gay voice as the rules dictated: "Action will be taken!" I must have paused too long, for Wunsiedel, who seldom raised his voice, shouted at me: "Answer! Answer, you know the rules!" And I answered, under my breath, reluctantly, like a child who is forced to say: I am a naughty child. It was only by a great effort that I managed to bring out the sentence: "Action will be taken," and hardly had I uttered it when there really was some action: Wunsiedel dropped to the floor. As he fell he rolled over onto his side and lay right across the open doorway. I knew at once, and I confirmed it when I went slowly around my desk and approached the body on the floor: he was dead.

Shaking my head I stepped over Wunsiedel, walked slowly along the corridor to Broschek's office, and entered without knocking. Broschek was sitting at his desk, a telephone receiver in each hand, between his teeth a ballpoint pen with which he was making notes on a writing pad, while with his bare feet he was operating a knitting machine under the desk. In this way he helps to clothe his family. "We've had some action," I said in a low voice.

Broschek spat out the ballpoint pen, put down the two receivers, reluctantly detached his toes from the knitting machine.

"What action?" he asked.

"Wunsiedel is dead," I said.

"No," said Broschek.

"Yes," I said, "come and have a look!"

"No," said Broschek, "that's impossible," but he put on his slippers and followed me along the corridor.

"No," he said, when we stood beside Wunsiedel's corpse, "no, no!" I did not contradict him. I carefully turned Wunsiedel over onto his back, closed his eyes, and looked at him pensively.

I felt something like tenderness for him, and realized for the first time that I had never hated him. On his face was that expression which one sees on children who obstinately refuse to give up their faith in Santa Claus, even though the arguments of their playmates sound so convincing.

"No," said Broschek, "no."

"We must take action," I said quietly to Broschek. "Yes," said Broschek, "we must take action."

Action was taken: Wunsiedel was buried, and I was delegated to carry a wreath of artificial roses behind his coffin, for I am equipped with not only a penchant for pensiveness and inactivity but also a face and figure that go extremely well with dark suits. Apparently as I walked along behind Wunsiedel's coffin carrying the wreath of artificial roses I looked superb. I received an offer from a fashionable firm of funeral directors to join their staff as a professional mourner. "You are a born mourner," said the manager, "your outfit would be provided by the firm. Your face—simply superb!"

I handed in my notice to Broschek, explaining that I had never really felt I was working to capacity there; that, in spite of the thirteen telephones, some of my talents were going to waste. As soon as my first professional appearance as a mourner was over I knew: This is where I belong, this is what I am cut out for.

Pensively I stand behind the coffin in the funeral chapel, holding a simple bouquet, while the organ plays Handel's Largo, a piece that does not receive nearly the respect it deserves. The cemetery café is my regular haunt; there I spend the intervals between my professional engagements, although sometimes I walk behind coffins which I have not been engaged to follow, I pay for flowers out of my own pocket and join the welfare worker who walks behind the coffin of some homeless person. From time to time I also visit Wunsiedel's grave, for after all I owe it to him that I discovered my true vocation, a vocation in which pensiveness is essential and inactivity my duty.

It was not till much later that I realized I had never bothered to find out what was being produced in Wunsiedel's factory. I expect it was soap.

Translated by Leila Vennewitz

Bonn Diary

Monday

Unfortunately I arrived too late to go out again or pay any calls; it was 2330 hours when I got to the hotel, and I was tired. So I had to be satisfied with looking out of the hotel window at the city lying there scintillating with life—bubbling, throbbing, boiling over, one might say: there are vital forces hidden there just waiting to be released. The city is still not all it might be. I smoked a cigar, abandoning myself wholly to this fascinating electric energy; I wondered whether I should phone Inna, finally resigned myself with a sigh and had one more look through my important files. Toward midnight I went to bed: I always find it hard to go to bed here. This city is not conducive to sleep.

Night jottings

Strange dream, very strange: I was walking through a forest of monuments, straight rows of them; in little clearings there were miniature parks, each with a monument in the center; all the monuments were alike, hundreds, thousands of them: a man standing "at ease," an officer to judge by the creases in his soft boots, yet the chest, face and pedestal of each monument were covered with a cloth—suddenly all the monuments were unveiled simultaneously, and I realized, without any particular surprise, that I was the man standing on the pedestal; I shifted my position on the pedestal, smiled, and now that the covering had dropped off I could read my name thousands of times over: Erick van Mackarka-Muff I laughed, and the laugh echoed back to me a thousand times from my own mouth.

Tuesday

Filled with a deep sense of happiness, I fell asleep again, woke refreshed, and laughed as I looked at myself in the mirror: it is only here in the capital that one has dreams like that. Before I had finished shaving, the first call from Inna. (That's what I call my old friend Inniga von Schekel-Pehnunz, a member of the new nobility but an old family: her father, Ernst von Schekel, was raised to the aristocracy by Wilhelm II only two days before the latter abdicated, but I have no qualms about regarding Inna as a friend of equal rank.)

On the phone Inna was—as always—sweet, managed to squeeze in some gossip and in her own way gave me to understand that the project which was the main reason for my visit to the capital was coming along very well. "The corn is ripe," she said softly, and then, barely pausing: "The baby's being christened today." She hung up quickly, to prevent me from asking questions in my impatience. Deep in thought I went down to the breakfast room: had she really meant the laying of the foundation stone? My frank, forthright soldierly nature still has difficulty understanding Inna's cryptic remarks.

Again in the breakfast room this abundance of virile faces, most of them well-bred: I passed the time by imagining which man would be suitable for which post, an old habit of mine; before I had even shelled my egg I had already found first-rate material for two regimental staffs and one divisional staff, and there were still some candidates left over for the general staff; playing games in my head, so to speak—just the thing for a veteran observer of human nature like myself. The memory of my dream enhanced my pleasant mood: strange, to walk through a forest of monuments and to see oneself on every pedestal. I wonder whether the psychologists have really plumbed all the depths of the self?

I ordered my coffee to be brought to the lobby, smoked a cigar and observed the time with a smile: 0956 hours—would Heffling be punctual? I had not seen him for six years, we had corresponded occasionally (the usual exchange of post cards one has with inferiors in the ranks)

I actually found myself feeling nervous about Heffling's punctuality; the trouble with me is, I am inclined to regard everything as symptomatic: Heffling's punctuality became for me the punctuality per se of the ranks. I remembered with a touch of emotion what my old divisional chief, Welk von Schnomm, used to say: "Macho, you are and always will be an idealist."

(Memo: renew the standing order for upkeep of Schnomm's grave.)

Am I an idealist? I fell into a reverie, until Heffling's voice roused me: I looked first at the time—two minutes after ten (I have always allowed him this microscopic reserve of privilege)—then at him: how fat the fellow's got, grossly fat around the neck, hair getting thin, but still that phallic sparkle in his eyes, and his "Present, Colonel!" sounded just like old times. "Heffling!" I cried, slapping him on the shoulder and ordering a double schnapps for him. He stood at attention as he took the drink from the waiter's tray; I drew him by the sleeve over to the corner, and we were soon deep in reminiscences: "Remember the time at Schwichi-Schwalo-che, the ninth. . . .

It is heart-warming to observe how powerless the vagaries of fashion are to corrode the wholesome spirit of the people: the homespun virtues, the hearty male laugh, and the never-failing readiness to share a good dirty story, are still to be found. While Heffling was telling me some variations of the familiar subject in an undertone, I noticed Murcks-Maloche had entered the lobby and—without speaking to me, as arranged—had disappeared into the rear of the restaurant. By a glance at my wristwatch I indicated to Heffling that I was pressed for time, and with the sound instincts of the simple man he understood immediately that he had to leave. "Come and see us some time, Colonel, my wife would be delighted." Laughing and joking we walked side by side to the porter's desk, and I promised Heffling I would come and see him. Perhaps an opportunity would offer for a little adventure with his wife; every now and again I feel the urge to partake of the husky eroticism of the lower classes, and one never knows what arrows Cupid may be holding in store in his quiver.

I sat down beside Murcks, ordered some Hennessy and, as soon as the waiter had gone, said in my straightforward fashion:

"Well, fire away."

"Yes, we've made it." He laid his hand on mine and whispered: "I'm so glad, Macho, so glad."

"I'm pleased too," I said warmly, "that one of the dreams of my youth has come to pass. And in a democracy too."

"A democracy in which we have the majority of Parliament on our side is a great deal better than a dictatorship."

I felt constrained to stand up; I was filled with solemn pride; historic moments have always moved me deeply.

"Murcks," I said, choking back the tears, "is it really true then?"

"It's true, Macho," he said.

"It's all settled?"

"It's all settled—you're to give the dedication address today. The first course of instruction is starting right away. Those enrolled are still being put up in hotels, till the project can be officially declared open."

"Will the public—will it swallow it?"

"It'll swallow it—the public will swallow anything," said Murcks.

"On your feet, Murcks," I said, "let's drink a toast, let's drink to the spirit to which this building is dedicated: to the spirit of military memories."

We clinked glasses and drank.

I was too moved to undertake any serious business that morning; I went restlessly up to my room, from there to the lobby, wandered through this enchanting city, after Murcks had driven off to the Ministry. Although I was in civilians, I had the impression of a sword dangling at my side; there are some sensations which are really only appropriate when one is in uniform. Once again, while I was strolling through the city, looking forward to my tête-à-tête with Inna, uplifted by the certainty that my plan had become reality—once again I had every reason to recall one of Schnomm's expressions: "Macho, Macho," he used to say, "you've always got your head in the clouds." He had said it when there were only thirteen men left in my regiment and I had four of those men shot for mutiny.

In honor of the occasion I permitted myself an aperitif at a café not far from the station; I looked through some newspapers, glanced at a few editorials on defense policy, and tried to imagine what Schnomm—if he were still alive—would have said had he read the articles. "Those Christians—" he would have said, "who would have thought it of them!"

At last it was time to go to the hotel and change for my rendez-vous with Inna: her signal on the car horn—a Beethoven motif—made me look out of the window; she waved up at me from her lemon-yellow car: lemon-yellow hair, lemon-yellow dress, black gloves. With a sigh, after blowing her a kiss, I went to the mirror, tied my tie, and went downstairs; Inna would be the right wife for me, but she has been divorced seven times and, not unnaturally, is skeptical about the institution of marriage; besides, we are separated by a deep gulf in background and outlook: she comes from a strict Protestant family, I from a strict Catholic one—all the same, numbers link us together symbolically: she has been divorced seven times, I have been wounded seven times. Inna!! I still can't quite get used to being kissed on the street. . . .

Inna woke me at 1617 hours: she had some strong tea and ginger biscuits ready, and we quickly went once more through the files on Hürlanger-Hiss, the unforgotten field marshal to whose memory we planned to dedicate the building.

While I was examining the Hürlanger files once more, my arm around Inna's shoulder, lost in daydreams of her gift of love, I heard the band music: melancholy overtook me, for, like all the other experiences of this day, to listen to this music in civilian clothes was truly an ordeal.

The band music and Inna's nearness diverted my attention from the files; however, Inna had filled me in verbally so that I was fully equipped to give my speech. The doorbell rang as Inna was pouring out my second cup of tea; I jumped, but Inna smiled reassuringly. "An important guest," she said, returning from the hall, "a guest whom we cannot possibly receive in here." There was a twinkle in her eye as she gestured toward the rumpled bed in all its delightful disarray of love. "Come along," she said. I got out of bed, followed her in a kind of daze, and was genuinely surprised to find myself face to face in her living room with the Minister of Defense. His frank, rugged countenance was shining. "General von Machorka-Muff," he said, with a beaming smile, "welcome to the capital!"

I could not believe my ears. With a twinkle in his eye the Minister handed me my commission.

I think, looking back, I must have swayed for a moment and suppressed a few tears; but actually I am not quite sure what was going on inside me; all I remember is hearing myself say: "But Your Excellency—the uniform—half an hour before the ceremony starts. . . ." With a twinkle in his eye—what an admirable man he is, what sterling qualities!—he glanced at Inna, Inna twinkled back at him, drew aside a chintz curtain dividing off one corner of the room, and there it was, there hung my uniform, with all my decorations on it.

. . . Events, emotions followed so thick and fast that looking back all I can do is give their sequence in note-form:

We offered the Minister some refreshment and he had a glass of beer while I changed in Inna's room.

Drive to the building site, which I was viewing for the first time: I was extraordinarily moved by the sight of this piece of land on which my pet project is to become reality: the Academy for Military Memoirs, where every veteran from the rank of major up is to be given the opportunity of committing his reminiscences to paper, through conversations with old comrades and cooperation with the Ministry's Department of Military History; my own feeling is that a six-week course should suffice, but Parliament is willing to subsidize a three-month course. I was also thinking of having a few healthy working-class girls housed in a special wing, to sweeten the evening leisure hours of the comrades who are plagued with memories. I have gone to a great deal of trouble to find appropriate inscriptions. The main wing is to bear in gold lettering the inscription: ME-MORIA DEXTERA EST; while over the girls' wing, which will also contain the bathrooms, will be the words: BALNEUM ET AMOR MARTIS DECOR. However, on the way there the Minister hinted that I should not mention this part of my plan just yet; he was afraid—perhaps rightly so—of opposition from some of his fellow members of Parliament, although—as he put it with a chuckle—no one could complain of lack of liberalization!

There were flags all around the building site, the band was playing: I used to have a comrade, as I walked beside the Minister toward the platform. Since with his usual modesty the Minister de-

clined to open proceedings, I stepped up at once onto the dais, sur-
veyed the row of assembled comrades, and, encouraged by a wink
from Inna, began to speak:

"Your Excellency, comrades! This building, which *is* to bear the
name Hürlanger-Hiss Academy for Military Memoirs, needs no
justification. But a justification is required for the name Hürlanger-
Hiss, a name which for many years—to this very day, I would say—
has been regarded as dishonored. You all know the disgrace attach-
ing to this name: when the army of Field Marshal Emil von
Hürlanger-Hiss was obliged to retreat at Schwichi-Schwaloche,
Hürlanger-Hiss could report a loss of only 8,500 men. According
to the calculations of Tapir's specialists in retreat—Tapir, as you
know, was our private name for Hitler—his army should, with the
proper fighting spirit, have had a loss of 12,300 men. You are also
aware, Your Excellency and comrades, of the insulting treatment to
which Hürlanger-Hiss was subjected: he was transferred in disgrace
to Biarritz, where he died of lobster poisoning. For years—a total
of four-teen years—this dishonor has attached to his name. All the
data on Hürlanger army fell into the hands of Tapir's underlings,
later into the hands of the Allies, but today, today," I cried, pausing
so as to let my next words sink in, "today it can be taken as a
proven fact, and I am prepared to make the material public, it can
be taken as proven fact that our great Field Marshal's army suffered
losses at Schwichi-Schwaloche of a total of 14,700 men: it can
therefore be assumed beyond any doubt that his army fought with
unexampled courage, and his name is now cleared of all blemish."

While I let the deafening applause pour over me and modestly
diverted the ovation from myself to the Minister, I had a chance to
observe from the faces of my comrades that they too were surprised
by this information; how discreetly Inna had carried on her
research!

To the strains of See'st thou the dawn in eastern skies I took the
trowel and stone from the mason and set the cornerstone in place;
it contained a photograph of Hürlanger-Hiss together with one of
his shoulder-straps.

At the head of my comrades I marched from the building site to
the villa, "The Golden Shekel," which Inna's family has put at our
disposal until the academy has been completed. Here we had a
brisk round of drinks, a word of thanks from the Minister, and a

telegram from the Chancellor was read out, before the social hour began.

The social hour was opened by a concerto for seven drums, played by seven former generals; with the consent of the composer, a captain with musical aspirations, it was announced that it would be known as the Hürlanger-Hiss Memorial Septet. The social hour was an unqualified success: songs were sung, stories told, confidences exchanged, old quarrels forgotten.

Wednesday

We had just an hour to get ready for the church service; in relaxed marching order we made our way just before 0730 hours to the cathedral. Inna stood beside me in church, and I felt encouraged when she whispered that she recognized a colonel as her second husband, a lieutenant-colonel as her fifth, and a captain as her sixth. "And your eighth," I whispered in her ear, "will be a general." My mind was made up; Inna blushed; she did not hesitate when after it was over I took her into the vestry to introduce her to the prelate who had conducted the service. "Indeed, my dear child," the priest said, after we had discussed the church's position, "since none of your former marriages was solemnized in church, there is no obstacle to you and General von Machorka. Muff having a church wedding."

It was under these auspices that we had breakfast, in a gay mood, à deux; Inna was elated, I had never seen her quite like that. "I always feel like this," she said, "when I am a bride." I ordered champagne.

We decided to keep our engagement a secret for the time being, but as a little celebration we drove up to the Petersberg, a lovely hill a few miles outside Bonn, where Inna's cousin, whose maiden name was Pelf, had invited us for lunch. Inna's cousin was adorable.

The afternoon and evening were devoted entirely to love, the night to sleep.

Thursday

I still can't quite get used to the idea that I am living and working here; it must be a dream! Gave my first lecture this morning: "Reminiscence as a Historical Duty."

Annoying interlude at midday. Murcks-Maloche came to see me at the villa on behalf of the Minister to report that the opposition had expressed itself dissatisfied with our academy project.

"Opposition?" I asked, "what's that?"

Murcks enlightened me. I was astounded. "Let's get this straight," I said impatiently, "do we have the majority or don't we?"

"We do," said Murcks.

"Well then," I said. Opposition—a strange word, I don't like it at all; it is such a grim reminder of times that I thought were over and done with.

Inna, when I told her at teatime about my annoyance, consoled me.

"Erich," she said, putting her little hand on my arm, "no one has ever opposed our family."

Translated by Leila Vennewitz

When the War Broke Out

I was leaning out of the window, my arms resting on the sill. I had rolled up my shirt sleeves and was looking beyond the main gate and guardroom across to the divisional headquarters telephone exchange, waiting for my friend Leo to give me the prearranged signal: come to the window, take off his cap, and put it on again. Whenever I got the chance I would lean out of the window, my arms on the sill; whenever I got the chance I would call a girl in Cologne and my mother—at army expense—and when Leo came to the window, took off his cap, and put it on again, I would run down to the barrack square and wait in the public callbox till the phone rang.

The other telephone operators sat there bareheaded, in their undershirts, and when they leaned forward to plug in or unplug, or to push up a flap, their identity disks would dangle out of their undershirts and fall back again when they straightened up. Leo was the only one wearing a cap, just so he could take it off to give me the signal. He had a heavy, pink face, very fair hair, and came from Oldenburg. The first expression you noticed on his face was guilelessness; the second was incredible guilelessness, and no one paid enough attention to Leo to notice more than those two expressions; he looked as uninteresting as the boys whose faces appear on advertisements for cheese.

It was hot, afternoon; the alert that had been going on for days had become stale, transforming all time as it passed into stillborn Sunday hours. The barrack square lay there blind and empty and I was glad I could at least keep my head out of the camaraderie of my roommates. Over there the operators were plugging and unplugging, pushing up flaps, wiping off sweat, and Leo was sitting there among them, his cap on his thick fair hair.

All of a sudden I noticed the rhythm of plugging and unplugging had altered; arm movements were no longer routine, mechanical, they became hesitant, and Leo threw his arms up over his head three times: a signal we had not arranged but from which I could tell that something out of the ordinary had happened. Then I saw an operator take his steel helmet from the switchboard and put it on; he looked ridiculous, sitting there sweating in his undershirt, his identity disk dangling, his steel helmet on his head—but I couldn't laugh at him; I realized that putting on a steel helmet meant something like "ready for action," and I was scared.

The ones who had been dozing on their beds behind me in the room got up, lit cigarettes, and formed the two customary groups: three probationary teachers, who were still hoping to be discharged as being "essential to the nation's educational system," resumed their discussion of Ernst Jünger; the other two, an orderly and an office clerk, began discussing the female form; they didn't tell dirty stories, they didn't laugh, they discussed it just as two exceptionally boring geography teachers might have discussed the conceivably interesting topography of the Ruhr valley. Neither subject interested me. Psychologists, those interested in psychology, and those about to complete an adult education course in psychology may be interested to learn that my desire to call the girl in Cologne became more urgent than in previous weeks; I went to my locker, took out my cap, put it on, and leaned out of the window, my arms on the sill, wearing my cap: the signal for Leo that I had to speak to him at once. To show he understood, he waved to me, and I put on my tunic, went out of the room, down the stairs, and stood at the entrance to headquarters, waiting for Leo.

It was hotter than ever, quieter than ever, the barrack squares were even emptier, and nothing has ever approximated my idea of hell as closely as hot, silent, empty barrack squares. Leo came very quickly; he was also wearing his steel helmet now, and was displaying one of his other five expressions that I knew: dangerous for everything he didn't like. This was the face he sat at the switchboard with when he was on evening or night duty, listened in on secret official calls, told me what they were about, suddenly jerked out plugs, cut off secret official calls so as to put through an urgent secret call to Cologne for me to talk to the girl; then it would be my turn to work the switchboard, and Leo would first call his girl in

Oldenburg, then his father; meanwhile Leo would cut thick slices from the ham his mother had sent him, cut these into cubes, and we would eat cubes of ham. When things were slack, Leo would teach me the art of recognizing the caller's rank from the way the flaps fell; at first I thought it was enough to be able to tell the rank simply by the force with which the flap fell—corporal, sergeant, etc—but Leo could tell exactly whether it was an officious corporal or a tired colonel demanding a line; from the way the flap fell, he could even distinguish between angry captains and annoyed lieutenants— nuances that are very hard to tell apart, and as the evening went on, his other expressions made their appearance: fixed hatred; primor- dial malice. With these faces he would suddenly become pedantic, articulate his "Are you still talking?", his "Yessirs," with great care, and with unnerving rapidity switch plugs so as to turn an official call about boots into one about boots and ammunition, and the other call about ammunition into one about ammunition and boots, or the private conversation of a sergeant major with his wife might be suddenly interrupted by a lieutenant's voice saying, "I in- sist the man be punished, I absolutely insist." With lightning speed Leo would then switch the plugs over so that the boot partners were talking about boots again and the others about ammunition, and the sergeant major's wife could resume discussion of her stomach trouble with her husband. When the ham was all gone, Leo's relief had arrived, and we were walking across the silent barrack square to our room, Leo's face would wear its final expression: foolish, in- nocent in a way that had nothing to do with childlike innocence.

Any other time I would have laughed at Leo, standing there wearing his steel helmet, that symbol of inflated importance. He looked past me, across the first, the second barrack square, to the stables; his expressions alternated from three to five, from five to four, and with his final expression he said, "It's war, war, war— they finally made it." I said nothing, and he said, "I guess you want to talk to her?"

"Yes," I said.

"I've already talked to mine," he said. "She's not pregnant. I don't know whether to be glad or not. What d'you think?"

"You can be glad," I said. "I don't think it's a good idea to have kids in wartime."

"General mobilization," he said, "state of alert, this place is soon going to be swarming—and it'll be a long while before you and I can go off on our bikes again." (When we were off duty we used to ride our bikes out into the country, onto the moors, the farmers' wives used to fix us fried eggs and thick slices of bread and butter.) "The first joke of the war has already happened," said Leo. "In view of my special skills and services in connection with the telephone system, I have been made a corporal. Now go over to the public callbox, and if it doesn't ring in three minutes I'll demote myself for incompetence."

In the callbox I leaned against the Münster Area phone book, lit a cigarette, and looked out through a gap in the frosted glass across the barrack square; the only person I could see was a sergeant major's wife, in Block 4, I think. She was watering her geraniums from a yellow jug; I waited, looked at my wristwatch: one minute, two, and I was startled when it actually rang, and even more startled when I immediately heard the voice of the girl in Cologne: "Maybach's Furniture Company." And I said, "Marie, it's war, it's war"—and she said, "No." I said, "yes it is." Then there was silence for half a minute, and she said, "Shall I come?", and before I could say spontaneously, instinctively, "Yes, please do," the voice of what was probably a fairly senior officer shouted, "We need ammunition, and we need it urgently." The girl said, "Are you still there?" The officer yelled, "God damn it!" Meanwhile I had had time to wonder about what it was in the girl's voice that had sounded unfamiliar, ominous almost: her voice had sounded like marriage, and I suddenly knew I didn't feel like marrying her. I said, "We're probably pulling out tonight." The officer yelled, "God damn it, God damn it!" (evidently he couldn't think of anything better to say), the girl said, "I could catch the four o'clock train and be there just before seven," and I said, more quickly than was polite, "It's too late, Marie, too late"—then all I heard was the officer, who seemed to be on the verge of apoplexy. He screamed, "Well, do we get the ammunition or don't we?" And I said in a steely voice (I had learned that from Leo), "No, no, you don't get any ammunition, even if it chokes you." Then I hung up.

It was still daylight when we loaded boots from railway cars onto trucks, but by the time we were loading boots from trucks onto railway cars it was dark, and it was still dark when we loaded boots from railway cars onto trucks again; then it was daylight again, and we loaded bales of hay from trucks onto railway cars, and it was still daylight, and we were still loading bales of hay from trucks onto railway cars; but then it was dark again, and for exactly twice as long as we had loaded bales of hay from trucks onto railway cars, we loaded bales of hay from railway cars onto trucks. At one point a field kitchen arrived, in full combat rig. We were given large helpings of goulash and small helpings of potatoes, and we were given real coffee and cigarettes which we didn't have to pay for; that must have been at night, for I remember hearing a voice say: Real coffee and cigarettes for free, the surest sign of war. I don't remember the face belonging to this voice. It was daylight again when we marched back to barracks, and as we turned into the street leading past the barracks, we met the first battalion going off. It was headed by a marching band playing "Must I Then," followed by the first company, then their armored vehicles, then the second, third, and finally the fourth with the heavy machine guns. On not one face, not one single face, did I see the least sign of enthusiasm. Of course, there were some people standing on the sidewalks, some girls too, but not once did I see anybody stick a bunch of flowers onto a soldier's rifle; there was not even the merest trace of a sign of enthusiasm in the air.

Leo's bed was untouched. I opened his locker (a degree of familiarity with Leo which the probationary teachers, shaking their heads, called "going too far"). Everything was in its place: the photo of the girl in Oldenburg, she was standing, leaning against her bicycle, in front of a birch tree; photos of Leo's parents; their farmhouse. Next to the ham there was a message: "Transferred to area headquarters. In touch with you soon. Take all the ham, I've taken what I need. Leo." I didn't take any of the ham, and closed the locker; I was not hungry, and the rations for two days had been stacked up on the table: bread, cans of liver sausage, butter, cheese, jam, and cigarettes. One of the probationary teachers, the one I liked least, announced that he had been promoted to Pfc and appointed room senior for the period of Leo's absence; he began to distribute the rations. It took a very long time; the only thing I was interested in was the cigarettes, and these he left to the last because he was a nonsmoker. When I finally got the cigarettes, I tore open the pack, lay down on the bed in my clothes, and smoked; I watched the others eating. They spread liver sausage an inch thick on the bread and discussed the "excellent quality of the butter," then they drew the blackout blinds and lay down on their beds. It was very hot, but I didn't feel like undressing. The sun shone into the room through a few cracks, and in one of these strips of light sat the newly promoted PFC sewing on his PFC's chevron. It isn't so easy to sew on a PFC's chevron: it has to be placed at a certain prescribed distance from the seam of the sleeve; moreover, the two open sides of the chevron must be absolutely straight. The probationary teacher had to take off the chevron several times; he sat there for at least two hours, unpicking it, sewing it back on, and he did not appear to be running out of patience. Outside, the band came marching by every forty minutes, and I heard the "Must I Then" from Block 7. Block 2, from Block 9, then from over by the stables—it would come closer, get very loud, then softer again; it took almost exactly three "Must I Thens" for the PFC to sew on his chevron, and it still wasn't quite straight. By that time I had smoked the last of my cigarettes and fell asleep.

That afternoon we didn't have to load either boots from trucks onto railway cars or bales of hay from railway cars onto trucks; we had to help the quartermaster sergeant. He considered himself a genius at organization; he had requisitioned as many assistants as there were items of clothing and equipment on his list, except that for the groundsheets he needed two; he also required a clerk. The two men with the groundsheets went ahead and laid them out, flicking the corners nice and straight, neatly on the cement floor of the stable. As soon as the groundsheets had been spread out, the first man started off by laying two neckties on each groundsheet; the second man, two handkerchiefs; I came next with the mess kits. While all the articles for which, as the sergeant said, size was not a factor were being distributed, he was preparing, with the aid of the more intelligent members of the detachment, the objects for which size was a factor: tunics, boots, trousers, and so on. He had a whole pile of paybooks lying there. He selected the tunics, trousers, and boots according to measurements and weight, and he insisted everything would fit, "unless the bastards have got too fat as civilians." It all had to be done at great speed, in one continuous operation, and it was done at great speed, in one continuous operation, and when everything had been spread out the reservists came in, were conducted to their groundsheets, tied the ends together, hoisted their bundles onto their backs, and went to their rooms to put on their uniforms. Only occasionally did something have to be exchanged, and then it was always because someone had got too fat as a civilian. It was also only occasionally that something was missing: a shoe-cleaning brush or a spoon or fork, and it always turned out that someone else had two shoe-cleaning brushes or two spoons or forks, a fact which confirmed the sergeant's theory that we did not work mechanically enough, that we were "still using our brains too much." I didn't use my brain at all, with the result that no one was short a mess kit. While the first man of each company being equipped was hoisting his bundle onto his shoulder, the first of our own lot had to start spreading out the next groundsheet. Everything went smoothly. Meanwhile the newly promoted PFC sat at the table and wrote everything down in the paybooks; most of the time he had only to enter a one in the paybook, except with the neckties, socks, handkerchiefs, undershirts, and underpants, where he had to write a two.

In spite of everything, though, there were occasionally some dead minutes, as the quartermaster sergeant called them, and we were allowed to use these to fortify ourselves; we would sit on the bunks in the grooms' quarters and eat bread and liver sausage, sometimes bread and cheese or bread and jam, and when the sergeant had a few dead minutes himself he would come over and give us a lecture about the difference between rank and appointment. He found it tremendously interesting that he himself was a quartermaster sergeant—"that's my appointment"—and yet had the rank of a corporal, "that's my rank." In this way, so he said, there was no reason, for example, why a PFC should not act as a quartermaster sergeant, indeed even an ordinary private might; he found the theme endlessly fascinating and kept on concocting new examples, some of which betokened a well-nigh treasonable imagination. "It can actually happen, for instance," he said, "that a PFC is put in command of a company, of a battalion even."

For ten hours I laid mess kits on groundsheets, slept for six hours, and again for ten hours laid mess kits on groundsheets; then I slept another six hours and still had heard nothing from Leo. When the third ten hours of laying out mess kits began, the PFC started entering a two wherever there should have been a one, and a one wherever there should have been a two. He was relieved of his post, and now had to layout neckties, and the second probationary teacher was appointed clerk. I stayed with the mess kits during the third ten hours too. The sergeant said he thought I had done surprisingly well.

During the dead minutes, while we were sitting on the bunks eating bread and cheese, bread and jam, bread and liver sausage, strange rumors were beginning to be peddled around. A story was being told about a rather well-known retired general who received orders by phone to go to a small island in the North Sea where he was to assume a top-secret, extremely important command. The general had taken his uniform out of the closet, kissed his wife, children, and grandchildren good-bye, given his favorite horse a farewell pat, and taken the train to some station on the North Sea, and from there hired a motorboat to the island in question. He had been foolish enough to send back the motorboat before ascertaining the nature of his command; he was cut off by the rising tide and—so the story went—had forced the farmer on the island at pistol point to risk his life and row him back to the mainland. By afternoon there was already a variation to the tale: some sort of a struggle had taken place in the boat between the general and the farmer, they had both been swept overboard and drowned. What I couldn't stand was that this story—and a number of others—was considered criminal all right, but funny as well, while to me they seemed neither one nor the other. I couldn't accept the grim accusation of sabotage, which was being used like some kind of moral tuning fork, nor could I join in the laughter or grin with the others. The war seemed to deprive what was funny of its funny side.

At any other time the "Must I Thens" that ran through my dreams, my sleep, and my few waking moments, the countless men who got off the streetcars and came hurrying into the barracks with their cardboard boxes and went out again an hour later with "Must I Then"; even the speeches we sometimes listened to with half an ear, speeches in which the words "united effort" were always occurring—all this I would have found funny, but everything which would have been funny before was not funny any more, and I could no longer laugh or smile at all the things which would have seemed laughable; not even the sergeant, and not even the PFC, whose chevron was still not quite straight and who sometimes laid out three neckties on the groundsheet instead of two.

It was still hot, still August, and the fact that three times sixteen hours are only forty-eight, two days and two nights, was something I didn't realize until I woke up about eleven on Sunday and for the first time since Leo had been transferred was able to lean out of the window, my arms on the sill. The probationary teachers, wearing their walking-out dress, were ready for church, and looked at me in a challenging kind of way, but all I said was "Go ahead, I'll follow you," and it was obvious that they were glad to be able to go without me for once. Whenever we had gone to church they had looked at me as if they would like to excommunicate me, because something or other about me or my uniform was not quite up to scratch in their eyes: the way my boots were cleaned, the way I had tied my tie, my belt or my haircut; they were indignant not as fellow soldiers (which, objectively speaking, I agree would have been justified), but as Catholics. They would rather I had not made it so unmistakably clear that we were actually going to one and the same church; it embarrassed them, but there wasn't a thing they could do about it, because my paybook is marked RC.

This Sunday there was no mistaking how glad they were to be able to go without me. I had only to watch them marching off to town, past the barracks, clean, upright, and brisk. Sometimes, when I felt bouts of pity for them, I was glad for their sakes that Leo was a Protestant: I think they simply couldn't have borne it if Leo had been a Catholic too.

The office clerk and the orderly were still asleep; we didn't have to be at the stable again till three that afternoon. I stood leaning out of the window for a while, till it was time to go, so as to get to church just in time to miss the sermon. Then, while I was dressing, I opened Leo's locker again: to my surprise it was empty, except for a piece of paper and a big chunk of ham. Leo had locked the cupboard again to be sure I would find the message and the ham. On the paper was written "This is it—I'm being sent to Poland—did you get my message?" I put the paper in my pocket, turned the key in the locker, and finished dressing; I was in a daze as I walked into town and entered the church, and even the glances of the three probationary teachers, who turned round to look at me and then back to the altar again, shaking their heads, failed to rouse me completely. Probably they wanted to make sure quickly whether I hadn't come in after the Elevation of the Host so they could apply for my excommunication; but I really had arrived before the Elevation, so there was nothing they could do; besides, I wanted to remain a Catholic. I thought of Leo and was scared, I thought too of the girl in Cologne and had a twinge of conscience, but I was sure her voice had sounded like marriage. To annoy my roommates, I undid my collar while I was still in church.

After Mass I stood outside leaning against the church wall in a shady corner between the vestry and the door, took off my cap, lit a cigarette, and watched the faithful as they left the church and walked past me. I wondered how I could get hold of a girl with whom I could go for a walk, have a cup of coffee, and maybe go to a movie; I still had three hours before I had to layout mess kits on groundsheets again. It would be nice if the girl were not too silly and reasonably pretty. I also thought about dinner at the barracks, which I was missing now, and that perhaps I ought to have told the office clerk he could have my chop and dessert.

I smoked two cigarettes while I stood there, watching the faithful standing about in twos and threes, then separating again, and just as I was lighting the third cigarette from the second a shadow fell across me from one side, and when I looked to the right I saw that the person casting the shadow was even blacker than the shadow itself: it was the chaplain who had read Mass. He looked very kind, not old, thirty perhaps, fair and just a shade too well fed. First he looked at my open collar, then at my boots, then at my bare head, and finally at my cap, which I had put next to me on a ledge from where it had slipped off onto the paving; last of all he looked at my cigarette, then into my face, and I had the feeling that he didn't like anything he saw there. "What's the matter?" he finally asked. "Are you in trouble?" And hardly had I nodded in reply to this question, when he said, "Do you wish to confess?" Damn it, I thought, all they ever think of is confession, and only a certain part of that even. "No," I said, "I don't wish to confess." "Well then," he said, "what's on your mind?" He might just as well have been asking about my stomach as my mind. He was obviously very impatient, looked at my cap, and I felt he was annoyed that I hadn't picked it up yet. I would have liked to turn his impatience into patience, but after all it wasn't I who had spoken to him, but he who had spoken to me, so I asked—to my annoyance, somewhat falteringly—whether he knew of some nice girl who would go for a walk with me, have a cup of coffee, and maybe go to a movie in the evening; she didn't have to be a beauty queen, but she must be reasonably pretty, and if possible not from a good family, as these girls are usually so silly. I could give him the address of a chaplain in Cologne where he could make inquiries, call up if necessary, to satisfy himself I was from a good Catholic home. I talked a lot, toward the end a bit more coherently, and noticed how his face altered: at first it was almost kind, it had almost looked benign, that was in the early stage when he took me for a highly interesting, possibly even fascinating case of feeble-mindedness and found me psychologically quite amusing. The transitions from kind to almost benign, from almost benign to amused were hard to distinguish, but then all of a sudden—the moment I mentioned the physical attributes the girl was to have—he went purple with rage. I was scared, for my mother had once told me it is a sign of danger when overweight people suddenly go purple in the face. Then he began to shout at me, and shouting has always put me on edge. He shouted that I looked a mess, with my "field tunic" undone, my boots unpolished, my cap lying next to me "in the dirt, yes, in the dirt," and how undisciplined I was, smoking one cigarette after another, and whether perhaps I couldn't tell the difference between a Catholic priest and a pimp. With my nerves strung up as they were, I had stopped being scared of him, I was just plain angry. I asked him what my tie, my boots, my cap, had to do with him, whether he thought maybe he had to do my corporal's job, and "Anyway," I said, "you fellows tell us all the time to come to you with our troubles, and when someone really tells you his troubles, you get mad." "you fellows, eh?" he said, gasping with rage. "Since when are we on such familiar terms?" "We're not on any terms at all," I said. I picked up my cap, put it on without looking at it, and left, walking straight across the church square. He called after me to at least do up my tie, and I shouldn't be so stubborn; I very nearly turned round and shouted that he was the stubborn one, but then I remembered my mother telling me it was all right to be frank with a priest but you should try to avoid being impertinent—and so, without looking back. I went on into town. I left my tie dangling and thought about Catholics; there was a war on, but the first thing they looked at was your tie, then your boots. They said you should tell them your troubles, and when you did, they got mad.

I walked slowly through town, on the lookout for a café where I wouldn't have to salute anyone: this stupid saluting spoiled all cafés for me. I looked at all the girls I passed, I turned round to look at them, at their legs even, but there wasn't one whose voice would not have sounded like marriage. I was desperate. I thought of Leo, of the girl in Cologne, I was on the point of sending her a telegram; I was almost prepared to risk getting married just to be alone with a girl. I stopped in front of the window of a photographer's studio, so I could think about Leo in peace. I was scared for him. I saw my reflection in the shop window—my tie undone and my black boots unpolished. I raised my hands to button up my collar, but then it seemed too much trouble, and I dropped my hands again. The photographs in the studio window were very depressing. They were almost all of soldiers in walking-out dress; some had even had their pictures taken wearing their steel helmets, and I was wondering whether the ones in steel helmets were more depressing than the ones in peaked caps when a sergeant came out of the shop carrying a framed photograph: the photo was fairly large, at least twenty-four by thirty, the frame was painted silver, and the picture showed the sergeant in walking-out dress and steel helmet. He was quite young, not much older than I was, twenty-one at most; he was just about to walk past me, he hesitated, stopped, and I was wondering whether to raise my hand and salute him, when he said, "Forget it—but if I were you I'd do up your collar, and your tunic too. The next guy might be tougher than I am." Then he laughed and went off, and ever since then I have preferred (relatively, of course) the ones who have their pictures taken in steel helmets to the ones who have their pictures taken in peak caps.

Leo would have been just the person to stand with me in front of the photo studio and look at the pictures; there were also some bridal couples, first communicants, and students wearing colored ribbons and fancy fobs over their stomachs, and I stood there wondering why they didn't wear ribbons in their hair; some of them wouldn't have looked bad in them at all. I needed company and had none.

Probably the chaplain thought I was suffering from lust, or that I was an anticlerical Nazi; but I was neither suffering from lust nor was I anticlerical or a Nazi. I simply needed company, and not male company either, and that was so simple that it was terribly complicated; of course there were loose women in town as well as prostitutes (it was a Catholic town), but the loose women and the prostitutes were always offended if you weren't suffering from lust.

I stood for a long time in front of the photo studio. To this day I still always look at photo studios in strange cities; they are all much the same, and all equally depressing, although not everywhere do you find students with colored ribbons. It was nearly one o'clock when I finally left, on the lookout for a café where I didn't have to salute anyone, but in all the cafés they were sitting around in their uniforms, and I ended up by going to a movie anyway, to the first show at one-fifteen. All I remember was the newsreel: some very ignoble-looking Poles were maltreating some very noble-looking Germans. It was so empty in the movie that I could risk smoking during the show; it was hot that last Sunday in August 1939.

When I got back to barracks, it was way past three. For some reason the order to put down groundsheets at three o'clock and spread out mess kits and neckties on them had been countermanded; I came in just in time to change, have some bread and liver sausage, lean out of the window for a few minutes, listen to snatches of the discussion about Ernst Jünger and the other one about the female form. Both discussions had become more serious, more boring; the orderly and the office clerk were now weaving Latin expressions into their remarks, and that made the whole thing even more repulsive than it was in the first place.

At four we were called out, and I had imagined we would be loading boots from trucks onto railway cars again or from railway cars onto trucks, but this time we loaded cases of soap powder, which were stacked up in the gym, onto trucks, and from the trucks we unloaded them at the parcel post office, where they were stacked up again. The cases were not heavy, the addresses were typewritten. We formed a chain, and so one case after another passed through my hands; we did this the whole of Sunday afternoon right through till late at night, and there were scarcely any dead minutes when we could have had a bite to eat. As soon as a truck was fully loaded, we drove to the main post office, formed a chain again, and unloaded the cases. Sometimes we overtook a "Must I Then" column, or met one coming the other way; by this time they had three bands, and it was all going much faster. It was late, after midnight, when we had driven off with the last of the cases, and my hands remembered the number of mess kits and decided there was very little difference between cases of soap powder and mess kits.

I was very tired and wanted to throw myself on the bed fully dressed, but once again there was a great stack of bread and cans of liver sausage, jam and butter, on the table, and the others insisted it be distributed; all I wanted was the cigarettes, and I had to wait till everything had been divided up exactly, for of course the Pfc left the cigarettes to the last again. He took an abnormally long time about it, perhaps to teach me moderation and discipline and to convey his contempt for my craving; when I finally got the cigarettes, I lay down on the bed in my clothes and smoked and watched them spreading their bread with liver sausage, listened to them praising the excellent quality of the butter, and arguing mildly as to whether the jam was made of strawberries, apples, and apricots, or of strawberries and apples only. They went on eating for a long time, and I couldn't fall asleep. Then I heard footsteps coming along the passage and knew they were for me: I was afraid and yet relieved, and the strange thing was that they all, the office clerk, the orderly, and the three probationary teachers who were sitting round the table, stopped their chewing and looked at me as the footsteps drew closer. Now the PFC found it necessary to shout at me: he got up and yelled, calling me by my surname, "Damn it, take your boots off when you lie down."

There are certain things one refuses to believe, and I still don't believe it, although my ears remember quite well that all of a sudden he called me by my surname; I would have preferred it if we had used surnames all along, but coming so suddenly like that it sounded so funny that, for the first time since the war started, I had to laugh. Meanwhile the door had been flung open and the company clerk was standing by my bed; he was pretty excited, so much so that he didn't bawl me out, although he was a corporal, for lying on the bed with my boots and clothes on, smoking. He said, "you there, in twenty minutes in full marching order in Block 4, understand?" I said "Yes" and got up. He added, "Report to the sergeant major over there," and again I said "Yes" and began to clear out my locker. I hadn't realized the company clerk was still in the room. I was just putting the picture of the girl in my trouser pocket when I heard him say, "I have some bad news, it's going to be tough on you, but it should make you proud too; the first man from this regiment to be killed in action was your roommate, Corporal Leo Siemers."

I had turned round during the last half of this sentence, and they were all looking at me now, including the corporal. I had gone quite pale, and I didn't know whether to be furious or silent. Then I said in a low voice, "But war hasn't been declared yet, he can't have been killed—and he wouldn't have been killed," and I shouted suddenly, "Leo wouldn't get killed, not him . . . you know he wouldn't." No one said anything, not even the corporal, and while I cleared out my locker and crammed all the stuff we were told to take with us into my pack, I heard him leave the room. I piled up all the things on the stool so I didn't have to turn around; I couldn't hear a sound from the others, I couldn't even hear them chewing. I packed all my stuff very quickly; the bread, liver sausage, cheese, and butter I left in the locker and turned the key. When I had to turn around, I saw they had managed to get into bed without a sound; I threw my locker key onto the office clerk's bed, saying, "Clear out everything that's still in there, it's all yours." I didn't care for him much, but I liked him best of the five. Later on I was sorry I hadn't left without saying a word, but I was not yet twenty. I slammed the door, took my rifle from the rack outside, went down the stairs, and saw from the clock over the office door downstairs that it was nearly three in the morning. It was quiet and still warm that last Monday of August 1939. I threw Leo's locker key somewhere onto the barrack square as I went across to Block 4. They were all there, the band was already moving into position at the head of the company, and some officer who had given the "united effort" speech was walking across the square; he took off his cap, wiped the sweat from his forehead, and put his cap on again. He reminded me of a streetcar conductor who takes a short break at the terminus.

The sergeant major came up to me and said, "Are you the man from staff headquarters?" and I said "Yes." He nodded; he looked pale and very young, somewhat at a loss; I looked past him toward the dark, scarcely distinguishable mass. All I could make out was the gleaming trumpets of the band. "You wouldn't happen to be a telephone operator?" asked the sergeant major. "We're short one here." "As a matter of fact I am," I said quickly and with an enthusiasm that seemed to surprise him, for he looked at me doubtfully. "Yes, I'm one," I said, "I've had practical training as a telephone operator." "Good," he said, "you're just the man I need. Slip in somewhere there at the end, we'll arrange everything en route." I went over toward the right, where the dark gray was getting a little lighter; as I got closer, I even recognized some faces. I took my place at the end of the company. Someone shouted, "Right turn— forward march!" and I had hardly lifted my foot when they started playing their "Must I Then."

Translated by Leila Vennewitz

When the War Was Over

It was just getting light when we reached the German border: to our left, a broad river, to our right a forest; even from its edges you could tell how deep it was. Silence fell in the boxcar; the train passed slowly over patched-up rails, past shelled houses, splintered telegraph poles. The little guy sitting next to me took off his glasses and polished them carefully.

"Christ," he whispered to me, "d'you have the slightest idea where we are?"

"Yes," I said, "the river you've just seen is known here as the Rhine, the forest you see over there on the right is called the Reich Forest—and we'll soon be getting into Cleves."

"D'you come from around here?"

"No, I don't." He was a nuisance; all night long he had driven me crazy with his high-pitched schoolboy's voice. He had told me how he had secretly read Brecht, Tucholsky, and Walter Benjamin, as well as Proust and Karl Kraus; that he wanted to study sociology, and theology too, and help create a new order for Germany, and when we stopped at Nimwegen at daybreak and someone said we were just coming to the German border, he nervously asked us all if there was anyone who would trade some thread for two cigarette butts, and when no one said anything, I offered to rip off my collar tabs, known—I believe—as insignia, and turn them into dark-green thread. I took off my tunic and watched him carefully pick the things off with a bit of metal, unravel them, and then actually start using the thread to sew on his ensign's piping around his shoulder straps. I asked him whether I might attribute this sewing job to the influence of Brecht, Tucholsky, Benjamin, or Karl Kraus, or was it perhaps the subconscious influence of Jünger that made him restore his rank with Tom Thumb's weapon. He had flushed and said he was through with Jünger, he had written him off; now, as we approached Cleves, he stopped sewing and sat down on the floor beside me, still holding Tom Thumb's weapon.

"Cleves doesn't convey anything to me," he said, "not a thing. How about you?"

"Oh yes," I said, "Lohengrin, Swan margarine, and Anne of Cleves, one of Henry the Eighth's wives."

"That's right," he said, "Lohengrin—although at home we always ate Sanella. Don't you want the butts?"

"No," I said, "take them home for your father. I hope he'll punch you in the nose when you arrive with that piping on your shoulder."

"You don't understand," he said. "Prussia, Kleist, Frankfurt-on-the-Oder, Potsdam, Prince of Homburg, Berlin."

"Well," I said, "I believe it was quite a while ago that Prussia took Cleves—and somewhere over there on the other side of the Rhine there is a little town called Wesel."

"Oh, of course," he said, "that's right, Schill."

"The Prussians never really established themselves beyond the Rhine," I said, "they only had two bridgeheads: Bonn and Koblenz."

"Prussia," he said.

"Blomberg," I said. "Need any more thread?" He flushed and was silent.

The train slowed down, everyone crowded round the open sliding door and looked at Cleves. English guards on the platform, casual and tough, bored yet alert: we were still prisoners. In the street a sign: "To Cologne." Lohengrin's castle up there among the autumn trees. October on the Lower Rhine, Dutch sky; my cousins in Xanten, aunts in Kevelaer; the broad dialect and the smugglers' whispering in the taverns; St. Martin's Day processions, gingerbread men, Breughelesque carnival, and everywhere the smell, even where there was none, of honey cakes.

"I wish you'd try to understand," said the little guy beside me.

"Leave me alone," I said; although he wasn't a man yet, no doubt he soon would be, and that was why I hated him. He was offended and sat back on his heels to add the final stitches to his braid; I didn't even feel sorry for him: clumsily, his thumb smeared with blood, he pushed the needle through the blue cloth of his air force tunic. His glasses were so misted over I couldn't make out whether he was crying or whether it just looked like it. I was close to tears myself: in two hours, three at most, we would be in Cologne, and from there it was not far to the one I had married, the one whose voice had never sounded like marriage.

The woman emerged suddenly from behind the freight shed, and before the guards knew what was happening, she was standing by our boxcar and unwrapping a blue cloth from what I first took to be a baby: a loaf of bread. She handed it to me, and I took it; it was heavy, I swayed for a moment and almost fell forward out of the train as it started moving. The bread was dark, still warm, and I wanted to call out "Thank you, thank you," but the words seemed ridiculous, and the train was moving faster now, so I stayed there on my knees with the heavy loaf in my arms. To this day all I know about the woman is that she was wearing a dark headscarf and was no longer young.

When I got up, clasping the loaf, it was quieter than ever in the boxcar; they were all looking at the bread, and under their stares it got heavier and heavier. I knew those eyes, I knew the mouths that belonged to those eyes, and for months I had been wondering where the borderline runs between hatred and contempt, and I hadn't found the borderline; for a while I had divided them up into sewers-on and non-sewers-on, when we had been transferred from an American camp (where the wearing of rank insignia was prohibited) to an English one (where the wearing of rank insignia was permitted), and I had felt a certain fellow feeling with the non-sewers-on till I found out they didn't even have any ranks whose insignia they could have sewn on. One of them, Egelhecht, had even tried to drum up a kind of court of honor that was to deny me the quality of being German (and I had wished that this court, which never convened, had actually had the power to deny me this quality). What they didn't know was that I hated them, Nazis and non-Nazis, not because of their sewing and their political views but because they were men, men of the same species as those I had had to spend the last six years with; the words "man" and "stupid" had become almost identical for me.

In the background Egelhecht's voice said, "The first German bread—and he of all people is the one to get it."

He sounded as if he was almost sobbing. I wasn't far off it myself either, but they would never understand that it wasn't just because of the bread, or because by now we had crossed the German border, it was mainly because, for the first time in eight months, I had for one moment felt a woman's hand on my arm.

"No doubt," said Egelhecht in a low voice, "you will even deny the bread the quality of being German."

"Yes, indeed," I said, "I shall employ a typical intellectual's trick and ask myself whether the flour this bread is made of doesn't perhaps come from Holland, England, or America. Here you are," I said. "Divide it up if you like."

Most of them I hated, many I didn't care about one way or the other, and Tom Thumb, who was now the last to join the ranks of the sewers-on, was beginning to be a nuisance; yet I felt it was the right thing to do, to share this loaf with them, I was sure it hadn't been meant only for me.

Egelhecht made his way slowly toward me: he was tall and thin, like me, and he was twenty-six, like me; for three months he had tried to make me see that a nationalist wasn't a Nazi, that the words "honor," "loyalty," "fatherland," "decency," could never lose their value—and I had always countered his impressive array of words with just five: Wilhelm II, Papen, Hindenburg, Blomberg, Keitel. It had infuriated him that I never mentioned Hider, not even that May 1 when the sentry ran through the camp blaring through a megaphone, "Hider's dead, Hider's dead!" "Go ahead," I said, "divide up the bread."

"Number off," said Egelhecht. I handed him the loaf, he took off his coat, laid it on the floor of the boxcar with the lining uppermost, smoothed the lining, and placed the bread on it, while the others numbered off around us. "Thirty-two," said Tom Thumb, then there was a silence. "Thirty-two," said Egelhecht, looking at me, for it was up to me to say thirty-three; but I didn't say it. I turned away and looked out at the highway with the old trees: Napoleon's poplars, Napoleon's elms, like the ones I had rested under with my brother when we rode from Weeze to the Dutch border on our bikes to buy chocolate and cigarettes cheap.

I could sense that those behind me were terribly offended; I saw the yellow road signs: "To Kalkar," "To Xanten," "To Geldern," heard behind me the sounds of Egelhecht's tin knife, felt the offendedness swelling like a thick cloud. They were always being offended for some reason or other. They were offended if an English guard offered them a cigarette, and they were offended if he did not; they were offended when I cursed Hider, and Egelhecht was mortally offended when I did not curse Hider; Tom Thumb had secretly read Benjamin and Brecht, Proust, Tucholsky, and Karl Kraus, and when we crossed the German border he was sewing on his ensign's piping. I took the cigarette out of my pocket I had got in exchange for my staff Pfc chevron, turned around, and sat down beside Tom Thumb. I watched Egelhecht dividing up the loaf: first he cut it in half, then the halves in quarters, then each quarter again in eight parts. This way there would be a nice fat chunk for each man, a dark cube of bread which I figured would weigh about two to three ounces.

Egelhecht was just quartering the last eighth, and each man, every one of them, knew that the ones who got the center pieces would get at least a quarter to a half ounce extra, because the loaf bulged in the middle and Egelhecht had cut the slices all the same thickness. But then he cut off the bulge of the two center slices and said, "Thirty-three—the youngest starts." Tom Thumb glanced at me, blushed, bent down, took a piece of bread, and put it directly into his mouth. Everything went smoothly till Bouvier, who had almost driven me crazy with his planes he was always talking about, had taken his piece of bread; now it should have been my turn, followed by Egelhecht, but I didn't move. I would have liked to light my cigarette, but I had no matches and nobody offered me one. Those who already had their bread were scared and stopped chewing; the ones who hadn't got their bread yet had no idea what was happening, but they understood: I didn't want to share the loaf with them. They were offended, while the others (who already had their bread) were merely embarrassed. I tried to look outside: at Napoleon's poplars, Napoleon's elms, at the tree-lined road with its gaps, with Dutch sky caught in the gaps, but my attempt to look unconcerned was not successful. I was scared of the fight that was bound to start now; I wasn't much good in a fight, and even if I had been it wouldn't have helped, they would have beaten me up the way they did in the camp near Brussels when I had said I would rather be a dead Jew than a live German. I took the cigarette out of my mouth, partly because it felt ridiculous, partly because I wanted to get it through the fight intact, and I looked at Tom Thumb, who, his face scarlet, was squatting on his heels beside me. Then Gugeler, whose turn it would have been after Egelhecht, took his piece of bread, put it directly into his mouth, and the others took theirs. There were three pieces left when the man came toward me whom I scarcely knew—he had not joined our tent till we were in the camp near Brussels. He was already old, nearly fifty, short, with a dark, scarred face, and whenever we began to quarrel he wouldn't say a word, he used to leave the tent and run along beside the barbed-wire fence like someone to whom this kind of trotting up and down is familiar. I didn't even know his first name; he wore some sort of faded tropical uniform, and civilian shoes. He came from the far end of the boxcar straight toward me, stopped in front of me, and said in a surprisingly gentle voice, "Take the bread"—and when I didn't, he shook his head and said, "You fellows have one hell of a talent for turning everything into a symbolic event. It's just bread, that's all, and the woman gave it to you, the woman—here you are." He picked up a piece of bread, pressed it into my right hand, which was hanging down helplessly, and squeezed my hand around it. His eyes were quite dark, not black, and his face wore the look of many prisons. I nodded, got my hand muscles moving so as to hold on to the bread; a deep sigh went through the car; Egelhecht took his bread, then the old man in the tropical uniform. "Damn it all," said the old fellow, "I've been away from Germany for twelve years. You're a crazy bunch, but I'm just beginning to understand you." Before I could put the bread into my mouth the train stopped, and we got out.

Open country, turnip fields, no trees; a few Belgian guards with the lion of Flanders on their caps and collars ran along beside the train calling, "All out, everybody out!"

Tom Thumb remained beside me; he polished his glasses, looked at the station sign, and said, "Weeze—does this also convey something to you?"

"Yes," I said, "it lies north of Kevelaer and west of Xanten."

"Oh yes," he said, "Kevelaer—Heinrich Heine."

"And Xanten—Siegfried, in case you've forgotten."

Aunt Helen, I thought. Weeze. Why hadn't we gone straight through to Cologne? There wasn't much left of Weeze other than a spattering of red bricks showing through the treetops. Aunt Helen had owned a fair-sized shop in Weeze, a regular village store, and every morning she used to slip some money into our pockets so we could go boating on the river Niers or ride over to Kevelaer on our bikes; the sermons on Sunday in church, roundly berating the smugglers and adulterers.

"Let's go," said the Belgian guard. "Get a move on, or don't you want to get home?"

I went into the camp. First we had to file past an English officer who gave us a twenty-mark bill, for which we had to sign a receipt. Next we had to go to the doctor; he was a German, young, and grinned at us; he waited till twelve or fifteen of us were in the room, then said, "Anyone who is so sick that he can't go home today need only raise his hand." A few of us laughed at this terribly witty remark; then we filed past his table one by one, had our release papers stamped, and went out by the other door. I waited for a few moments by the open door and heard him say, "Anyone who is so sick that—," then moved on, heard the laughter when I was already at the far end of the corridor, and went to the next check point. This was an English corporal, standing out in the open next to an uncovered latrine. The corporal said, "Show me your paybooks and any papers you still have." He said this in German, and when they pulled out their paybooks, he pointed to the latrine and told them to throw the books into it, adding, "Down the hatch!" and then most of them laughed at this witticism. It had struck me anyway that Germans suddenly seemed to have a sense of humor, so long as it was foreign humor: in camp even Egelhecht had laughed at the American captain who had pointed to the barbed-wire entanglement and said, "Don't take it so hard, boys, now you're free at last."

The English corporal asked me too about my papers, but all I had was my release; I had sold my paybook to an American for two cigarettes. So I said, "No papers"—and that made him as angry as the American corporal had been when I had answered his question, "Hider youth, SA, or Party?" with "No." He had yelled at me and put me on KP, he had sworn at me and accused my grandmother of various sexual offenses the nature of which, due to my insufficient knowledge of the American language, I was unable to ascertain. It made them furious when something didn't fit into their stereotyped categories. The English corporal went purple with rage, stood up, and began to frisk me, and he didn't have to search long before he had found my diary. It was thick, cut from paper bags, stapled together, and in it I had written down everything that had happened to me from the middle of April till the end of September: from being taken prisoner by the American sergeant Stevenson to the final entry I had made in the train as we went through dismal AntWerp and I read on walls "Vive le Roil" There were more than a hundred paper-bag pages, closely written, and the furious corporal took it from me, threw it into the latrine, and said, "Didn't I ask you for your papers?" Then I was allowed to go.

We stood crowded around the camp gate waiting for the Belgian trucks which were supposed to take us to Bonn. Bonn? Why Bonn, of all places? Someone said Cologne was closed off because it was contaminated by corpses, and someone else said we would have to clear away rubble for thirty or forty years, rubble, ruins, "and they aren't even going to give us trucks, we'll have to carry away the rubble in baskets." Luckily there was no one near me who I had shared a tent or sat in the boxcar with. The drivel coming from mouths I did not know was a shade less disgusting than if it had come from mouths I knew. Someone ahead of me said, "But then he didn't mind taking the loaf of bread from the Jew," and another voice said, "Yes, they're the kind of people who are going to set the tone." Someone nudged me from behind and asked, "Four ounces of bread for a cigarette, how about it, eh?" and from behind he thrust his hand in front of my face, and I saw it was one of the pieces of bread Egelhecht had divided up in the train. I shook my head. Someone else said, "The Belgians are selling cigarettes at ten marks apiece." To me that seemed very cheap: in camp the Germans had sold cigarettes for a hundred and twenty marks apiece. "Cigarettes, anyone?" "Yes," I said, and put my twenty-mark bill into an anonymous hand.

Everyone was trading with everyone else. It was the only thing that seriously interested them. For two thousand marks and a threadbare uniform someone got a civilian suit, the deal was concluded, and clothes were changed somewhere in the waiting crowd, and suddenly I heard someone call out, "But of course the underpants go with the suit—and the tie too." Someone sold his wristwatch for three thousand marks. The chief article of trade was soap. Those who had been in American camps had a lot of soap—twenty cakes, some of them—for they had been given soap every week but never any water to wash in, and the ones who had been in the English camps had no soap at all. The green and pink cakes of soap went back and forth. Some of the men had discovered their artistic aspirations and shaped the soap into little dogs, cats, and gnomes, and now it turned out that the artistic aspirations had lowered the exchange value. Unsculptured soap rated higher than sculptured, a loss of weight being suspected in the latter.

The anonymous hand into which I had placed the twenty-mark bill actually reappeared and pressed two cigarettes into my left hand, and I was almost touched by so much honesty (but I was almost touched only till I found out that the Belgians were selling cigarettes for five marks; a hundred-percent profit was evidently regarded as a fair markup, especially among "comrades"). We stood there for about two hours, jammed together, and all I remember is hands: trading hands, passing soap from right to left, from left to right, money from left to right and again from right to left; it was as if I had fallen into a snakepit; hands from all sides moved every which way, passing goods and money over my shoulders and over my head in every direction.

Tom Thumb had managed to get close to me again. He sat beside me on the floor of the Belgian truck driving to Kevelaer, through Kevelaer, to Krefeld, around Krefeld to Neuss; there was silence over the fields, in the towns, we saw hardly a soul and only a few animals, and the dark autumn sky hung low. On my left sat Tom Thumb, on my right the Belgian guard, and we looked out over the tailboard at the road I knew so well: my brother and I had often ridden our bicycles along it. Tom Thumb kept trying to justify himself, but I cut him off every time, and he kept trying to be clever; there was no stopping him. "But Neuss," he said, "that can't remind you of anything. What on earth could Neuss remind anybody of?"

"Novesia Chocolate," I said, "sauerkraut, and Quirinus, but I don't suppose you ever heard of the Thebaic Legion."

"No, I haven't," he said, and blushed again.

I asked the Belgian guard if it was true that Cologne was closed off, contaminated by corpses, and he said, "No—but it's a mess all right; is that where you're from?"

"Yes," I said.

"Be prepared for the worst . . . do you have any soap left?"

"Yes, I have," I said.

"Here," he said, pulling a pack of tobacco out of his pocket. He opened it and held out the pale-yellow, fresh, fine-cut tobacco for me to smell. "It's yours for two cakes of soap—fair enough?"

I nodded, felt around in my coat pocket for the soap, gave him two cakes, and put the tobacco in my pocket. He gave me his sub-machine gun to hold while he hid the soap in his pockets; he sighed as I handed it back to him. "These lousy things," he said, "we'll have to go on carrying them around for a while yet. You fellows aren't half as badly off as you think. What are you crying about?"

I pointed toward the right: the Rhine. We were approaching Dormagen. I saw that Tom Thumb was about to open his mouth and said quickly, "For God's sake shut up, can't you? Shut up." He had probably wanted to ask me whether the Rhine reminded me of anything. Thank God he was deeply offended now and said no more till we got to Bonn.

In Cologne there were actually some houses still standing; some-where I even saw a moving streetcar, some people too, women even: one of them saved to us. From the Neuss-Strasse we turned into the Ring avenues and drove along them, and I was waiting all the time for the tears, but they didn't come; even the insurance buildings on the avenue were in ruins, and all I could see of the Hohenstaufen Baths was a few pale-blue tiles. I was hoping all the time the truck would turn off somewhere to the right, for we had lived on the Car-olingian Ring; but the truck did not turn. It drove down the Rings—Barbarossa Square, Saxon Ring, Salian Ring—and I tried not to look, and I wouldn't have looked if the truck convoy had not got into a traffic jam up front at Clovis Square and we hadn't stopped in front of the house we used to live in, so I did look.

The term "totally destroyed" is misleading: only in rare cases is it possible to destroy a house totally. It has to be hit three or four times and, to make certain, it should then burn down; the house we used to live in was actually, according to official terminology, totally destroyed, but not in the technical sense. That is to say, I could still recognize it; the front door and the doorbells, and I submit that a house where it is still possible to recognize the front door and the doorbells has not, in the strict technical sense, been totally destroyed. But of the house we used to live in there was more to be recognized than the doorbells and the front door. Two rooms in the basement were almost intact, on the mezzanine, absurdly enough, even three: a fragment of wall was supporting the third room that would probably not have passed a spirit-level test; our apartment on the second floor had only one room intact, but it was gaping open in front, toward the street; above this, a high, narrow gable reared up, bare, with empty window sockets. However, the interesting thing was that two men were moving around in our living room as if their feet were on familiar ground; one of the men took a picture down from the wall, the Terborch print my father had been so fond of, walked to the front, carrying the picture, and showed it to a third man who was standing down below in front of the house. This third man shook his head like someone who is not interested in an object being auctioned, and the man up above walked back with the Terborch and hung it up again on the wall; he even straightened the picture—I was touched by this mark of neatness— stepped back to make sure the picture was really hanging straight, then nodded in a satisfied way. Meanwhile the second man took the other picture off the wall: an engraving of Lochner's painting of the cathedral, but this one also did not appear to please the third man standing down below. Finally the first man, the one who had hung the Terborch back on the wall, came to the front, formed a megaphone with his hands, and shouted, "Piano in sight!" and the man below laughed, nodded, likewise formed a megaphone with hands, and shouted, "I'll get the straps." I could not see the piano, but I knew where it stood: on the right in the corner I couldn't see into and where the man with the Lochner picture was just disappearing.

"Whereabouts in Cologne did you live?" asked the Belgian guard.

"Oh, somewhere over there," I said, gesturing vaguely in the direction of the western suburbs.

"Thank God, now we're moving again," said the guard. He picked up his submachine gun, which he had placed on the floor of the truck, and straightened his cap. The lion of Flanders on the front of his cap was rather dirty. As we turned into Clovis Square, I could see why there had been a traffic jam: some kind of raid seemed to be going on. English military police cars were all over the place, and civilians were standing in them with their hands up, surrounded by a sizable crowd, quiet yet tense. A surprisingly large number of people in such a silent, ruined city.

"That's the black market," said the Belgian guard. "Once in a while they come and clean it up."

Before we were even out of Cologne, while we were still on the Bonn-Strasse, I fell asleep and I dreamed of my mother's coffee mill: the coffee mill was being let down on a strap by the man who had offered the Terborch without success, but the man below rejected the coffee mill; the other man drew it up again, opened the hall door, and tried to screw the coffee mill back where it had hung before, immediately to the left of the kitchen door, but now there was no wall there for him to screw it onto, and still the man kept on trying (this mark of tidiness touched me even in my dream). He searched with the forefinger of his right hand for the pegs, couldn't find them, and raised his fist threateningly to the gray autumn sky which offered no support for the coffee mill. Finally he gave up, tied the strap around the mill again, went to the front, let down the coffee mill, and offered it to the third man, who again rejected it, and the other man pulled it up again, untied the strap, and hid the coffee mill under his jacket as if it were a valuable object; then he began to wind up the strap, rolled it into a coil, and threw it down into the third man's face. All this time I was worried about what could have happened to the man who had offered the Lochner without success, but I couldn't see him anywhere; something was preventing me from looking into the corner where the piano was, my father's desk, and I was upset at the thought that he might be reading my father's diaries. Now the man with the coffee mill was standing by the living-room door trying to screw the coffee mill onto the door panel; he seemed absolutely determined to give the coffee mill a permanent resting place, and I was beginning to like him, even before I discovered he was one of our many friends whom my mother had comforted while they sat on the chair beneath the coffee mill, one of those who had been killed right at the beginning of the war in an air raid.

Before we got to Bonn, the Belgian guard woke me up. "Come on," he said, "rub your eyes, freedom is at hand," and I straightened up and thought of all the people who had sat on the chair beneath my mother's coffee mill: truant schoolboys whom she helped to overcome their fear of exams, Nazis whom she tried to enlighten, non-Nazis whom she tried to fortify—they had all sat on the chair beneath the coffee mill, had received comfort and censure, defense and respite. Bitter words had destroyed their ideals and gentle words had offered them those things which would outlive the times: mercy to the weak, comfort to the persecuted.

The old cemetery, the market square, the university. Bonn. Through the Koblenz Gate and into the park. "So long," said the Belgian guard, and Tom Thumb with his tired child's face said, "Drop me a line some time."

"All right," I said, "I'll send you my complete Tucholsky."

"Wonderful," he said, "and your Kleist too?"

"No," I said, "only the ones I have duplicates of."

On the other side of the barricade through which we were finally released, a man was standing between two big laundry baskets; in one he had a lot of apples, in the other a few cakes of soap. He shouted, "Vitamins, my friends, one apple—one cake of soap!" And I could feel my mouth watering. I had quite forgotten what apples looked like; I gave him a cake of soap, was handed an apple, and bit into it at once. I stood there watching the others come out; there was no need for him to call out now: it was a wordless exchange. He would take an apple out of the basket, be handed a cake of soap, and throw the soap into the empty basket; there was a dull thud when the soap landed. Not everyone took an apple, not everyone had any soap, but the transaction was as swift as in a self-service store, and by the time I had just finished my apple, he already had his soap basket half full. The whole thing took place swiftly and smoothly and without a word; even the ones who were very economical and very calculating couldn't resist the sight of the apples, and I began to feel sorry for them. Home was welcoming its homecomers so warmly with vitamins.

It took me a long time to find a phone in Bonn; finally a girl in the post office told me that the only people to get phones were doctors and priests, and even then only those who hadn't been Nazis. "They're scared stiff of the Nazi Werewolf underground," she said. "I s'pose you wouldn't have a cigarette for me?" I took my pack of tobacco out of my pocket and said, "Shall I roll one for you?", but she said no, she could do it herself, and I watched her take a cigarette paper out of her coat pocket and quickly and deftly roll herself a firm cigarette. "Who do you want to call?" she said, and I said, "My wife," and she laughed and said I didn't look married at all. I also rolled myself a cigarette and asked her whether there was any chance of selling some soap: I needed money, train fare, and didn't have a pfennig. "Soap," she said, "let's have a look." I felt around in my coat lining and pulled out some soap, and she snatched it out of my hand, sniffed it, and said, "Real Palmolive! That's worth—worth—I'll give you fifty marks for it." I looked at her in amazement, and she said, "yes, I know, you can get as much as eighty for it, but I can't afford that." I didn't want to take the fifty marks, but she insisted, she thrust the note into my coat pocket and ran out of the post office; she was quite pretty, with that hungry prettiness which lends a girl's voice a certain sharpness.

What struck me most of all, in the post office and as I walked slowly on through Bonn, was the fact that nowhere was there a student wearing colored ribbons; and the smells; everyone smelled terrible, all the rooms smelled terrible, and I could see why the girl was so crazy about the soap. I went to the station, tried to find out how I could get to Oberkerschenbach (that was where the one I married lived), but nobody could tell me; all I knew was that it was a little place somewhere in the Eifel district not too far from Bonn. There weren't any maps anywhere either, where I could have looked it up; no doubt they had been banned on account of the Nazi Werewolves. I always like to know where a place is, and it bothered me that I knew nothing definite about this place Oberkerschenbach and couldn't find out anything definite. In my mind I went over all the Bonn addresses I knew, but there wasn't a single doctor or a single priest among them; finally I remembered a professor of theology I had called on with a friend just before the war. He had had some sort of trouble with Rome and the Index, and we had gone to see him simply to give him our moral support; I couldn't remember the name of the street, but I knew where it was, and I walked along the Poppelsdorf Avenue, fumed left, then left again, found the house, and was relieved to read the name on the door.

The professor came to the door himself. He had aged a great deal, he was thin and bent, his hair quite white. I said, "you won't remember me, Professor. I came to see you some years ago when you had that stink with Rome and the Index—can I speak to you for a moment?" He laughed when I said stink, and said, "Of course," when I had finished, and I followed him into his study; I noticed it no longer smelled of tobacco, otherwise it was still just the same, with all the books, files, and house plants. I told the professor I had heard that the only people who got phones were priests and doctors, and I simply had to call my wife. He heard me out—a very rare thing—then said that, although he was a priest, he was not one of those who had a phone, for "you see," he said, "I am not a pastor." "Perhaps you're a Werewolf," I said. I offered him some tobacco, and I felt sorry for him when I saw how he looked at my tobacco; I am always sorry for old people who have to go without something they like. His hands trembled as he filled his pipe, and they did not tremble just because he was old. When he had at last got it lit—I had no matches and couldn't help him—he told me that doctors and priests were not the only people with phones. "These nightclubs they're opening up everywhere for the soldiers," they had them too, and I might try in one of these nightclubs; there was one just around the corner. He wept when I put a few pipefuls of tobacco on his desk as I left, and he asked me as his tears fell whether I knew what I was doing, and I said, yes, I knew, and I suggested he accept the few pipefuls of tobacco as a belated tribute to the courage he had shown toward Rome all those years ago. I would have liked to give him some soap as well, I still had five or six pieces in my coat lining, but I was afraid his heart would burst with joy; he was so old and frail.

"Nightclub" was a nice way of putting it, but I didn't mind that so much as the English sentry at the door of this nightclub. He was very young and eyed me severely as I stopped beside him. He pointed to the notice prohibiting Germans from entering this nightclub, but I told him my sister worked there, I had just returned to my beloved fatherland, and my sister had the house key. He asked me what my sister's name was, and it seemed safest to give the most German of all German girls' names, so I said, "Gretchen." Oh yes, he said, that was the blond one, and let me go in. Instead of bothering to describe the interior, I refer the reader to the pertinent "Fraulein literature" and to movies and TV. I won't even bother to describe Gretchen (see above). The main thing was that Gretchen was surprisingly quick on the uptake and, in exchange for a cake of Palmolive, was willing to make a phone call to the priest's house in Kerschenbach (which I hoped existed) and have the one I had married called to the phone. Gretchen spoke fluent English on the phone and told me her boyfriend would try to do it through the army exchange, it would be quicker. While we were waiting, I offered her some tobacco, but she had something better; I tried to pay her the agreed fee of a cake of soap in advance, but she said no, she didn't want it after all, she would rather not take anything, and I when I insisted on paying she began to cry and confided that one of her brothers was a prisoner of war, the other one dead, and I felt sorry for her, for it is not pleasant when girls like Gretchen cry. She even let on that she was a Catholic, and just as she was about to get her first communion picture out of a drawer the phone rang, and Gretchen lifted the receiver and said "Reverend," but I had already heard that it was not a man's voice. "Just a moment," Gretchen said, and handed me the receiver. I was so excited I couldn't hold the receiver; in fact, I dropped it, fortunately onto Gretchen's lap. She picked it up, held it against my ear, and I said, "Hello—is that you?"

"Yes," she said. "Darling, where are you?"

"I'm in Bonn," I said. "The war's over—for me."

"My God," she said, "I can't believe it. No—it's not true."

"It is true," I said, "it is—did you get my postcard?"

"No," she said, "for the lat eight months I haven't had the slightest idea where you were."

Those bastards," I said, "those dirty bastards. Listen, just tell me where Kerschenback is."

"I"—she was crying so hard she couldn't speak, I heard her sobbing and gulping till at last she was able to whisper—"at the station in Bonn, I'll meet you," then I could no longer hear her, someone said something in English that I didn't understand.

Gretchen put the receiver to her ear, listened a moment, shook her head, and replaced it. I looked at her and knew I couldn't offer her the soap now. I couldn't even say "Thank you," the words seemed ridiculous, I lifted my arms helplessly and went out.

I walked back to the station, in my ear the woman's voice which had never sounded like marriage.

Translated by Leila Vennewitz

The Staech Affair

The "AE" in Staech is pronounced like a long, faintly aspirated "a," as in *Bach*. It bothers the Inhabitants of the place—consisting almost entirely of Benedictine monks—to hear the "ae" pronounced as in aerobatics. Hence this preamble. There are some further antagonisms associated with the name "Staech" which I can only mention in passing. A heated dispute among onomatologists, for instance, some maintaining that the "ae" is an unmistakable sign of Germanic origin, while their opponents claim that the final "ch" is an unmistakable sign of Celtic origin. I plead the Celtic cause, knowing only too well how corruptible vowels are; and besides, there is the telltale dialect in and around Staech. Staech is located in the Rhineland. I must dispense with a definition of what constitutes Rhenish, restricting myself to the line of demarcation given to the Rhineland at the time of the Prussian occupation, which has persisted since 1815, and according to this line of demarcation Staech is located in the Rhineland. It is ancient, renowned, beautiful, idyllic; in the midst of tall trees, the incomparable gray of medieval Rhenish romanesque; a robust little river by the name of Brülle provides the landscape's essential ingredient of water. (Brülle is in no way related to the German verb hrüllen, to roar. Beware of jumping to false etymological conclusions! The name probably derives from hruhlen, in turn a local corruption of the amply familiar huhlen, to consort illicitly. It has almost been established that here, in the midst of these venerable forests, a medieval prelate built an abode for his concubine.)

Staech has two hotels—one luxury, one modest—a youth camp, and a hostel that is used for conferences. The most important feature is the Benedictine abbey. There one can play at being a temporary monk. Tranquillity, Gregorian chants, peace within and without. And then there are the monks in their noble garb, one or other of whom, at any given moment, either at prayer or meditation or in conversation with a guest, embellishes landscape or garden. Everything extremely simple, almost austere; the soil is tilled, orchards are tended. The climate is too harsh for wine.

I can forgo further details and merely point out that Staech is extolled by the protocol officials of the nearby capital as being "a sheer delight." A high-ranking—perhaps even the highest-ranking—official of the protocol department is said to have remarked, "What more can we ask for? The Occident in one of its most cultivated articulations is only fifty Mercedes-minutes away."

Indeed, Staech is virtually irreplaceable. Eleventh (possibly tenth or twelfth) century, gray Rhenish romanesque, Gregorian chants, the opportunity to become a temporary monk or to stay in a luxury hotel and at the same time participate in all the delights of the liturgy and the consolations of almost all the sacraments. An area— again I quote a protocol official—abounding in "positively unique opportunities for country rambles" in which, depending on the condition of the heart, lungs, or glands, one can spend half an hour, an entire hour, an hour and a half, three hours, in fact a whole day walking or hiking, equipped with a handy foolproof local map obtainable free of charge from the hall porter at the luxury hotel. The fact that in the luxury hotel one can also be a temporary husband or wife is familiar to cynics, who know that the management there is both discreet and broad-minded.

Only the protocol department is in a position to appreciate the invaluable role Staech performs for the benefit of wives of prominent visitors to the nation's capital. While their husbands get down to the nitty-gritty in the capital, the ladies enjoy being driven out to Staech in the protocol Mercedes. Departure is timed for the visitor to arrive in the morning for the Terce or Sext services and thus admire the nobly clad monks both aurally and visually (it is said that there have even been attempts at tactile perception). This is followed by light refreshments or lunch, and then, depending on time, mood, and stamina, a stroll through the truly magnificent woods, and in the afternoon attendance at Nones or Vespers, followed by tea and a drive back, filled with a deep spiritual peace, to the capital. And German as well as foreign politicians find Staech unique as a place of meditation and purification; some very strong-minded men have been seen humbly and tearfully kneeling there. Guests from the United States and Africa are particularly enchanted with Staech, it has even been claimed that spontaneous conversions have taken place there. And, needless to say, where Ora is demonstrated with such credibility, Labora is not forgotten either: brothers with rough hands, mud on their hands and feet, their habits sometimes even bespattered with cow dung, are to be seen from time to time, and the strange part about it is: these working monks are not merely on show, they are genuine.

One surprising aspect is that the monks are always so willing to leave this idyllic spot. The travel itch of the monks of Staech has not escaped the affectionate mockery of the good Rhenish people in the neighborhood: a well-to-do local wag with an unpaid debt of gratitude to the monks is said to have once presented them with a whole collection of suitcases for Christmas. The monks really do love to travel; they lecture, with and without slides, participate in conferences, seminars, panel discussions; some of them contribute as free-lance writers to the supplements of serious national journals, discussing matters of theology, religion, and Christianity; and they seize every opportunity of going off to Hamburg, Munich, or Frankfurt. Yes, they love to go away, these monks, and they are not always happy to come back. Some are motorized, most are not. Hence the nominal full strength, amounting at present to forty-seven monks and brothers, is seldom achieved.

There have been occasions when only eleven, and once only nine, were present at afternoon Nones. After one such service a very prominent lady from Thailand apprehensively asked the protocol official whether there was some contagion in the air and whether—she had been nourished on early nineteenth-century literature—the reverend gentlemen were "stricken." The official found himself obliged to seek an explanation from the abbot and was given the devastating information that only one was sick, the others were all away on their travels.

Since in this age of technology the number of salaried workers is perforce steadily increasing (farming, hotel staff, administration), Staech is not financially self-supporting. It is liberally subsidized by state and diocese; and, moreover, the fact that it is supported is taken for granted. Not once has this fact been challenged in the finance committee, not even by the most religiously emancipated of its members. Who would want to see Staech deprived of its subsidies? That would be like suggesting that Cologne Cathedral be sold as a quarry. Even rabid freethinkers, irreligious Socialists (there are still some of those about), have never thought of withholding approval of the funds earmarked for Staech. Paradoxically enough, in latter years a contrary trend has become noticeable: the representatives of the classic Christian parties are hesitating somewhat longer, whereas the others are consenting with almost embarrassing alacrity. Of one thing there can be no doubt: even the most pettifogging atheist in the capital would not refuse Staech his support. Staech is something it ought not to be: dependent on the state and on the diocese in whose territory it is located. Of course, state and diocese are in a way dependent on Staech, but who could ever plumb the depths of such dialectics of varying interdependence?

One thing is certain; the abbot collects, and not too badly either. But in return state and diocese want to see something, or rather: they feel there should be something to see and hear. What, after all, is the use of a vast abbey like that, with all its complex economy (which is more complex than its tradition), if, as happened one foggy autumn day during the visit of a (non-Catholic) queen, only fifteen nobly garbed monks were present and the choral singing, even though each one "gave it all he had," sounded thin? Moreover, the participants included two aged bedridden monks who had been pressed somewhat forcibly into service. The queen was disappointed, very disappointed. During the ensuing informal lunch at the hotel she looked almost miffed, like a girl who has been done out of a date. After all, Staech stands for something. At home the queen had requested a thorough briefing on the history, tradition, and function of Staech.

As was inevitable, the news of the choir's poor numerical showing reached the ears of the head of state. He—the head of state— was most annoyed and passed on his annoyance to the archbishop, who communicated the incident in a handwritten document beginning "Scandalum juisse . . ." to the order's abbot general in Rome: the latter took up the matter with Staech and insisted on a list of those present and those absent, with detailed information on the absent monks' reasons for travel. The inquiries were, naturally, somewhat protracted, and even after some pretty massive interpolations the results were meager. Only sixteen of the absent monks could come up with an adequate alibi: eight had been occupied in a completely bona fide pursuit—conducting religious exercises in a convent—and eight had been away on lecture tours for Christian educational projects, some with, some without, colored slides. Five of the younger monks had left to attend a writers' conference ("We must seek contacts with the progressive elements of our own country"), the topic of which had caused both head of state and bishop considerable raising of eyebrows: "Orgasm as Depicted in Contemporary German Literature." It turned out later that four of these young monks had found the topic boring and spent most of their time at the movies, and in the balcony at that, where they could smoke. The alibis for the remaining eleven monks remained obscure. Two had ostensibly gone off to another monastery with which Staech was on friendly terms, to consult some volumes of the Acta Sanctorum, those in the Staech library having been stolen during the years of postwar confusion; the two monks had never arrived at the other monastery and, what was more, stubbornly refused to say where they had actually been (as yet unclarified). One monk had gone to Holland, with a purpose but no destination: purpose—to study the changes in Dutch Catholicism. This objective was termed by the bishop "rather vague." The objective of four other monks was given as: the study of Bavarian and Austrian baroque; they may have been traipsing around anywhere between Wiirzburg and the Hungarian border, but they did bring back an alibi in the form of a pretty good crop of colored slides. One monk had gone to a North German university town ostensibly to encourage an eminent physicist in his desire to convert to Catholicism; what had actually happened (as the physicist himself subsequently told the head of state at a reception) was that the monk tried to prevent the conversion.

Well, there was trouble. The abbot could not be deposed, only voted out of office, and this was something the monks refused to do. They liked their abbot. For a while the abbot managed to curb the monks' travel itch. The next state visitor was a president from Africa, who turned out to be an expert, having been educated by Benedictines. There were thirty-two monks present, but even thirty-two monks do not make the Staech choir seem exactly overcrowded. The effect is roughly that of a hundred and fifty bishops inside St. Peter's: something like a sightseeing group of elderly sacristans. The head of state, amazed at the African guest's fund of knowledge about the order, expressed distinct annoyance to the head of protocol and raised the question of whether Staech was still fulfilling its function. . . . The result was a verbal confrontation between protocol officials and the diocesan secretariat.

The topic remained a secret, but some things inevitably leaked out: the curbing of travel itch at Staech had been followed by accesses of kleptomania and exhibitionism. Eleven of the younger monks had had to be consigned to a private psychiatric clinic. The abbot's request that notice of important state visits be given well in advance, in order that he might adjust the monks' travel movements accordingly, was refused. He was tersely informed that it was up to Staech to be "ready for action" at all times, since guests, such as journalists from the Eastern European bloc, often turned up at short notice, eager to see the sights.

What might be called the "Staech affair" ran on for about a year, when suddenly, one crisp but sunny spring day, head of state and bishop made an unannounced appearance. How these two old codgers had managed to keep their arrangements a secret was never divulged. Well-informed circles assume these must have been made during the solemn reading of the petition for beatification of the nun Huberta Dörffler; the two men had been seen whispering together. Both men had simply given orders after breakfast to "harness" their Mercedes 600s and be driven to Staech, where they had met, and, without first calling on the abbot, immediately entered the church, Terce having just begun. Present in the church were fourteen monks.

During the subsequent serving of light refreshments (bread, wine, olives), the abbot not only seemed relaxed, he was relaxed. He said that, after having managed to achieve almost a full complement during the visit of an eminent Scandinavian guest—forty-three monks in the choir!—he had been obliged to reopen the "safety valve." In reply to the bishop's sarcastic question as to what relevance the words "safety valve" had to the monastic rule, the abbot responded with a cordial invitation to have a look at the medical reports of the psychiatric clinic. The two gentlemen who had come to inflict a defeat on the abbot suffered one themselves. The abbot declared that he for his part couldn't care less about state visits, and that he found the politicians who from time to time fled to Staech in search of consolation and tranquillity a nuisance. He expressed his willingness, in the case of state visits of special importance, to allow alumni and minor orders to take part in choral prayer as guests dressed in monks' habits. Transportation for such auxiliary personnel, as well as the procurement of monks' habits, would be a matter for the Most Reverend Lord Bishop and/or the Right Honorable Herr President to arrange. "And should you wish," he added, with irreverent frankness, "to resort to actors, by all means do so! I decline any further responsibility."

At the next state visit (a Catholic dictator from southwestern Europe), seventy-eight monks could be counted in the Staech choir, by far the majority youthful. In the car, on his way back to the capital, the dictator remarked to his escort, "These Germans! There's no one like them! Even their new generation of ascetic young monks can't be beaten." What he never found out, and what could never be confirmed in the capital, was that sixty of the young monks had been students who had demonstrated there in protest against the dictator's visit and had been arrested; they had been promised release and, in return for a honorarium of forty marks (they had first demanded seventy but finally consented to forty), had been persuaded to have their hair cut.

Meanwhile people have been saying in the capital that the chief of protocol came to a verbal agreement with the chief of police: to be more generous in the arrest of student demonstrators during state visits and more generous in their release. Since a relationship exists between state visits and student demonstrations analogous to that between state visits and sightseeing tours of Staech, the Staech problem is regarded as solved. On the occasion of a visit of an Asian statesman, who then evinced an almost churlish lack of interest in monks, eighty-two monks could be counted. It seems there are now also some freeloaders, who obtain more accurate information on the dates of pending state visits than the abbot has as yet been able to do, and who then proceed to demonstrate rather too demonstratively (in the opinion of objective observers)—even investing now and again in a few tomatoes or eggs—in order to be arrested, then released, and acquire a free haircut plus forty marks and a copious lunch at Staech which, at the express wish of the abbot, is charged to diocesan rather than state funds.

Musically speaking, neither freeloaders nor students have so far presented any problem. Gregorian chants seem to come naturally to them. The only problems are those arising between the demonstrating groups, one group denouncing the other as "mercenary consumer-opportunists" and the latter denouncing the former as "abstract fantasists." The abbot of Staech gets along well with both groups, some of the young men—seven so far, apparently—have already entered the monastery as novices, and the fact that now and again during choir practice they slip a Ho Chi Minh into the Gregorian rhythm has so far gone unnoticed, even by a recently converted American statesman who, weary of NATO talk, spent a longer period at Staech than had been provided for by the protocol department. In a farewell communiqué he intimated that his visit to Staech had enriched his image of Germany by an important facet.

Translated by Leila Vennewitz

Till Death Us Do Part

In the draft from the swing door her first match went out, a second one broke on the striking surface, and it was nice of her attorney to offer her his lighter, shielding the flame with his hand.
Now at last she could smoke—both felt good, the cigarette and the
sunshine. It had taken barely ten minutes, an eternity, and perhaps
it was that eternity as well as the permanence of those endless corridors that put the hands of the clock out of action. And the crowds,
all those people looking for room numbers, reminded her of a summer clearance sale at Strössel's. What was the difference between
divorces and bath towels at a clearance sale? Lineups for both, only
that—so it seemed to her—in divorces the final decision was announced more speedily, and speed, after all, was what she had been
after. *Schröder vs. Schröder.* Divorced. *Naumann vs. Naumann.* Divorced. *Blutzger vs. Blutzger.* Divorced.

Was the nice lawyer really going to say at this point what he was
obliged to say? The only thing he could say? He said it: "Don't take
it so hard." Said it although he knew she wasn't taking it hard at
all, yet he had to say it, he said it nicely, and it was nice that he said
it nicely. And naturally he didn't have much time, had to hurry off
to the next case, appear again in court, line up again. *Klotz vs.
Klotz.* Divorced.

Things had been much the same at the clearance sale: waiting
politely, never impatient yet ever attentive until the woman who
was too old to wear out even a single new bath towel had decided
to take a whole dozen; then on to the next customer, who was
clutching three swimsuits. After all, even at Strössel's there was still
such a thing as personal service, not like at those discount stores
where they unload junk on the customers. After all, the attorney
couldn't go on standing beside her forever, there really not being

much more to say than "Don't take it so hard." Her position at the top of the steps reminded her acutely of another occasion, seven years ago, when she had stood at the top of the steps leading up to City Hall: parents, witnesses, parents-in-law, photographer, cute little trainbearers—Irmgard's, Ute's, and Oliver's kids; bouquets, the taxi decorated with white roses, the "Till death us do part" still ringing in her ears, and on by taxi to the second ceremony, and once again, this time in church, "Till death us do part."

And here was the bridegroom waiting for her again at the foot of these steps, elated at the successful outcome and a bit embarrassed but also visibly proud of his second success of the day: having managed to find, here at the very foot of the steps, in one of the most hopeless parking areas in town, a spot for his car. Successes of various kinds had played quite a role in the divorce proceedings.

Now it wasn't death but the court that had separated them, and the occasion had lacked all dignity. And if the court, in pronouncing the divorce, had established death, why then wasn't there a funeral? Catafalque, mourners, candles, funeral oration? Or at least the wedding in reverse? Cute little kids, this time maybe Herbert's—Gregor and Marika—who would unfasten her train, lift the bridal wreath off her head, exchange her white dress for a suit: a kind of nuptial striptease performed in public on the steps if there wasn't going to be a funeral?

She had known, of course, that he would be waiting for her here, to start another of those futile discussions, since death had now been established—futile because he couldn't grasp the fact that there was nothing more she wanted from him now that she had moved with their son into a small apartment, neither money, nor her share in the "Jointly acquired assets," nor even those six Louis—the how-many-th was it again?—chairs that were indisputably hers, inherited from her grandmother. One day he would probably unload them outside her door because he "simply couldn't stand disputed ownership." She wanted neither the chairs nor the set of Meissen porcelain (thirty-six pieces), nor any kind of a "property settlement." Nothing. After all, she had the boy, for the time being, since he was still living, unmarried, with that other woman—which one was it now, Lotte or Gaby? Not until he married Lotte or Gaby (or was it Connie?) would they have to "share" the boy (and there was no Solomon holding the sword over the child to be shared); all those nasty details about custody had been agreed upon, settled, and so there would be visiting rights, she would hand over the child to be stuffed and spoiled. ("Are you sure you don't want any more whipped cream?" and "Do you really like your new parka?" and "Of course I'll get you the model airplane.") For one day, for two, or a day and a half, and she would pick him up again. ("No, I really can't buy you a new parka, and I can't buy you a color TV for your first communion"—Or was it confirmation? "No.")

Another cigarette? Better not. Now that the nice attorney with the chic little lighter no longer stood at her side, that draft from the swing door would force her to light the new cigarette from the old, and little things like that would make her look more of a slut than ever and, when it came to the final decision about the child, would certainly count as a black mark against her. This habit of smoking on the street had already been noted in the divorce files; besides, since she had admitted to being guilty of adultery (before he had, which also had to be admitted), she had anyway been recorded in the court documents as a kind of slut. All that nattering about whether or why women shouldn't, couldn't, mightn't smoke on the street had been described by the opposing attorney as a "pseudo-emancipatory" affectation not appropriate to her "educational level."

A good thing he didn't come up the steps, that he restricted himself to beckoning gestures; a good thing, too, that he shook his head in disapproval when she did, after all, light that second cigarette—not from the first one but with a match that didn't go out, although the clearance sale kept the swing door in constant motion.

Despite the absence of either priest or registry official, of tearful mothers and mothers-in-law, of photographer and cute little kids, at least there might have been an undertaker who would have driven off with something—what?—in a coffin, cremated it, and somewhere—where?—secretly buried it.

Probably he was even missing an appointment for her sake (the merger negotiations with Hocker & Hocker, perhaps, where he had been appointed to solve personnel problems); but would he really miss the Hocker & Hocker negotiations for the sake of a few chairs? He couldn't grasp, simply couldn't, that she didn't hate him at all, that she wanted nothing from him, that he had not merely ceased to matter to her but had become a stranger, someone she had once known, once married, who had become someone else. They had been successful in everything: building a career and building a house. They had failed in only one thing: keeping death at bay. Nor was it only he who had died—she had died too; even her memory of him failed her. And perhaps the clerics and bureaucrats couldn't and wouldn't grasp the fact that this "Till death us do part" didn't mean physical death at all, much less a death before a physical death, that it meant only the entry of a total stranger into the conjugal bedroom insisting on rights he no longer possessed. The role of the court that issued this death certificate and called it a divorce was as irrelevant as that of the priest and the registry official: no one could revive the dead or make death reversible.

She threw down the cigarette, ground it out, and waved him away, finally and firmly. There was nothing further to discuss, and she knew exactly where he was intending to drive her: to the café out in Haydn Park, where at this hour the Turkish waitress would be placing miniature copper vases, each containing one tulip and one hyacinth, on the tables, and straightening the tablecloths; where—at this hour—somewhere in the background a vacuum cleaner was still being used. He had always called it the "café of Memories," condescendingly pronouncing it "quite good, not high class, certainly not smart." No, she repeated her final dismissive gesture, once, twice, until, shaking his head, he finally did get into his red car, maneuver out of his parking slot and, without waving to her again, drive off, "carefully but self-confidently," in his customary manner.

It was not yet nine-thirty, and now at last she could walk down the steps, buy a newspaper, and enter the café across the street. What a relief that he no longer barred her way down the steps! She was in no hurry, and there were a few things she wanted to think about. At twelve, when her son came home from school, she would give him a big pancake with some canned cherries, and some grilled tomatoes, he loved that. She would play with him, help him with his homework, and maybe go to a movie, maybe even to Haydn Park, to establish the final death of memory. Over canned cherries, pancake, and grilled tomatoes he would naturally ask her whether she was going to get married again. No, she would say, no. One death was enough for her. And would she be going back to work at Strössel's, where he was allowed to sit in the back room, do his homework, play with fabric swatches, and where that nice Mr. Strössel sometimes stroked his head in a friendly way? No. No.

The tablecloth at the café pleased her, felt good under her hands; it actually was pure cotton, old rose with silver stripes, and she thought of the tablecloths at the café in Haydn Park: maize-yellow, coarsely woven, those first ones had been, seven years ago: later came the green ones, with a printed daisy pattern, and finally the bright yellow ones, with no pattern at all but a fringed border, and he had always (and would have done so today) fidgeted with the fringe and tried to persuade her that she really did have a right to some kind of compensation, at least fifteen—maybe twenty—thousand marks that he could (and would) easily raise with a mortgage on the unencumbered house—after all, she had always been a "good although unfaithful spouse, careful and thrifty without being stingy" and had participated "quite positively and productively in the enhancement of their standard of living." As for those Louis chairs and the Meissen porcelain, she really was entitled to those. His fury at her refusal to take any of that had exceeded his fury over her lapse with Strössel; and finally he had (and would have done so today) ripped off some of the cheap fringe and thrown it on the floor—disapproving looks from the Turkish waitress, who was just arriving with tea and coffee, tea for him, coffee for her—further grounds for ominous remarks about her health and a scornful gesture toward the ashtray (which, incidentally, was ugly, dark brown, floor-colored—and which, she must admit, already contained three butts!).

Yes, coffee. Here she was, drinking coffee again, turning over the pages of the newspaper. Here in the café she could also smoke undisturbed, without inviting annoying glances or snide remarks. She thought of the shoving and chasing in the endless corridors of the courthouse, with all those hurrying people who had a sense of injury or had inflicted injury, who were owed rent or hadn't paid rent, where everything was decided and nothing clarified, by nice attorneys and nice judges who couldn't keep death at bay.

Again and again she caught herself smiling at the thought of the timing of the death that had separated them. It had started a year ago, when they were having dinner at the home of his boss, and he suddenly remarked that she was "involved in textiles," which sounded as if she were a carpet or fabric weaver or designer,

whereas she had simply been a saleswoman in a dry-goods store—
and how happy she had been there, her hands unfolding, refolding,
everything pleasing to the hands, the eyes and, when business was
quiet, tidying everything up, putting things back into drawers, onto
shelves and racks: towels, sheets, handkerchiefs, shirts, and socks,
and then one day that nice young man had turned up, the one who
had just died, and had asked to see some shirts, although he had no
intention of buying one or the money to do so—turned up simply
because he was looking for someone to whom he could spill out his
excitement over his success: three years after graduating from night
school ("I'm involved in electrotechnology," and all he'd been was
an electrician) he already had his degree and had been given a subject for his doctoral thesis. And now that phrase, "my wife's involved in textiles," which was supposed to sound at least like
applied arts if not art, and how angry, almost sick with rage, it had
made him when she said, "Yes, I was a saleswoman in a dry-goods
store, and I still help them out sometimes." In the car on the way
home not a word, not a syllable, icy silence, hands gripping the
steering wheel.

The coffee was surprisingly good, the newspaper boring ("industrial profits too low, wages too high"), and what she picked up from
the conversations around her all seemed to be about court cases.
("Facts twisted." "I can prove that the sofa belongs to me." "I'm
not going to let them take away my son."). Attorneys' gowns, attorneys' briefcases. An office messenger brought some files that were
solemnly opened, carefully scrutinized. And then the young waitress bringing her a second cup of coffee actually put a hand on her
shoulder and said, "Don't take it too hard. It'll pass. I cried my eyes
out for weeks—weeks, I tell you." She was ready to be angry, but
then she smiled and said, "It's already passed." And the waitress
went on, "And I was the guilty party too." Too? she thought. Am I
the guilty party, and if so how do I show it—because I smoke,
maybe? Drink coffee, read the paper, and smile? Yes, of course she
was guilty, she had refused to acknowledge the death soon enough
and had continued to live out those deadly months with him. Until
one day he brought home a new evening dress, bright red, very low-
cut, saying, "Wear this to the company dance tonight—I'd like you
to dance with my boss and show him everything you've got," but
she had worn her old silver-gray with the bead pattern she liked. A

month later, when he found out about the affair with Strössel, she remembered his fury when he said, "What you refused to show my boss you've now shown to yours."

Yes, so she had—not long after he had moved out of the bedroom into the guest room, and the next morning had come back into the bedroom with all that porn stuff and a whip and had started a terrible row about his sexual achievements, which she was denying him but which he urgently needed; they were in such stark contrast to his professional achievements that he was developing a neurosis, almost a psychosis; there was no way she could offer him this satisfaction, she had taken away the whip and locked the door after him. The stuff had turned her ice cold, and she blamed herself for still not acknowledging the death, taking the child, ordering a taxi, and driving away. In actual fact she had gone on to share in the remodeling of the house—guest room, guest bathroom, TV room, study, sauna, children's room—and it had been her idea to go to Strössel and ask for a discount, for bath and hand towels, sheets and pillowcases, drapery fabrics. Naturally she had felt a bit uneasy when Strössel looked deep into her eyes and increased the discount from twenty to forty percent; and when his eyes grew misty and he tried to grab her across the counter, she had murmured, "For heaven's sake, not here, not here," and Strössel got the wrong (or right) idea and thought that somewhere else she would be willing. She had actually gone upstairs with him, with that pudgy, bald bachelor who was twenty years older than she and blissful when she lay down with him. And meanwhile he had left the store open and the cash register unattended, and not even the unavoidable unbuttoning and buttoning of clothing had embarrassed her. And later when he packed up her purchases downstairs at the cash desk, he hadn't given her a discount but had made her pay the full retail price, and when he held the door open for her, he hadn't tried to kiss her. The opposing attorney had actually tried to have Strössel attest to her claim of "discount withheld after favors granted," but then her nice attorney had succeeded in keeping Strössel out of it. Yes, she had gone back to Strössel several times. "Not to make purchases?" "No." "How often?" She didn't know, really she didn't. She hadn't counted. Marriage had never been spoken of, the word "love" never mentioned. It was that soft, deeply moved and moving bliss of Strössel's that made her afraid of sinking back onto a rose-colored pillow.

No, she couldn't go back to him, and his old-fashioned store would have been the right place for her, where she knew every case and box, every shelf and drawer, knew the stocks that genuinely did consist of only wool and cotton; she and her hands, that were infallible when it came to spotting any adulteration by even the tiniest synthetic thread. No, she couldn't work in one of those "cheap and nasty" stores either, as Strössel always called them. No, she wouldn't marry again, be present again when a living person died and once again a death separated her. She supposed the time had come when husbands became brutally obscene, and lovers, in an old-fashioned way that was almost too rose-colored, became tender and blissful.

"See?" said the waitress when she paid her bill. "Now we're feeling a bit better, aren't we? After all, you're still a young woman, nice-looking too, and"—here it came—"you've got all your life before you and your son'll stick by you!" She smiled at the waitress again as she left the café. She would bake her son a hazelnut cake, buy the ingredients on the way home, and if he asked her, "Do I really have to go to that woman?" (Connie, Gaby, Lotte?), she would say, "No!" And then there was still the firm of Haunschiider, Krermm & Co., Strössel's old competitors, where the infallibility of her hands would be equally in demand. Only that it was more of a mail-order house, and she wouldn't so often be able to unfold a shirt and smooth it out, as she had done for that attractive young man who had just received his degree and been given the subject for his doctoral thesis. Perhaps instead of cherries she would buy some smoked herring, he liked that just as much, and he would stand beside her while it turned crisp in the pan, while the pancake dough enfolded it and turned golden-brown. She could probably become a buyer at Haunschiider, Krermm & Co.; she knew she could rely on her hands, no adulterating thread would get past them.

Translated by Leila Vennewitz

Rendezvous with Margret; or, Happy Ending

The journey there was pleasant: the Rhine still under early-morning mist; weeping willows, barges, sirens, the trip taking precisely as long as I needed for my breakfast. Coffee and rolls acceptable, eggs fried; no baggage, just cigarettes, newspaper, matches, return ticket, ballpoint pen, wallet, and handkerchief, and the certainty of seeing Margret again. After so many years, after several abortive meetings, after knowing her for more than forty years, I had been surprised and stirred by something I had never seen before: her handwriting, strong yet graceful, and the words, written on the death announcement with surprising firmness: "do come—it would give me so much pleasure to see you again." The small "d" in "do" made me suspect that she had never come to terms with the capital "D"; we all have a letter or two that we stumble over.

On arrival I got rid of my largest piece of baggage, the newspaper. I left it behind in the dining car and reached the cemetery in good time after my own fashion: too late for the Largo, the De Profundis, and the incense in the chapel, too late also to join the cortège. I was just in time to see the acolytes taking off their vestments and bundling them under their arms as they walked away. The taller one unscrewed the processional cross into three sections, packing it away in a case obviously designed for that purpose, and as they got into the waiting taxi they all lit cigarettes: priest, driver, and acolytes. The driver offered the priest a light, the younger acolyte did the same for the older one, and at that point one of them must have made a joke: I saw them all laugh, saw the older acolyte coughing with laughter and cigarette smoke, and I had to laugh too, when I thought of the sacristy cupboards where in another five minutes they would be putting away their paraphernalia: oak, baroque, three hundred years old, the pride of the parish of St. Francis Xavier, which in 1925 had been renamed St. Peter Canisius; and it wasn't I, it was the deceased who had just been buried, on whose coffin clods of earth were still falling, he who had saved the day in 1945 by his inspired recollection of the depth of those cupboards where, behind the neat piles of altar linen and various sacred utensils, we had hidden cigarettes and coffee stolen from the Americans when they left their Jeeps unattended or invited us in groups to a kind of Werewolf-reeducation. It was he, not I, who, with the corrupt cunning of the European, had correctly sized up the Americans' naive awe of ecclesiastical institutions, and for years I had wondered why, instead of claiming credit for this inspiration, he had always ascribed it to me. Much later, long after I had left home, it dawned on me that a story of that kind would have done no service to his respectability, whereas it "fitted" me, although I never really had that idea nor ever would have.

I approached the Zerhoff family grave with circumspection, avoiding the paths on which I would have encountered men with and without top hats, ladies with and without Persian lamb coats, former schoolmates and knights of Catholic orders, schoolmates as knights of Catholic orders. I walked along the familiar path between the rows of graves to our own family grave, where the last burial—my father's—had taken place five years ago; it had been insinuated that he had died brokenhearted because neither of his two sons had begotten a male heir in any woman's womb; well, he had no female heir either. The burial plot was well cared for, the lease paid; the gravel was truly snow-white, the beds of pansies heart-shaped, the pansies in turn—nine or eleven to a bed—planted in the shape of a heart. The names of Mother, Father, and Josef on the lectern-shaped marble gravestones; above Josef's name, the inevitable iron cross; the gravestones of long-dead ancestors overgrown with ivy and, rising above all the graves, the simple, classicistic, vaguely Puritan cross, to which had later been added a scroll proclaiming in neo-Gothic script: "Love never endeth." A gravestone was ready for me, too, the last bearer of the name; the dash after my name and birth date, that graphic "to," had something ominous about it. Who would continue to pay the (not inconsiderable) lease when my earthly days were done? Margret, probably. She was a woman in good health, well off, childless, a tea drinker, a moderate smoker, and in the melody of her handwriting, particularly in the small "d," I could perceive a long life for her.

I stood behind the tamarisk hedge, now grown quite dense, that separated the Zerhoff burial plot from ours, and then I saw her: she seemed more attractive than ever, more so than the girl of fifteen with whom I had lain in the grass, more so than the woman of twenty, thirty, and thirty-five with whom I had had those embarrassing and abortive reunions, the last one fifteen years ago in Sinzig when she turned on her heel outside the hotel room and drove away; she hadn't even allowed me to take her to the station. She must be close to fifty now, her thick, rather coarse blond hair had turned an attractive gray, and black suited her.

As children we had often had to come out here on summer evenings to water the flowers: my brother Josef, Margret, myself, and her brother Franzi, into whose grave the last members of the cortege were just then throwing their flowers or their shovelfuls of earth; the familiar drumming of earth on wood, the impact of the bunches of mimosa like the alighting of a bird. Often we had spent our streetcar money on ice cream, setting out on the long homeward journey on foot and, in the summer heat, soon regretting our recklessness, but invariably Josef had produced some hidden "reserves" and paid our fares home, and on the streetcar, relieved and tired, we would argue about whether he had paid for our ice cream or our fares.

I still had to fight back my tears when I thought of Josef, and I still didn't know, after thirty-four years I didn't know, whether it was his death or his last wish that brought tears to my eyes. At the very end of the platform, beyond the station roof, before the arrival of the leave train, we had once again discussed ways and means of not returning to the front, fever, accident, medical certificates—and in the end it was Margret who broke the taboo and spoke of—what do they call it?—"desertion," and Father had stamped his foot in rage and said, "There is no such thing as desertion in our family!" and Josef had laughed and said, "Where to? Am I supposed to swim across the Channel or to Sweden, or across Lake Constance to Switzerland—and Vladivostok, you know, is a pretty long way off," and he was already standing on the steps, the stationmaster had blown his whistle, when he leaned, down once more and said clearly, more to me than to my father, "Please, no priests at my grave, no mumbo jumbo at any memorial service." He was nineteen, had given up the study of theology, and Margret was at that time considered almost his fiancée. We never saw him again. We winced, I more than my father, Margret less, as if whipped by his last words; and of course, when the news of his death arrived, I reminded Father of Josef's last wish, not repeating his words, I was too scared to do that, but simply saying, "you know what he asked for, what his last wish was." But Father had waved me away and, I need hardly say, not done as Josef had asked. They had indeed had their memorial service, with incense, Latin, and catafalque; in solemn pomp they had executed their precise choreography, in their black, gold-embroidered brocade robes, and they had even rounded up a choir of theology students who sang something in Greek. The Eastern Churches were already becoming very fashionable. I have never entered a church since, except as an acolyte and in my later capacity as salesman of devotional supplies; and when Franzi Zerhoff and I had assisted at solemn requiems, they had sometimes reminded me, in their heavy, gold-embroidered brocade robes, of Soviet marshals with their bulky gold shoulder pieces and their chests covered with about a hundred and fifty decorations. Always plenty of Latin, male choir in red-and-white sashes, top hats trembling in their hands, and the air trembling with the vehemence of their chest tones.

Margret's mouth was surprisingly small and still not hard under her austere nose; she was slimmer, only her wrists revealed traces of plumpness. There she stood, dignified, erect, shaking hands, nodding, yet she had kept that swift, ephemeral, springy quality. The gray around her head reminded me of the whitish-gray dust in her hair when we staggered out of the burning house and lay down in the garden on the grass, came together on that June night after saying good-bye to Josef, when so many values and so much that was valuable had been destroyed; and I thought of the dust in her kisses, in her tears, of our irresponsible laughter when Father also came staggering out of the house and saw us lying there, and how our dust-powdered faces screwed up with laughter when he twisted the key to his safe in the air as if it, the air, contained his securities and all that notarized stuff; and of course he didn't know, none of us knew, that in this so charmingly conventional war degrees of heat would build up that venerable safes could not withstand. And in the end, when later they were poking through the debris, he had found nothing but ashes in his molten safe, and it had been Margret, not I (who was of course familiar with such sayings), who told him, "Memento, quia pulvis es et . . .", but she did not complete the sentence. For a time we were inseparable, but we never came together again, not even with a kiss, not even with a handclasp.

Margret turned toward me and, in a kind of bitter joy, her woman's face changed to the face of that girl who, with me, had scorned accepted values on that June night—or had I then embraced the Margret of today, had I at last caught up with her, she with me? Had Josef's curse at last truly united us? I thought of him, of the whiplash with which he had changed the course of my life, and I realized here, at last, that that was what he had wanted: to change the course of my life, away from gold brocade, male choirs, family graves, real and potential knights of Catholic orders. Perhaps that was the only thing he had learned in that gloriously conventional war, and today, here, facing Margret, I had no reason to bear a grudge against him on that score. I bore no grudge against anyone, not even against my father, who later became very silent, almost humble, and who always looked so expectantly at me when Margret came over from next door. We used to go to the movies, to the theater, for walks, we had long discussions—but we never got as far as even a handclasp, even a flicker of memory. I carried on as an acolyte, regarding it as a job (tips and free meals); I got into the black market, finished high school, left home, and, via the black market, ended up in the devotional-supplies business when I was asked to get hold of a Leonardo da Vinci print for a Moselle vintner's first communion in exchange for butter, and did so. I had a few affairs, and I imagine Margret did, too.

I was standing close enough to be able to read the word "Blackbird," from Margret's lips. I nodded, withdrew, and headed for the "Blackbird," where funeral receptions have been held since time immemorial. I only had to go back to the exit, cross the street, and walk for five minutes through Douglas firs. At the "Blackbird" they were already busy cutting up limp rolls, spreading them with butter, adding slices of sausage or cheese, and decorating them with mayonnaise. I wondered whether Aunt Marga was still alive, she had always insisted on having blood sausage with onion rings, as greedily as if she were starving, although everyone knew that not even she had any idea of the extent of her fortune. The coffee machine was steaming, brandy snifters were being placed on trays, freshly opened bottles beside them (Margret was sure to have firmly insisted on a price "by the bottle"), bottles of mineral water were being snapped open, flowers stuck in little vases. Still the same old, old-fashioned routine.

I recognized the priest, who had arrived without the acolytes and was sitting in a corner smoking a cigar with a contented, off-duty expression. He nodded at me. Not because he recognized me, we had never met. He looked like a nice fellow, I sat down at his table and asked him about the special carrying case for the collapsible cross: in my days as an acolyte we used to have to lug the whole cross around, and it had always been a problem getting it into a car without smashing a window or knocking top hats off heads. And I knew of a few rural communities where the old processional cross was still in use. He told me the name of the company, I jotted it down on my return ticket, then we both speculated as to why people continued to put up with those limp rolls. I told him that even as children we had called those sandwiches "Blackbird pasteboard with mayonnaise," whether we were present as mourners or acolytes or—as frequently happened—as mourning acolytes. They were behind the times, there should be "Hawaiian Toast" or something, and sherry, not brandy, and not Persian lamb coats but mink, and instead of the lousy coffee—why did it always have to be so lousy everywhere?—they should have ordered mocha, which did sometimes turn out like reasonably good coffee.

I glanced at my return ticket, where I had noted the trains: 14:22, 15:17, then none till 17:03; it was now just on eleven, and if I wanted to take Margret along, if I wanted, after thirty-four years, to touch her hair that evening, I supposed I would have to stay on a while and run the risk of encountering a former schoolmate or two among the red-and-white sashes, maybe even among the Catholic knights: one of them was sure to shout the opening lines of The Odyssey—in Greek, of course—into my ear, to prove that his classical education had not failed to leave its mark on him. Another, although we had graduated from high school more than thirty years ago and not seen each other since, taking it for granted that I would fully agree, would start moaning about modern times, about his spoiled brats, the Socialists, the general moral decline, and how he was working himself to death in his practice while his third or fourth apartment building was costing him more and more due to this damned inflation. I was prepared to endure this; I knew this kind of talk from funerals I had attended not as a mourner but professionally: I also have an agency for gravestones, and my top hat counts as professional clothing and is tax-deductible. It couldn't take all that long: if we missed the 14:22 we would certainly catch the 15:17.

I was in luck, it was Bertholdi who sat down beside me. I recalled that in eight years of school I hadn't exchanged so much as forty words with him. There had been simply no occasion to do so, and I had reason to regret this now. He was a very nice fellow, without that bitter-sour expression that seems inevitable with successful as well as unsuccessful men at the start of the last third of their lives. Bertholdi asked how my business was going, and when I told him that I had been selling devotional supplies for some years now, he remarked that it must be hard going in this post–Vatican Council era. I agreed that business had taken a beating, but I could also report a certain upswing, and when he mentioned "Lefebvre?" I nodded but also shook my head. His shrewd question could be answered only partially in the affirmative: there was also, I said, independently of the person he had named, a return to the traditional that expressed itself in top hats, bridal trains, elaborate celebrations of first communions, confirmations, and weddings, and in its wake helped the sale of modern devotional supplies, well-crafted icon copies, for instance, in fact anything smacking of the Eastern Churches.

Because he spoke so nicely about his wife and children, I volunteered the information that, together with some business associates, I was engaged in opening up a new market for good icon reproductions: the Soviet Union, which we were supplying—illegally, of course—with excellent reproductions that were mounted over there on old wood panels, preferably worm-eaten, and painted over by skilled craftsmen, and for which there was a good demand. Since artists, craftsmen, and dealers naturally preferred foreign currency, quite a few of these reproductions were finding their way back via the tourist black market. Not exactly sharing in the profits, but doing its best to help, was an organization calling itself "Pictures for the Eastern Churches"; too many Soviet citizens in all the republics had sold off their family icons and now, caught up in the religious wave, found themselves without images. And, inwardly uneasy because Margret was still moving around and had not yet sat down, I went on to tell Bertholdi the trade's classic story of that long-dead colleague who, putting his trust in the religious currents prevalent during World War I, found himself stuck with some 10,000 portraits of Pope Benedict XV and lacked the financial and mental resources to save his business by profiting from the long reigns of the two Piuses. When asked by Bertholdi whether I would still invest much in Paul VI, I said," As a contemporary, perhaps; as a dealer in devotional supplies, no," adding that the only pope who had remained in demand after his death was John XXIII.

Bertholdi thanked me for this insight into the "subtleties" of my business and returned the compliment with an autobiographical sketch: he was a senior official in the educational system, complained neither of his children nor of the youth of today, spoke affectionately of his wife, laughingly discussed his pension with all its probable progressions and deductions; he hoped, he was confident, that he would be able to take early retirement so that he would finally have time to read Proust and Henry James. At last Margret came and sat down beside me, beckoned to a waitress to bring me a little pot of mocha, placed her hand on my arm, and said, "I remember how you hate bad coffee, and"—she didn't take away her hand—"Just now, when I saw you standing there, it occurred to me, after all these years it occurred to me, that he didn't curse God at all."

"No," I said, "it was only those cursed by God whom he cursed. And that curse was the blessing that he gave us."

Willi Offermann, seated across from us next to the priest, tried to bait me by speaking of Jerusalem and the Holy Sepulcher, and of people who had no religion yet lived very well off it. Did he mean me, or the dealers in devotional supplies in Jerusalem? Do I have no religion and live very well off it? Both questions filled me with doubts. True, I did live off it, but not as well as he seemed to believe, not even my gravestone agency brought in as much, although I can offer the latest designs and good African stones; and sometimes when I was checking a new shipment of rosaries (for which there was no longer much demand, at least not at the moment, in spite of Lefebvre), I would grasp one and recite the entire rosary. So as not to be looking constantly at Margret, who had got up again to tell a waiter carrying a plate of onion rings and slices of blood sausage to take it over to where Aunt Marga was indeed sitting, I looked at Offermann's wife: she was next to the priest and leaning across him in an effort to calm down her husband on the other side when Offermann suddenly raised his voice and started abusing the "Red scum!"—which was nonsense, because he hadn't seen me for thirty-one years and could have no idea whether I was red or green; besides, a minimum of logic should have told him that no sensible dealer in devotional supplies—and that's what I was—would ever vote for any party without the prefix "Christian." This was so obvious that he could have saved himself his uninformed provocation; I behaved as if he certainly couldn't mean me and smiled at his wife, who looked so nice that he couldn't possibly have deserved her.

Then Margret was beside me again, pouring mocha and remembering that I took whipped cream with it; she had brought over a little dish of it. She smelled of soap, toilet water, and perspiration, a smell that I perceived as familiar—yet it couldn't possibly be familiar to me. It was as if we had spent these thirty-four years together, her years becoming mine, a common tally of the years: some things neglected but nothing missed. I found her much more beautiful than on that June night; actually she had never been a beauty, she had always seemed like a girl who had been bicycling too fast and broken into a sweat, yet she had never been on a bicycle. As I looked at her she became younger and younger, until I could see her playing ball on the path between our two houses, flushed, eager, yet quiet, and she was, after all, the first and only woman from whose lips I had heard the word "desertion."

She kept her hand on my arm, and Offermann grew even angrier, prophesying doom, and seeming to hold me, me personally, responsible for the simultaneous decline in morals and faith; and not even when he spoke of my brother Josef ("Of course, if your brother Josef were still alive, but then the best always get killed!") did I allow myself to be provoked into saying something like You didn't get killed either, nor did Margret—who turned pale and whose hand on my arm was trembling. Finally Offermann attacked the priest, whom he accused of being too passive, and it was I who, in order to calm him down, whispered the opening lines of The Odyssey to him across the table. That actually had an effect: his face relaxed, and his wife smiled at me gratefully; the priest was relieved. I had looked at the time and found it was only twelve o'clock and that we would be able to catch the 14:22, and during my Homer recitation I thought of coffee and cakes on the train, thought of the crowded dining car, which was now moving beside the Rhine toward the Lorelei rock, and that probably they still served nothing but that seed cake that was enough to choke a person. But it was a long time since I had last ridden in the dining car in the afternoon, I merely remembered that Margret liked that damn cake. Once, on the train to Sinzig, she had told me it reminded her of a deceased aunt of whom she had been very fond. I beckoned to the waitress and asked her to order me a taxi for a quarter to two.

Translated by Leila Vennewitz

PART TWO

THE LOST HONOR OF KATHARINA BLUM

The Lost Honor of Katharina Blum; or, How Violence Develops and Where It Can Lead

The characters and action in this story are purely fictitious. Should the description of certain journalistic practices result in a resemblance to the practices of the Bild-Zeitung, such resemblance is neither intentional nor fortuitous, but unavoidable.

1

For the following account there are a few minor sources and three major ones; these will be named here at the beginning and not referred to again. Major sources are: the transcripts of the police interrogation; Hubert Blorna (attorney); and Peter Hach (public prosecutor, also high-school and university classmate of Hubert Blorna). It Was Hach who—in Confidence, needless to say-supplemented the transcripts and reported certain measures taken by the Police investigators as well as the results of their inquiries absent from the transcripts: not, we hasten to add, for official purposes but solely for private use. Hach was genuinely affected by the concern and frustration suffered by his friend Blorna, who could find no explanation for the whole affair and yet, "when I Come to think about it," found it "not inexplicable, but almost logical." Since the case of Katharina Blum will, in any event, remain more or less fictitious, because of the attitude of the accused and the very awkward position of her defense counsel Blorna, such minor and very human lapses in conduct as those committed by Hach may be not only understandable but forgivable.

The minor sources, some of greater and some of lesser significance, need not be mentioned here, since their respective implication, involvement, relevancy, bias, bewilderment, and testimony will all emerge from this report.

2

If this report—since there is such frequent mention of sources—should at times be felt to be "fluid," we beg the reader's forgiveness: it has been unavoidable. To speak of "sources" and "fluidity" is to preclude all possibility of composition, so perhaps we should instead introduce the concept of "bringing together," of "conduction," a concept that should be clear to anyone who as a child (or even as an adult) has ever played in, beside, or with puddles, draining them, linking them by channels, emptying, diverting, and rerouting them until the entire available puddlewater-potential is brought together in a collective channel to be diverted onto a different level or perhaps even duly rerouted in orderly fashion into the gutter or drain provided by the local authorities. The sole objective here, therefore, is to effect a kind of drainage. Clearly a due process of order! So whenever this account appears to be in a fluid state in which differences in and adjustments to level playa part, we ask the reader's indulgence, since there will always be stop-pages, blockages, siltings, unsuccessful attempts at conduction, and sources "that can never come together," not to mention subterranean streams, and so on, and soon.

3

The first facts to be presented are brutal: on Wednesday, February 20, 1974, on the eve of the traditional opening of Carnival, a young woman of twenty-seven leaves her apartment in a certain city at about 6:45 P.M. to attend a dance at a private home.

Four days later, after a dramatic—there is no getting around the word (and here we have an example of the various levels that permit the stream to flow)—turn of events, on Sunday evening at almost the same hour (to be precise, at about 7:04 P.M.) she rings the front door bell at the home of Walter Moeding, Crime Commissioner, who is at that moment engaged, for professional rather than private reasons, in disguising himself as a sheikh, and she declares to the startled Moeding that at about 12:15 noon that day she shot and killed Werner Tötges, reporter, in her apartment, and would the Commissioner kindly give instructions for her front door to be broken down and the reporter to be "removed"; for her part, she has spent the hours between 12:15 noon and 7:00 P.M. roaming around town in search of a remorse that she has failed to find; furthermore, she requests that she be arrested, she would like to be where her "dear Ludwig" is.

Moeding, to whom the young person is known from various interrogations and who feels a certain sympathy toward her, does not doubt her statement for a moment; he drives her in his own car to police headquarters, informs his superior, Chief Crime Commissioner Beizmenne, of the situation, has the young woman escorted to a cell, and fifteen minutes later meets Beizmenne outside her front door, where a police commando breaks down the door and finds the young woman's statement confirmed.

Let there not be too much talk about blood here, since only necessary differences in level are to be regarded as inevitable; we would therefore direct the reader to television and the movies and the appropriate musicals and gruesicals; if there is to be something fluid here, let it not be blood. Perhaps attention should merely be drawn to certain color effects: the murdered Tötges was wearing an improvised sheikh costume concocted from a rather worn sheet, and the effect of a lot of blood on a lot of white is well known; a pistol is then sure to act almost like a spray gun, and since in this instance the costume was made out of a large square of white cotton, modern painting or stage effects would seem to be more appropriate here than drainage. So be it. Those are the facts.

4

For a time it was considered not unlikely that Adolf Schönner, press photographer, who was also found shot but not until Ash Wednesday, in a wooded area to the west of the festive city, was likewise a victim of Blum; later, however, when a certain chronological order had been established for the course of events, this "proved to be unfounded." A cab driver stated later that he had driven Schönner disguised as a sheikh and a young female person dressed as an Andalusian woman to this very wood. But Tötges had been shot Sunday noon, whereas Schönner had not been killed until Tuesday noon. Although it was soon discovered that the murder weapon found beside Tötges could not possibly be the weapon with which Schönner was killed, suspicion continued to rest on Blum for several hours, notably on account of motive. If she could be said to have had grounds for taking revenge on Tötges, she had at least equal grounds for taking revenge on Schönner. But the police did concede that Blum was very unlikely to have possessed two weapons. In committing her crime, Blum had gone to work with a cool intelligence; when she was asked whether she had shot Schönner too, her answer took the form of a cryptic question: "Yes, come to think of it, why not him too?" Then, however, the police gave up suspecting her of Schönner's murder, especially since her alibi proved on examination to be virtually water-tight. No one who knew Katharina Blum or who, in the course of the investigation, became acquainted with her character, doubted that, if she had murdered Schönner, she would have admitted it without equivocation. In any event, the cab driver, who had driven the couple to the wood ("I'd be more inclined to describe it as kind of overgrown bushes," he said) did not recognize Blum from photographs. "Hell," he said, "these cute kids with their brown hair, between five foot five and five foot eight, age twenty-four to twenty-seven—there's a million of them during Carnival."

In Schönner's apartment no trace was found of Blum, or of anything pointing to the Andalusian woman. Other press photographers and friends of Schönner's knew only that on Tuesday, around noon, he had left a bar frequented by reporters "with some broad or other."

5

One of the leading Carnival officials, a wine and champagne dealer who took pride in his successful labors to restore Carnival jollity, was manifestly relieved that it was Monday and Wednesday respectively before both deeds became known. "A thing like that, just when the festive season's beginning—and you can forget about the Carnival spirit and business. If it gets out that fancy dress is being misused for criminal purposes, the whole mood's done for right there and business is ruined. That sort of thing's a real sacrilege. High spirits and a good time need trust, that's what they're built up on."

6

The news behaved somewhat oddly after the murder of two of its journalists. Wild excitement! Headlines. Front page. Special editions. Death notices of gigantic proportions. As if—if there's going to be any shooting in the world at all—the murder of a journalist were something special, more important than the murder of a bank manager, bank employee, or bank robber.

It is necessary to mention this excessive attention paid by the press to the event because it applies not only to the News: other newspapers also treated the murder of a reporter as something wicked, terrible, well-nigh ceremonial, one might almost say as a ritual murder. There was even mention of a "victim of his profession," and, of course, the News clung tenaciously to the version that Schönner had also been one of Blum's victims. Even if one is bound to admit that Tötges would probably not have been shot had he not been a reporter (but, for example, a shoemaker or a baker), the attempt should have been made to discover whether it would not have been more appropriate to speak of a death that resulted from a profession; for an explanation will emerge as to why someone as intelligent and coolheaded as Blum not only planned the murder but also carried it out and, at the critical moment—one which she herself had engineered—not only seized the pistol but put it to use.

7

Let us proceed at once from this lowest of all levels to higher planes. Away with the blood. Let the excitement in the press be forgotten.

Katharina Blum's apartment has meanwhile been cleaned up, the ruined rugs have landed on the garbage dump, and the furniture has been wiped and put back in place: all this at the expense and on the instructions of Blorna as empowered by his friend Hach, although it is far from certain whether Blorna will be appointed official custodian.

When all is said and done, in five years this Katharina Blum has invested seventy thousand marks in cash in a self-owned apartment worth altogether a hundred thousand marks. Hence—to quote her brother, who is at present serving a minor jail sentence—"there's lots of goodies worth swiping." But then who would be responsible for the interest and amortization on the remaining thirty thousand marks, even if a not inconsiderable increase in value is taken into account? There would be liabilities as well as assets. Be that as it may, by now Tötges has been buried (with disproportionate pomp and ceremony, in the opinion of many). Strangely enough, Schönner's death and funeral were accorded less display and attention. Why, one may ask? Because he was not a "victim of his profession" but more likely the victim of a crime passionnel? The sheikh costume is in the police vaults, likewise the pistol (an 8mm); only Blorna knows the origin of the pistol, whereas the attempts of the police and the public prosecutor's office to find this out have been fruitless.

8

Inquiries into Blum's activities during the four days in question progressed nicely enough at first, and it was only when attempts were made to gather information about the Sunday that they were brought up short.

On the Wednesday afternoon Blorna personally paid Katharina Blum two full weeks' wages at 1.80 marks per week, one for the current week, the other for the week to come, since he was leaving that same afternoon for a skiing vacation with his wife. Katharina had not only promised the Blornas, she had positively sworn that she really would take a vacation this time and enjoy herself during Carnival instead of picking up extra work, the way she had in every previous year during the festive season. She had delightedly told the

Blornas that she had been invited that evening to a small private dance at the home of her godmother, friend, and confidante, Else Woltersheim, and that she was looking forward to it very much, it had been such a long time since she had had an opportunity to dance. And Mrs. Blorna had said: "Never mind, Katie, when we come back we'll give another party, then you can dance again." For as long as she had been living in the city, i.e., for the past five or six years, Katharina had frequently complained of the lack of opportunity "just to go dancing somewhere." There were, she told the Blornas, those dumps where sex-starved students went looking for a free pickup, then there were those Bohemian-type places that were too wild for her tastes, and as for those church dances, nothing would induce her to go to those.

There was no difficulty in establishing that on Wednesday afternoon Katharina had worked for a further two hours at the home of Mr. and Mrs. Hiepertz, where she sometimes helped out at their request. Since the Hiepertzes were also leaving town during Carnival and going to see their daughter in Lemgo, Katharina had driven the elderly couple to the station in her Volkswagen. Despite the parking problem she had insisted on accompanying them to the platform and carrying their bags. ("Not for the money, oh no, we can't offer a thing for a kindness like that, she would be very hurt," Mrs. Hiepertz explained.)

It was confirmed that the train left at 5:30 P.M. If one was prepared to allow Katharina from five to ten minutes to find her car in the midst of the early Carnival crowds, and a further twenty to twenty-five minutes to reach her suburban apartment, so that she could not have entered it until between 6:00 and 6:15 P.M., not a single minute remained unaccounted for, provided one was fair enough to grant that she must have washed, changed, and had a bite to eat, for by 7:25 P.M. she had already turned up at Miss Woltersheim's party, not in her own car but by streetcar, and she was dressed neither as a Bedouin nor as an Andalusian but merely wore a red carnation in her hair, red stockings and shoes, a high-necked blouse of honey-colored raw silk, and a plain tweed skirt of the same color. It may appear unimportant whether Katharina went to the party in her car or by streetcar, but it must be mentioned here because in the course of the investigation it turned out to be of considerable significance.

9

From the moment she entered the Woltersheim apartment the investigation was facilitated because from 7:25 P.M. onward Katharina was, without realizing it, under police observation. Throughout the entire evening, from 7:30 to 10:00 P.M., before leaving the apartment with him, she had danced "exclusively and fervently," as she later stated, with one Ludwig Götten.

10

We must not forget to pay tribute at this point to Peter Hach, the public prosecutor, for it is he alone whom we have to thank for the information—bordering on police-court gossip—that Commissioner Erwin Beizmenne had the Woltersheim and Blum telephones tapped from the moment Blum left the Woltersheim apartment with Götten. This was done in a manner that may be worth mentioning: in such cases Beizmenne would call up the appropriate superior and say: "I need my little plugs again. Two of them this time."

11

Götten, it seems, made no calls from Katharina's apartment. At least, Hach knew of none. One thing is certain: Katharina's apartment was under strict observation, and when by 10:30 Thursday morning there had been no phone calls and Götten had not left the apartment, Beizmenne was beginning to lose both his patience and his nerve, and a detachment of eight heavily armed police officers broke into the apartment, storming it with the most intensive precautionary measures, searched it, but found no trace of Götten, all they found being Katharina, "looking extremely relaxed, almost happy," standing at her kitchen counter drinking coffee from a large mug and taking a bite from a slice of white bread and butter and honey. She aroused suspicion in that she did not appear surprised but rather quite composed, "not to say triumphant." She was wearing a green cotton house-coat embroidered with daisies, with nothing underneath, and when she was asked by Commissioner Beizmenne ("quite roughly," she said later) what had happened to Götten, she said she didn't know when Ludwig had left the apartment: she had woken up at 9:30 A.M. and he was already gone. "Without saying good-bye?" "Yes."

12

Here we should inquire into a hotly disputed question put by Beizmenne, a question repeated by Hach, withdrawn, repeated again, and again withdrawn. Blorna considers this question important because he believes that, if it was in fact asked, it was from this and only from this that Katharina's bitterness, sense of humiliation, and fury may have stemmed. Since Blorna and his wife describe Katharina as being extremely sensitive, almost prudish, in sexual matters, the mere possibility must be considered that Beizmenne might—in fury, too, over the disappearance of Götten, whom he thought he had in his grasp—have asked the controversial question. Beizmenne allegedly asked the maddeningly composed Katharina as she leaned against her counter: "Well, did he fuck you?" whereupon Katharina apparently not only blushed but said triumphantly: "No, I wouldn't call it that."

It may be safely assumed that, if Beizmenne did ask the question, from that moment on any feelings of trust between him and Katharina were out of the question. However, the absence of any relationship of mutual trust between the two—although there is evidence to show that Beizmenne, who is said to be "not all that bad," tried to establish such a relationship—should not be regarded as conclusive proof that he did in fact ask the fateful question. In any event, Hach, who was present when the apartment was searched, is regarded by his friends and acquaintances as "sex-starved" and it is quite likely that such a crude idea occurred to him on seeing the extremely attractive Blum girl leaning so casually against her counter, and that he would have liked to ask her that very question or perform the crudely specified activity with her.

13

The apartment was then thoroughly searched, and a few objects were confiscated, notably anything in writing. Katharina Blum was permitted to get dressed in the bathroom in the presence of a woman police officer by the name of Pletzer. Even so, the bathroom door had to remain slightly ajar and was kept under the close scrutiny of two armed police officers. Katharina was permitted to take her handbag with her, and since the possibility of arrest could not be excluded she was allowed to take along her night things, toilet articles, and something to read. Her library consisted of four love stories, three detective novels, plus a biography of Napoleon and one of Queen Christina of Sweden. All these books emanated from a book club. Because she kept on asking, "But why, why, what have I done wrong?" she was finally informed politely by Pletzer the policewoman that Ludwig Götten was a wanted man who had been nearly convicted of bank robbery and was suspected of murder and other crimes.

14

When, at about 11:25 A.M., Katharina Blum was finally taken from her apartment for questioning, it was decided not to handcuff her after all. Beizmenne had been inclined to insist on handcuffs, but after a brief dialogue between Policewoman Pletzer and Beizmenne's assistant Moeding he agreed to waive this. Since that day marked the opening of Carnival, numerous people living in the building had not gone to work or started out yet for the annual saturnalian parades, festivities: etc., so that some three dozen occupants of the ten-story apartment building were standing around in the lobby wearing topcoats, house-coats, and bathrobes, and Schönner the press photographer was standing just in front of the elevator when Katharina Blum, walking between Beizmenne and Moeding, flanked by armed police officers, emerged from the elevator. She was photographed repeatedly from the front, from behind, and from the side, and finally—since in her shame and confusion she kept trying to hide her face and so got all tangled up with her handbag, toilet articles, and a plastic bag containing two books and writing materials—with disheveled hair and an angry face.

15

Half an hour later, after her rights had been explained to her and she had been given a chance to freshen up a bit, the questioning began in the presence of Beizmenne, Moeding, Policewoman Pletzer, and the public prosecutors Korten and Hach. The interrogation was recorded:

"My name is Katharina Brettloh, née Blum. I was born on March 2, 1947, at Gemmelsbroich in the District of Kuir. My father was Peter Blum, a miner. He died when I was six, at the age of thirty-seven, of a lung injury received during the war. After the war my father again worked in a slate quarry and was suspected of suffering from pneumoconiosis. After his death my mother had to fight for her pension because the welfare office and the miners' local could not agree. I had to start doing housework at an early age because my father was often sick, which meant reduced pay, and my mother took on a number of jobs as a cleaning woman. I had no difficulty in school, although even while I was still there I had to do a lot of housework, not only at home but also in the homes of neighbors and others living in the village, where I used to lend a hand at baking, cooking, preserving, and slaughtering. I also did a lot of housework and helped with the harvest.

"After I left school in 1961 my godmother, Else Woltersheim, of Kuir, helped me to obtain a position as a maid at the Gerbers butcher shop in Kuir, where I sometimes had to help out by serving in the store too. With the aid and financial support of my godmother, Miss Woltersheim, I attended a home-economics school at Kuir where my godmother was an instructor and from which I graduated with very good grades. From 1966 to 1967 I worked as housekeeper at the all-day kindergarten attached to the Koeschler Company in neighboring Oftersbroich, and after that I was employed as a domestic aide by Dr. Kluthen, who had a medical practice in Oftersbroich, where I only stayed a year because the doctor was making more and more passes at me and his wife did not like that. I didn't like it myself. It disgusted me.

"In 1968, when I was unemployed for a few weeks and helping my mother in the house and sometimes helping out at meetings and bowling sessions of the Gemmelsbroich Fife & Drum Band, my older brother Kurt introduced me to Wilhelm Brettloh, a textile worker, whom I married a few months later. We lived in Gemmelsbroich, where on weekends when there were a lot of tourists I sometimes helped in the kitchen at Kloog's restaurant, and sometimes as a waitress behind the counter. After six months I already felt an insuperable aversion to my husband. I don't wish to go into details.

I left my husband and moved to town. I was divorced as the guilty party on grounds of willful desertion and resumed my maiden name.

"First I lived at Miss Woltersheim's, until after a few weeks I found a position living in as housekeeper and general help in the home of Mr. Fehnern, certified accountant. Mr. Fehnern made it possible for me to attend night school and adult-education courses and to qualify as a certified housekeeper. He was very kind and very generous, and I continued to work for him after I had passed my exams. At the end of 1969 Mr. Fehnern was arrested in connection with substantial tax evasions that had been discovered among large companies for which he had been working. Before he was taken away he handed me an envelope containing three months' salary and asked me to continue looking after things, he would soon be back, he said. I stayed on another month, looked after his employees, who were working in his office under the supervision of tax officials, kept the house clean and the garden tidy, and took care of the laundry. I used to take clean laundry to Mr. Fehnern in the detention jail, and food too, especially Ardennes pâté, which I had learned how to make at the Gerbers butcher shop in Kuir. Later on the office was closed, the house confiscated, and I had to give up my room. Apparently they had found evidence of embezzlement and forgery against Mr. Fehnern, and he was sent to a regular prison, where I continued to visit him. I also wanted to give him back the two months' salary, but he simply would not hear of it. Very soon I found a position with Dr. and Mrs. Blorna, whom I had met through Mr. Fehnern.

"The Blornas live in a house in the new 'South Side' development. Although they offered me a room there, I declined. I longed to be independent at last and to pursue my career more on my own. Dr. and Mrs. Blorna were very gracious to me. Mrs. Blorna—she is a member of a large architectural firm—helped me buy my own apartment in the suburb to the south that was advertised as 'Elegant Riverside Residences.' In their respective capacities of corporation lawyer and architect, Dr. and Mrs. Blorna were familiar with the project. With Dr. Blorna I calculated the financing, interest, and amortization for a two-room apartment with kitchen and bath on the eighth floor, and since by then I had been able to save 7,000 marks and Dr. and Mrs. Blorna guaranteed my bank loan of 30,000 marks, I was soon able to move into my apartment, early in 1970. At first my minimum monthly payment amounted to about 1,100 marks, but since Dr. and Mrs. Blorna deducted nothing for my board, and Mrs. Blorna even gave me something to take home every night in the way of food and drink, I could live very economically and was able to amortize my loan more quickly than had first been calculated.

"For four years I have been in sole charge of the Blorna household. My working hours are from seven in the morning till about four-thirty in the afternoon, when I have finished the housecleaning and shopping and completed preparations for the evening meal. I also take care of all the laundry. Between four-thirty and five-thirty I look after my own apartment and after that usually work another hour and a half to two hours for the elderly Hiepertz couple. In both homes I am paid extra for work on Saturdays and Sundays. In my free time I sometimes work for Kloft's the caterers, or I help out at receptions, parties, weddings, dances, and so on, usually on my own for a fixed fee but sometimes commissioned by Kloft's. My work there consists of job-pricing and general organization, but sometimes I do duty as cook or waitress. My gross income averages 1,800 to 2,300 marks a month. In the eyes of the income-tax department I am self-employed. I pay my taxes and insurance myself. All these things—tax returns, etc.—are looked after free of charge by Dr. Blorna's office. Since the spring of 1972 I have owned a 1968 Volkswagen which Werner Klormer, a chef employed at Kloft's, let me have at a good price. It was getting too difficult for me to reach my various places of work by public transportation. With my car I became sufficiently mobile to work at receptions and parties held in hotels farther away."

16

It took from 11:00 A.M. to 12:30 P.M. and, following a one-hour break, from 1:30 to 5:45 P.M. to conclude this part of the interrogation. During the lunch break Katharina Blum refused to accept coffee and a cheese sandwich from the police, nor did earnest and kindly attempts on the part of Policewoman Pletzer and Moeding, Beizmenne's assistant, succeed in altering her attitude. It was clearly impossible for her—as Hach told it—to distinguish between official and personal relations, to understand the necessity for the interrogation. When Beizmenne, who was enjoying his coffee and sandwiches and, collar unbuttoned and tie loosened, not only looked paternal but began to behave paternally, Katharina Blum insisted on being taken back to her cell. It is a matter of record that the two police officers who had been detailed to guard her urged her to accept coffee and sandwiches, but she obstinately shook her head, remained seated on her bunk, smoked a cigarette and, with wrinkled nose and an unmistakable expression, clearly conveyed her disgust at the vomit-spattered toilet in the cell. Later, at the urgings of the police-woman and the two young policemen, she permitted the former to take her pulse, and when this proved to be normal she condescended to have a slice of cake and a cup of tea brought from a nearby café, insisting, however, on paying for them out of her own pocket, although one of the young policemen, the one who had guarded her bathroom door that morning while she was dressing, was prepared to "treat" her. The opinion of the two policemen and Mrs. Pletzer on this episode with Katharina Blum: no sense of humor.

17

The recording of the witness's personal background was resumed at 1:30 P.M. and continued until 5:45 P.M. Beizmenne would have been glad to curtail it, but Blum insisted on every detail, and consent to this was given by the two public prosecutors. Eventually Beizmenne also agreed to this procedure—at first reluctantly, later (astutely enough) on account of disclosures relating to the background, which in his eyes was becoming important.

At about 5:45 P.M. the question of continuing or suspending the interrogation was raised, of whether Blum should be released or escorted to a cell. At about 5:00 P.M. she had actually been induced to accept another pot of tea and a sandwich (ham); furthermore, she consented to carry on with the interrogation, Beizmenne having promised to release her when it was over. The next subject was her relationship with Else Woltersheim. She was her godmother, said Katharina Blum, she had always taken an interest in her, she was a distant cousin of her mother's; Miss Woltersheim had got in touch with her as soon as she moved to town.

"I was invited to this private dance on February 20. It was supposed to take place on the twenty-first, the beginning of Carnival, but the date was put forward because Miss Woltersheim had some professional commitments for that date. It was the first time I had danced in four years. I wish to correct that statement: on various occasions, perhaps, two, three or possibly four times, I had danced at the Blornas after helping out at their parties. At the end of the evening, when I had finished tidying up and doing the dishes, when the coffee was served and Dr. Blorna had taken over the bar, they would call me in and I would dance in the living room with Dr. Blorna and other guests, gentlemen with university, business, or political connections. After a while I was not all that keen to go along with this idea, and finally I stopped altogether: often the men had had too much to drink and made advances to me. To be more precise: ever since I've had my own car I have declined to join in the dancing. Before that I had to rely on one of the gentlemen taking me home. Sometimes I danced with that gentleman"—she pointed to Hach, who actually blushed—"over there." She was not asked whether Hach had been among those who made advances to her.

18

The prolonged nature of the interrogation was explained by the fact that Katharina Blum was remarkably meticulous in checking the entire wording and in having every sentence read aloud to her as it was committed to the record. For example, the advances mentioned in the foregoing paragraph were first recorded as "amorous," the original wording being that "the gentlemen became amorous," which Katharina Blum indignantly rejected. A regular argument as to definition ensued between her and the public prosecutors, and between her and Beizmenne, with Katharina asserting that "becoming amorous" implied reciprocity whereas "advances" were a one-sided affair, which they had invariably been. Upon her questioners observing that surely this wasn't that important and it would be her fault if the interrogation lasted longer than usual, she said she would not sign any deposition containing the word "amorous" in-

stead of "advances." For her the difference was of crucial significance, and one of the reasons why she had separated from her
husband was that he had never been amorous but had consistently
made advances. Similar arguments ensued over the word "gracious," as applied to the Blornas. The record contained the words
"nice to me," Blum insisted on the word "gracious," and when the
word "kind" was suggested instead, "gracious" being considered
somewhat old-fashioned, she became indignant and declared that
"niceness" and "kindness" had nothing to do with "graciousness,"
and it was with graciousness that she felt the Blornas had always
treated her.

19

Meanwhile the occupants of the building had been questioned;
most of them had little or nothing to tell about Katharina Blum.
They had occasionally met in the elevator and passed the time of
day, they knew that the red Volkswagen belonged to her, some had
thought she was a private secretary, others—that she was a buyer
in a department store; she had always been smartly turned out,
pleasant, although a bit on the reserved side. Among the occupants
of the five other apartments on the eighth floor, where Katharina
lived, there were only two who had more detailed information to
give. One was the owner of a hairdressing salon, a Mrs. Schmill,
the other a retired employee of the electricity works by the name of
Ruhwiedel, and the startling thing was that both statements included the assertion that from time to time Katharina had received
or brought home a gentleman visitor. Mrs. Schmill maintained that
this visitor had come regularly, maybe every two or three weeks,
an athletic-looking gentleman of about forty, from an "obviously
superior" background, whereas Mr. Ruhwiedel described the visitor as a fairly young fellow who had sometimes entered Miss
Blum's apartment alone and sometimes accompanied by Miss
Blum. And this, moreover some eight or nine times during the past
two years, "those are only the visits I observed—naturally I can't
tell you anything about the ones I did not observe." When Katharina was confronted with these statements later that afternoon and
required to make response to them, it was Hach who, even before

actually putting the question, tried to make things easy for her by suggesting that these visitors might have been the guests who had occasionally driven her home from the Blornas. Katharina, blushing deeply from humiliation and anger, asked tartly whether it was against the law to receive male visitors, and since she refused to make use of the way out he had so kindly prepared for her, or refused to recognize it as such, Hach told her, also a bit tartly, that she must realize that a very serious case was being examined, i.e., the case of Ludwig Götten, a case that had numerous ramifications and had been occupying the police and the public prosecutor's office for more than a year, so now he was going to ask her whether the visits, which she was evidently not denying, had always been from one and the same person. And at this point Beizmenne intervened roughly, saying: "So you've known Götten for two years!"

Katharina was so taken aback by this remark that she was at a loss for an answer; she merely looked at Beizmenne and shook her head, and the answer she stammered out—a surprisingly mild "No, no, I met him only yesterday"—did not sound very convincing. Upon now being ordered to identify the visitor she shook her head "almost in horror" and refused to give any names.

Here Beizmenne resumed his paternal role and tried to persuade her, saying there was nothing wrong in having a boyfriend who— and here he made a crucial psychological error—rather than making advances had perhaps been amorous with her; after all, she was divorced and no longer bound by marriage vows, and it was not even—third crucial error!—reprehensible for amorousness occasionally to result in certain material benefits. And at this Katharina Blum finally dug in her heels. She refused to make any further statement and insisted on being taken either home or to a cell. To the surprise of all those present, Beizmenne, subdued and weary—by this time it was 8:40 P.M.—said he would have her taken home by a police officer. But then, when she had already risen and was gathering up her handbag, toilet articles, and the plastic bag, he suddenly barked the question at her: "How in the world did that amorous Ludwig of yours get out of the building last night? Every entrance, every exit, was guarded—you must have known a way and shown it to him, and I'm going to get to the bottom of it. Good night!"

20

Moeding, Beizmenne's assistant, who drove Katharina home, later
reported that he was very concerned about the young woman's condition and feared she might resort to something desperate: she was
absolutely shattered, done for, and oddly enough it was only in this
state that she had revealed, or maybe developed, a sense of humor.
Driving through town with her, he said, he had jokingly asked her
whether it wouldn't have been nice to go somewhere where they
could have had a drink and dance, with no embarrassment, no ulte-
rior motive, and she had nodded and said that wouldn't be bad at
all, might even be nice, and then, when they stopped outside her
building and he offered to take her up to her apartment, she had
said, sarcastically: "Hm, better not, I have enough gentlemen visitors, as you know—but thanks just the same."

Throughout the evening and half the night Moeding tried to con-
vince Beizmenne that Katharina Blum should be taken into custody
for her own protection, and when Beizmenne asked him whether he
might be in love he said, No, he just liked her, and she was his own
age, and he didn't believe in Beizmenne's theory of a major conspiracy in which Katharina was involved. What he did not report,
but Blorna was informed of by Miss Woltersheim, was the two
pieces of advice Moeding gave Katharina, who did not object
to his accompanying her through the lobby as far as the elevator:
somewhat risky advice that might have cost him dearly and, moreover, endangered the lives of himself and his colleagues, for what
he said to Katharina as they stood by the elevator was: "Don't
touch the phone, and don't look at the news tomorrow," from
which it was not clear whether he meant the News or simply the
news.

21

It was at about 3:30 on the afternoon of the same day (Thursday,
February 21, 1974) that Blorna was for the first time putting on his
skis at his winter resort in preparation for a cross-country run.
From this moment on the vacation to which he had been looking

forward for so many weeks was ruined. How glorious the walk had been last evening, shortly after their arrival, tramping for two hours through the snow with Trude, then the bottle of wine by the fireside and the deep sleep beside the open window: lingering over their first breakfast, and again lounging on the terrace for a few hours, warmly wrapped up, and just then, at the very moment when he was planning to set out, this fellow from the News had turned up and, with no preamble, started quizzing him about Katharina. Did Blorna consider her capable of committing a crime? "What do you mean?" he replied, "I'm an attorney and I know that all kinds of people are capable of committing a crime. What crime are you talking about? Katharina? Out of the question, what in the world gave you that idea? What makes you think such a thing?"

On finally being told that a wanted man was known to have spent the night in Katharina's apartment and that since about eleven that morning she had been the object of intensive questioning, his first thought was to fly home and be by her side, but the fellow from the News—did he really look that unsavory, or did Blorna get that impression later?—said, Well, things weren't really as bad as all that and couldn't Dr. Blorna tell him a bit about her character? And when he refused, the fellow told him that was a bad sign and could be misconstrued, for to refuse to comment on her character in a case of this kind—and this was a front-page story—was a clear implication of a bad character, and Blorna, by now furious and irritated in the extreme, said: "Katharina is a very intelligent, cool, level-headed person," and was annoyed because that wasn't true either and nowhere near conveying what he had wanted to say and ought to have said. He had never had anything to do with newspapers, let alone the News, and when the fellow drove off again in his Porsche Blorna unfastened his skis and knew he could forget about his vacation. He went upstairs and found Trude lying on the balcony, snugly tucked up and dozing in the sun. He told her what had happened. "Why don't you call her?" she said, and he made three, four, five attempts to reach her by telephone, but each time the operator's voice came back saying "Your party does not answer." He tried again around eleven that night, but again there was no answer. He drank a lot and slept badly.

22

On Friday morning when he appeared for breakfast around 9:30 looking thoroughly out of sorts, Trude held out the News to him. Katharina on the front page. Huge photo, huge type. KATHARINA BLUM: OUTLAW'S SWEETHEART REFUSES INFORMATION ON MALE VISITORS

Ludwig Götten, the outlaw and murderer who has been sought by the police for a year and a half, could have been arrested yesterday if his mistress, Katharina Blum, a domestic, had not destroyed all traces of him and covered his escape. It is assumed by the police that the Blum woman has been involved in the conspiracy for some time. (For further details see back page: MALE VISITORS.)

On the back page he saw that the News had transformed his statement that Katharina was intelligent, cool, and level-headed into "ice-cold and calculating," and his general observations on crime now read that she was "entirely capable of committing a crime."

The pastor of Gemmelsbroich had the following to say: "I wouldn't put anything past her. Her father was a Communist in disguise, and her mother, whom on compassionate grounds I employed for a time as a charwoman, stole the sacramental wine and carried on orgies in the sacristy with her lovers."

For the last two years the Blum woman has regularly received male visitors. Was her apartment a conspiracy hangout, a gang's headquarters, an arms cache? How did the 27-year-old domestic come by an apartment worth an estimated 110,000 marks? Did she share in the loot from the bank holdups? The police are pursuing their inquiries. The office of the public prosecutor is working around the clock. More details tomorrow. THE *NEWS* IS ALWAYS WHERE THE ACTION IS! Complete story in tomorrow's Weekend edition.

That afternoon, at the airport, Blorna reconstructed the swift sequence of events that followed: 10:25: Phone call from Lüding, very worked up, urging me to return at once and get in touch with Alois, who was equally worked up. Alois, described by Lüding as quite beside himself—since I have never seen him like that I consider it unlikely—at present attending a conference of Christian businessmen at Bad Bedelig where he is the main speaker and has to lead the discussion.

10:40: Call from Katharina asking me whether I had really said what was in the News. Glad to be able to set her right and explain what had happened, and she said (as far as I remember) something like: "I believe you, I really do, I know now the way these bastards work. This morning they even ferreted out my mother, 'who is a very sick woman, as well as Brettloh and some other people.'" On my asking her where she was she said: "At Else's, and now I have to go back for more questioning."

11:00: Call from Alois, whom for the first time in my life—and I've known him for twenty years—I heard in a state of agitation and alarm. Told me I must return at once to represent him in a very delicate matter, he had to give his paper now, then have lunch with the businessmen, after that lead the discussion, and in the evening attend an informal get-together, but he could be at our place some time between 7:30 and 9:30 and would still have time to drop in at the informal get-together.

11:30: Trude also feels we should leave immediately and stand by Katharina. I can tell from her ironical smile that she already has a theory (probably correct, as always) as to Alois's problems. 12:15: Reservations made, packing done, bill paid. After a vacation lasting barely forty hours, in taxi en route to I. At the airport in I, waited from 2 to 3 p.m. for fog to lift. Long talk with Trude about Katharina, of whom, as Trude knows, I am very, very fond. Also discussed how we had encouraged Katharina not to be so supersensitive but to forget her unhappy childhood and unfortunate marriage. How we had tried to overcome her pride in money matters and to arrange for cheaper credit from our own funds than she could get from the bank. Even when we explained that, if she gave us 9 per cent instead of the 14 per cent she has to pay the bank, we would lose nothing and she would save quite a bit, she was not convinced. How much we owe Katharina! Since she has been running our home in her quiet, pleasant manner, not only have our expenses gone down but the extent to which she has freed us for our professional lives is almost impossible to express in terms of money. She has released us from the chaos that for five years had been weighing so heavily on our marriage and our professional lives.

Decide about 4:30 that the fog doesn't look as if it's going to lift and so to take the train. On Trude's advice I do not call Alois Sträubleder. Taxi to station, where we just manage to catch the 5:45 for Frankfurt. Wretched journey—nausea, frayed nerves. Even Trude serious and worried. She has a sense of foreboding. In spite of utter exhaustion changed trains in Munich, managed to get a sleeper. We both anticipate trouble, with and over Katharina, problems with Lüding and Sträubleder.

23

Right on Saturday morning, on arriving at the station in the still celebrating city, rumpled and wretched as the couple was: right there on the platform is the News, once again with Katharina on the front page, now shown walking down the steps of police headquarters accompanied by a plain-clothes police officer. MURDERER'S MOLL WON'T TALK! NO HINT AS TO GÖTTEN'S WHEREABOUTS! POLICE ON FULL ALERT.

Trude bought the rag, and in silence they took a cab. As he was paying the driver while Trude was opening the front door, the driver pointed to the News, saying: "You're in there too, I recognized you right off. You're that broad's attorney, and her boss too, right?" Blorna overtipped the man who, with a grin that seemed less gloating than his tone of voice, carried their bags and skis into the hall and gave them a pleasant "So long now."

Trude had already plugged in the coffee-maker and was washing her hands in the bathroom. The News lay on the table in the living room together with two telegrams, one from Lüding and the other from Sträubleder. Lüding's: "Your failure to contact me disappointing to say the least. Lüding." Sträubleder's: "Fail to understand your letting me down like this. Expect immediate call. Alois."

It was just on 8:15, almost the very hour at which Katharina normally served their breakfast: how attractively she always set the table, with flowers, freshly laundered tablecloth and napkins, various kinds of bread, honey, eggs, and coffee, and, for Trude, toast and marmalade.

Even Trude waxed almost sentimental as she brought in the coffee, a few slices of rye crisp, some butter and honey. "It'll never be the same, never. They'll destroy that girl. If not the police, then the News, and when the News has finished with her it'll be the public. Here, read this first, then phone those gentlemen visitors." He read:

> The News, in its unceasing efforts to keep its readers fully abreast of events, has been successful in gathering further information throwing light on the character of Blum and her murky past. News reporters managed to ascertain the whereabouts of Miss Blum's invalid mother, who began by complaining that her daughter had not been to see her for a long time. Then, when confronted by the irrefutable facts, she said: "It was bound to come to this, it was bound to end like this." Miss Blum's former husband, Wilhelm Brettloh, a respectable textile worker who divorced his wife on grounds of willful desertion, was even more eager to supply the News with information: "Now," he said, barely managing to restrain his tears, "now I know why she walked out on me. Why she threw me over. That's what was going on. I see it all now. Our modest happiness was not enough for her. She was ambitious, and how is an honest, modest workingman ever to come by a Porsche? Maybe" (he added sagely) "you can pass my advice along to your readers: That's how false ideas about socialism are bound to end. I ask you and your readers: How does a housemaid come by such wealth? Not honestly, that's for sure. Now I know why I was always scared by her radical views, her hostility to the Church, and I bless Our Lord's wisdom in not sending us children. Now when I learn that she prefers the caresses of a murderer and a thief to my straightforward affection, that part is explained too. And yet I feel bound to cry out to her: My little Katharina, if only you had stayed with me! As the years went by we too would one day have been able to own a home and a small car, I could hardly have offered you a Porsche, merely such modest happiness as can be offered by an honest workingman who doesn't trust the unions. Ah, Katharina!"

Also on the back page, under the heading: RETIRED COUPLE HORRIFIED BUT NOT SURPRISED. Blorna found a column marked in red:

> Berthold Hiepertz, retired high-school principal, and his wife Mrs. Erna Hiepertz, appeared horrified to learn of Blum's activities but not "especially surprised." In Lemgo a woman reporter from the News called on the couple at the home of their married daughter, director of a sanatorium in that town, and Mr. Hiepertz, teacher of classical languages and history in whose home Blum had worked for

three years, stated: "In every respect a very radical person who cleverly succeeded in deceiving us."

(Hiepenz, whom Blorna telephoned later, swore that what he had actually said was: "If Katharina is a radical, then she is radical in her helpfulness, her organizing ability, and her intelligence—or I am very much mistaken in her, and I have had forty years' experience as a teacher and have seldom been deceived.")

(Continued from page 1:)

Miss Blum's former husband, now a completely broken man, on whom the News called during a rehearsal by the Gemmelsbroich Fife & Drum Corps, turned aside to conceal his tears. The other corps members, to quote Mr. Meffels, retired farmer, also turned aside in horror from Katharina, who had always acted so strangely and always pretended to be so easily shocked. The innocent Carnival pleasures of an honest workingman might well be said to have been clouded. And finally a picture of Blorna and Trude, in their garden beside the swimming pool. Caption: "What is the role of Mrs. Blorna, once known as 'Trude the Red,' and her husband, who sometimes describes himself as 'Leftist'? Dr. Blorna, highly paid corporation lawyer, with his wife Trude beside the swimming pool at their luxury home."

24

This is the moment for a kind of backing-up process, for what is known in movies and literature as a flashback: from the Saturday morning when Dr. and Mrs. Blorna, travel-worn and somewhat desperate, returned from their vacation, to the Friday morning when Katharina was once again taken to police headquarters for questioning, this time by Policewoman Pletzer and an older police officer who was only lightly armed, and she was picked up not from her own apartment but from Miss Woltersheim's, to which Katharina had driven around five o'clock that morning, this time in her car. The policewoman made no bones about knowing she would find Katharina at Miss Woltersheim's rather than at her own home. (In all justice we must not fail to recall the sacrifices and ordeals endured by Dr. and Mrs. Blorna: breaking off of their vacation, cab drive to the airport near I. Waiting in the fog. Cab to railway station. Catching the Frankfurt train plus changing at Munich. Being rattled about in the sleeper and, early in the morning, having hardly arrived home, already confronted by the News! Later—too late, of course—Blorna regretted that, instead of trying to telephone Katharina, who he knew was being questioned, he had not called Hach.)

What struck all those participating in Katharina's second interrogation on Friday—once again Moeding, Policewoman Pletzer, Public Prosecutors Korten and Hach, and Anna Lockster, stenographer (who was irritated by Blum's linguistic sensitivity and called her "stuck-up"—what struck all of these people was Beizmenne's mood of high good humor. He entered the room rubbing his hands, treated Katharina with great consideration, apologized for "certain incivilities" that stemmed from his own personality rather than his office, it was just that he was rather a rough diamond, and then started by picking up the itemized list that had been drawn up of all the confiscated articles. These were as follows:

(1) One small, well-worn green notebook, containing nothing but telephone numbers; these had meanwhile been checked out and revealed nothing of a compromising nature. Katharina Blum had evidently been using this notebook for almost ten years. A handwriting expert who had been trying to trace Götten by his handwriting (Götten had been, among other things, an army deserter and had worked in an office, thus leaving a number of handwriting traces) had described the development of Katharina's handwriting as a classic example: the girl who at sixteen had made a note of the telephone number of Gerbers the butcher, at seventeen the number of Dr. Kluthen, physician, at twenty while working for Mr. Fehnern—and later—the numbers and addresses of caterers, restaurateurs, and those working in her own line of business.

(2) Bank statements in which every transaction in her savings account had been meticulously identified by her own handwritten marginal notes. Each sum credited or debited to the account—all correct and not one of them suspicious. The same applied to her entries and notes, contained in a small file, on the state of her commitments to the Haftex company, from which she had bought her apartment at "Elegant Riverside Residences." In addition her tax declarations, assessments, and payments had been thoroughly examined and checked out by an accountant, and nowhere could that

expert discover any "substantial concealed amount." Beizmenne had considered it important to examine her financial transactions especially over the two preceding years, which he facetiously referred to as the "male visitor period." Nothing. However, it transpired that Katharina remitted 150 marks to her mother every month, and that she had a standing order with the firm of Kolter in Kuir for the care of her father's grave in Gemmelsbroich. The furniture she had bought, her household utensils, clothes, underwear, gasoline bills—all checked out and nowhere a discrepancy. In handing back the files to Beizmenne, the accountant remarked: "All I can say is, if she's released and is ever looking for a job—tip me off, will you? This is what we're always looking for and can never find." Nor did the Blum telephone bills yield any grounds for suspicion. It was apparent from them that she almost never made long-distance calls.

Further it was noted that now and again Katharina Blum had remitted small sums of 15 to 30 marks to her brother Kurt, then serving a sentence for breaking and entering, to augment his pocket money. Blum paid no church taxes. As shown by her financial records, she had left the Catholic Church at the age of nineteen in 1966.

(3) A second small notebook with various entries, mainly figures, contained four columns: one for the Blorna household with amounts for grocery shopping and expenditures on cleaning materials, dry cleaning, laundry. From these entries it was clear that Katharina did all the ironing herself. The second column was for the Hiepertz home with similar details and accounts. A third was for her own home, which she evidently ran on a very modest budget; there were months when she had spent scarcely 30 to 50 marks on food. However, she did seem to go quite often to the movies—she had no television set—and occasionally to buy herself chocolate bars and even a box of chocolates.

The fourth column itemized income and expenditure in connection with the extra jobs she took on and involved the purchase and laundering of uniforms as well as a proportion of the running expenses for her Volkswagen. At this point—the figures for gasoline—Beizmenne interrupted with an amiability that surprised everyone and asked her to account for the relatively high figures for gasoline, figures which, incidentally, tallied with the noticeably high figure on her odometer. It had been ascertained, he said, that the distance to the Blornas and back was about 6 kilometers, to the Hiepertzes and back about 8, to Miss Woltersheim's about 4, and if one were to reckon an average of one extra job a week (a generous estimate) and allow 20 kilometers for that (which was also generous and amounted to about 3 kilometers for each weekday) one would arrive at roughly 21 to 22 kilometers per day. And it must be considered that she did not visit Miss Woltersheim every day, but never mind about that. In other words, one arrived at some 8,000 kilometers a year, whereas when she—Katharina Blum—had acquired the VW six years ago the written agreement with Klormer the chef showed that at that time the car had had 56,000 kilometers on it. If one were to add six times 8,000 to that figure, her odometer should now show somewhere in the neighborhood of 104,000 to 105,000, whereas the actual figure was 162,000. Now it was known that from time to time she went to visit her mother in Gemmelsbroich and later at the sanatorium in Kuir-Hochsackel, and no doubt also her brother in jail—but the distance to Gemmelsbroich or Kuir-Hochsackel was about 50 kilometers there and back and to her brother about 60, and if one were to reckon one, or, to be generous, two visits a month (and her brother had been in jail only for the last year and a half, before that he had lived with their mother in Gemmelsbroich), well then—still calculating on the basis of six years—one would arrive at a further 7,000 to 8,000 kilometers, and there still remained a figure of between 45,000 and 50,000 unexplained, i.e., unaccounted for. So where had she driven to so often? Had she—he really didn't want to offer crude suggestions again, but she must understand his question—had she perhaps been meeting one or more persons somewhere—and, if so, where?

Fascinated, also shocked, not only Katharina Blum but all those present listened to Beizmenne's calculation presented in a mild voice, and it seemed as if Katharina, while Beizmenne was presenting these figures to her, did not even feel anger, merely a tension made up of shock and fascination, because, as he was speaking, she was not searching for an explanation of the 50,000 kilometers: she was trying to figure out where and when she had driven why and where to. On sitting down at the start of the interrogation she had been surprisingly approachable, almost "relaxed," she had even seemed a bit nervous and had accepted some tea without even in-

sisting on paying for it herself. And now, when Beizmenne had finished with his questions and calculations, a deathly silence—to
quote many, almost all, of those present—reigned, as if there were
a feeling that someone, on the basis of a discovery which (had it not
been for the gasoline bills) might easily have been overlooked, had
now actually penetrated an intimate secret of Katharina Blum,
whose life up to that moment had appeared to be an open book.

"Yes," said Katharina Blum, and from now on her statement
was recorded and exists in the transcript, "that's right, that
amounts to—I've just worked it out quickly in my head—almost 25
kilometers a day. I never gave a thought to it, nor to the cost either,
but sometimes I would just drive off, simply get in the car and drive,
with no destination in mind—or rather, somehow there always did
turn out to be a destination, I mean I would drive in a direction that
just seemed to suggest itself, south toward Coblenz, or west toward
Aachen, or down to the Lower Rhine. Not every day. I can't say
how often or at what intervals. Usually when it was raining and I
had finished work and was by myself. No, I wish to correct that
statement: it was only when it was raining that I went for drives like
that. I don't know why exactly. You must remember that sometimes, when I didn't have to go to the Hiepertzes and had no extra
job lined up, I would be home by five o'clock with nothing to do. I
didn't always want to go and see Else, especially since she's become
so friendly with Konrad, and to go to the movies alone isn't always
all that safe for a woman on her own. Sometimes I would go and
sit in a church, not for religious reasons but because you can be
quiet there, but these days you find people buttonholing you in
churches too, and they're not always laymen either. I do have a few
friends, of course: Werner Klormer, for instance, from whom I
bought my Volkswagen, and his wife, and some of the other staff
at Kloft's, but it is rather difficult, and usually embarrassing, to turn
up alone without automatically, or I should say, unconditionally,
falling in with every suggestion that offers. And so then I would just
get into the car, turn on the radio, and drive off, always on secondary roads, always in the rain, and the roads I liked best were the
ones with trees—sometimes I got as far as Holland or Belgium,
would have a cup of coffee or a beer there, and drive home again.
Yes. Now that you ask me I see it all. So—if you ask me how often, I
would say: two or three times a month—sometimes less, sometimes

maybe more often, and usually for several hours, until at about nine or ten, sometimes not till eleven, I would come home, dead tired. It may have been partly fear too: I know too many lonely women who spend their evenings getting drunk in front of the TV."

The gentle smile with which Beizmenne absorbed this explanation, without comment, gave no hint as to what was going on in his mind. He merely nodded, and if he rubbed his hands again it must have been because Katharina Blum's information had confirmed one of his theories. For a while everything was very quiet, as if those present were surprised or embarrassed; it seemed as if for the first time Blum had revealed something personal and intimate. After that the itemization of the remaining confiscated articles was swiftly disposed of.

(4) One photograph album containing snapshots of persons who were all easily identified. Katharina Blum's father, who looked ailing and bitter and far older than he could have been. Her mother who, it was disclosed, was dying of cancer. Her brother. Katharina herself, at four, at six, as a First Communicant at ten, as a bride of twenty; her husband; the Gemmelsbroich pastor, neighbors, relatives, various photos of Else Woltersheim; then an older man, not immediately identifiable, who looked rather jolly and turned out to be Mr. Fehnern, the guilty accountant. Not a single picture of anyone who could be made to link up with Beizmenne's theories.

(5) A passport issued in the name of Katharina Brettloh née Blum. In connection with this item, she was asked questions about travel, and it turned out that she had never "been on a real trip" and, except for a few days when she had been off sick, had always worked. She had received her vacation pay from the Fehnerns and the Blornas, but she had either gone on working or taken extra jobs.

(6) One old chocolate box. Contents: some letters, scarcely a dozen, from her mother, brother, husband, Miss Woltersheim. None containing the slightest indication that bore on the suspicion resting upon her. The box also contained a few loose snapshots of her father as a private in the German Army and of her husband in the uniform of the Fife & Drum Corps, a few torn-off calendar pages with mottoes, and a sizable handwritten collection of her own recipes plus a pamphlet entitled "The Use of Sherry in Sauces."

(7) One binder containing certificates, diplomas, and records, all her divorce papers, and the certified documents relating to her condominium apartment.

(8) Three bunches of keys. These had been checked out and found to be house and closet keys to her own apartment, the Blornas' home, and the Hiepertzes'.

It was established and recorded that no suspicious clue had been found among the above-mentioned articles; Katharina Blum's explanation of her gas consumption and the kilometers she had driven was accepted without comment.

Only now did Beizmenne draw from his pocket a ruby ring, set with diamonds, that he had apparently been keeping there loose, for he polished it on his jacket sleeve before holding it out to Katharina.

"Do you recognize this ring?"

"Yes," she said, without hesitation or embarrassment.

"Does it belong to you?"

"Yes."

"Do you know what it is worth?"

"Not exactly. It can't be much."

"Well now," said Beizmenne pleasantly, "we have had it appraised, and as a precautionary measure not only by our expert here in the building but also, so as to be sure and not do you an injustice, by a local jeweler. This ring is worth between eight and ten thousand marks. You didn't know that? I am prepared to believe you, but I must still ask you to explain where you got it. In the context of an inquiry concerning a criminal convicted of robbery and strongly suspected of murder, a ring of this kind is no trivial matter, nor is it a private and personal matter such as a few hundred kilometers or driving around for hours in the rain. Now from whom did you receive this ring? From Götten or the gentleman visitor, or perhaps Götten was the gentleman visitor? And if not: where did you drive to as a 'lady visitor,' if I may use the term facetiously—in the rain for thousands of kilometers? It would be a simple matter for us to find out from which jeweler the ring was obtained, and whether it was bought or stolen, but I would like to give you a chance—I do not, you see, consider you directly involved in a criminal capacity, merely naive and a little too romantic. How do you propose to explain to me—to us—that you, a person known to be easily shocked, almost prudish, a person whose friends have nicknamed 'the nun,' who avoids discotheques because of the depraved goings-on there, who gets a divorce because her husband 'made advances' to her—how do you propose to explain that you (so you say) did not meet this man Götten until the day before yesterday and yet that very day—one might say, post haste—took him home and there very rapidly became, well, shall we say, intimate with him? What do you call that? Love at first sight? Infatuation? Amorous feelings? Don't you see that there are certain inconsistencies there which do not altogether preclude suspicion? And there is something else." He put his hand in his jacket pocket and drew out a rather large white envelope from which he extracted a somewhat fancy, mauve, cream-lined envelope of normal dimensions. "This empty envelope which, together with the ring, we found in your night-table drawer, is postmarked February 12, 1974, 6:00 P.M., Düsseldorf Station Post Office—and addressed to you. For Heaven's sake," Beizmenne said in conclusion, "if you have had a boyfriend who visited you from time to time and whom you sometimes drove to see, who wrote you letters and sometimes gave you presents—go ahead and tell us, it's not a crime! It would only incriminate you if there were some connection with Götten."

It was clear to everyone in the room that Katharina recognized the ring but had not known its value; that here again the sensitive subject of male visitors was being raised. Was she ashamed because she saw a threat to her reputation, or did she see a threat to someone else whom she did not want to implicate in the affair? This time she only blushed slightly. Would she not admit to having received the ring from Götten because she knew it would not have been very convincing to try and present Götten as that kind of cavalier? She remained calm, "subdued" almost, as she testified:

"It is true that at Miss Woltersheim's party I danced exclusively and fervently with Ludwig Götten, whom I saw for the first time in my life and whose surname I did not discover until I was being questioned by the police on Thursday morning. I felt a great tenderness for him and he for me. I left Miss Woltersheim's apartment around ten o'clock and drove with Ludwig Götten to my apartment.

"As to the origin of the ring I cannot—correction: I do not wish to—give any information. Since it did not come into my possession in any irregular manner, I do not feel obliged to account for its origin. The sender of the envelope produced for my inspection is unknown to me. I take it to be one of the usual specimens of advertising material. I am by this time quite well known in the catering business. Why an advertisement should be sent to me with no sender's name in a fancy lined envelope is something I cannot explain. I would merely like to point out that some firms in the food business are anxious to project a glamorous image."

On then being asked why on that particular day, although she was obviously—and by her own admission—so fond of driving, why on that particular day she had taken the streetcar to Miss Woltersheim's, Katharina Blum said she had not known whether she would have a lot to drink or a little, and it had seemed safer not to take her own car. When asked whether she drank a lot or even sometimes became intoxicated, she said, No, she did not drink much and she had never been intoxicated, and only once—and that had been in the presence and at the instigation of her husband at a social evening of the Fife & Drum Corps—had she been made intoxicated, and that had been with some aniseed stuff that tasted like lemonade. Later she had been told that this somewhat expensive stuff was very popular for getting people drunk. When it was pointed out to her that this explanation—of having feared she might have too much to drink—did not hold water since she never drank much, and did she not realize that it must look as if she had had a regular assignation with Götten and so had known she would not need her car but would drive home in his, she shook her head, saying it was exactly as she had stated. She had certainly felt in the mood for drinking a bit more than usual, but in the end she had not done so.

One further point remained to be clarified before the lunch break: Why had she no savings book or checkbook? Maybe she did have a checking account somewhere after all? No, the only account she had was the one at the savings bank. Every sum at her disposal, even the smallest, she immediately applied to her loan, on which the interest was so high; sometimes this interest amounted to almost double the interest on her savings, and on a checking account there was hardly any interest at all. Besides, she found it too expensive and too complicated to use checks. All her running expenses, for her home and for her car, she paid in cash.

25

Certain blockages, also definable as tensions or pressures, are, of course, unavoidable inasmuch as not all sources can be diverted and/or rerouted at one go and all at once, so that dry land is immediately exposed. However, unnecessary tensions are to be avoided, and we will now try to explain why on this Friday morning not only Beizmenne but also Katharina behaved in such a mild, not to say subdued manner, Katharina seeming even nervous or intimidated. While it was true that the News, which a friendly neighbor had pushed under Miss Woltersheim's front door, had aroused anger, exasperation, indignation, shame, and fear in both women, the immediately ensuing telephone conversation with Blorna had mitigated these emotions; and since, shortly after the two horrified women had skimmed through the News and Katharina had telephoned Blorna, Policewoman Pletzer had arrived and frankly admitted that naturally Katharina's apartment was being kept under surveillance and that was how she knew she would find Katharina here, and now unfortunately they had to go—Miss Woltersheim too, unfortunately—to police headquarters for questioning, the shock caused by the News gave way temporarily before Policewoman Pletzer's candid, pleasant manner, and Katharina was once again able to dwell on something that had occurred during the night and that had made her very happy: Ludwig had called her, and from there!

He had been so sweet, and that was why she had told him nothing of all this trouble because she didn't want him to feel he was the cause of any unhappiness. Nor did they mention love, she had expressly forbidden him to do that even on the way home with him in the car. No, no, she was fine, of course she would rather be with him and stay with him forever or at least for a long time, preferably forever and ever, of course, and she would rest up during Carnival and never, never again dance with any other man but him, and never anything but Latin American, and only with him, and what were things like where he was? The accommodation was fine, and he had everything he needed, and since she had forbidden him to mention love all he wanted to say was that he liked her very, very, very much, and one day—he didn't yet know when, it might be months or even a couple of years—he would come for her and take her away, he didn't yet know where to. And so on, the way people do chat on the phone when they feel a great affection for one another. No mention of intimacies, let alone any word about that event which Beizmenne (or, as becomes increasingly likely: Hach) had so crudely specified. And so on. Merely the things this kind of tender loving couple finds to say to each other. For quite some time. Ten minutes. Maybe even more, Katharina told Else. Perhaps, as far as the actual vocabulary of the two young lovers is concerned, one may also refer to certain modern movies in which a good deal of chitchat plus a good deal of seemingly inconsequential chitchat goes on in telephone conversations—often over great distances.

The telephone conversation between Katharina and Ludwig had, moreover, been the cause of Beizmenne's relaxed and pleasant mood of leniency; and although he thought he knew why Katharina had dropped all that stubborn standoffish attitude, she, of course, could not suspect that his cheerful mood stemmed from the same event, although not for the same reason. (This notable and note-worthy process should prompt us to telephone more often—even, if need be, without tender whisperings—since we can never know who may derive pleasure from such a call.) But Beizmenne knew the reason for Katharina's nervousness, for he was also aware of a further telephone call, an anonymous one.

The reader is asked not to explore the sources of confidential in-formation contained in this chapter: it is merely that the amateur-ishly erected earth wall of a subsidiary puddle has been breached and the water drawn off and/or caused to flow out before the weak retaining wall collapses and all that pressure and tension is drained away.

26

To avoid any misunderstanding it must be noted that naturally both Else Woltersheim and Blorna were aware that Katharina had com-mitted an offense by helping Götten to slip out unseen from her apartment; indeed, the fact that she had provided him with an es-cape route made her an accessory to certain criminal acts, even if in this case not the relevant ones! Else Woltersheim told her this point-blank, shortly before Policewoman Pletzer came to pick them both up for questioning, Blorna seized the first opportunity to draw Katharina's attention to the criminal nature of her action. Nor should Katharina's remark to Miss Woltersheim about Götten be withheld: "But don't you see—he was simply the One who was to come, and I would have married him and had children with him—even if I had had to wait years till he got out of jail!"

27

The interrogation of Katharina could thus be considered at an end; she had merely to be available for a possible confrontation with statements made by the other Woltersheim guests. For it was now necessary to clarify a question that, in the context of Beizmenne's theory of a prearranged assignation and conspiracy, was sufficiently important: How had Ludwig Götten come to be a guest at the Woltersheim dance?

Katharina Blum was told that she could decide whether to go home or to wait in some place of her choice, but she declined to go home, saying that events had spoiled the apartment for her once and for all, and that she preferred to wait in a cell until Miss Woltersheim had been questioned, and then to go home with her. Only now did Katharina take the two issues of the News from her handbag and ask whether the government—as she put it—could not do something to protect her from this filth and to restore her lost honor. She was now well aware that her interrogation was perfectly justified, although she could not quite see the point of this "going into every last intimate detail," but she could not understand how details arising out of the interrogation—the gentlemen visitors, for instance—could ever have come to the knowledge of the News, and all those lying and fraudulent statements. At this point Hach, the public prosecutor, intervened, saying that, in view of the enormous public interest in the Götten case, it had, of course, been necessary to issue a statement for the press; as yet there had been no press conference, but owing to the excitement and apprehension generated by Götten's escape—which Katharina must remember she had made feasible—it would hardly be possible to avoid one. Moreover, the mere fact of knowing Götten had made her a "public figure" and thus the object of justifiable public interest. She was free to bring a private suit on the grounds of insulting and possibly libelous details in the newspaper reports and, if it should turn out that there had been "leaks" in official circles, she could rest assured that the police authorities would bring charges against a person or persons unknown and support her in the restitution of her rights.

Katharina Blum was then escorted to a cell. It was not considered necessary to put her under strict guard; she was assigned a fairly young woman police assistant, Renate Zündach, who stayed with her, unarmed, and reported later that throughout the whole period—some two and a half hours—Katharina Blum had done nothing but read the two issues of the News over and over again. Tea, sandwiches—she refused them all, not aggressively but in "quite a pleasant, rather apathetic way." Every attempt to discuss clothes, movies, dancing, which she, Renate Zündach, tried to initiate in order to take Blum's mind off her problems, had been repulsed by Katharina. Then, Zündach reported, in order to help Blum, who seemed positively hypnotized by the News, she had asked her colleague Hüften to relieve her for a few minutes and had gone off to the archives, returning with clippings from other newspapers in which Blum's involvement and interrogation, and her potential role, had been reported quite matter-of-factly. They carried brief accounts on the third or fourth page that did not even give Blum's full name, referring merely to a certain Katharina B., a domestic. In the Review, for example, there had been a mere ten-line report, with no picture, in which mention was made of the unfortunate involvement of a completely blameless person. All this—she had placed fifteen newspaper clippings in front of Blum, she said—failed to console her: Katharina had merely asked: "Who reads those anyway? Everyone I know reads the News!"

28

In order to clarify how Götten came to be at the Woltersheim dance, the first to be questioned was Else Woltersheim herself, and from the outset it became clear that, in her attitude toward the entire body of men by whom she was being questioned, Miss Woltersheim was, if not downright hostile, certainly more hostile than Blum. She stated that she had been born in 1930, was thus forty-four, unmarried, occupation housekeeper–cateress. Before testifying about the affair itself she gave her opinion, in an "unemotional, dry-as-dust tone of voice, which lent more strength to her indignation than if she had shouted or screamed abuse," on the treatment of Katharina Blum by the News as well as on the fact that details from the interrogation were evidently being leaked to that kind of publication. She realized that Katharina's role had to be examined, but she wondered if "the destruction of a young life," as was now taking place, could be justified. She had known Katharina, she went on, since the day she was born, and could already observe the havoc being wrought in her since yesterday. She was no psychologist, but the fact that Katharina had obviously lost all interest in her apartment, of which she had been so fond and for which she had worked so hard, was, in her opinion, alarming.

It was not easy to interrupt Miss Woltersheim's torrent of complaint, it was too much even for Beizmenne, and only when he broke in to reproach her for admitting Götten into her home did she say that she hadn't even known his name, he hadn't introduced himself nor had anyone introduced him to her. All she knew was that, on the Wednesday in question, at around 7:30 P.M., he had turned up in the company of Hertha Scheumel, who had come with her friend Claudia Sterm, who in turn was in the company of a man dressed as a sheikh of whom all she knew was that they called him Karl and who later in the evening behaved in a distinctly odd manner. There could be no question of any prearranged meeting with this man Götten, nor had she ever heard his name before, and she knew all about Katharina's life down to the last detail. On being confronted with Katharina's statement about her "mystery drives," she had perforce to admit that she had known nothing about them, and this dealt a crucial blow to her claim to familiarity with every detail of Katharina's life. On the subject of the gentlemen visitors she became embarrassed, saying that, since Katharina had apparently said nothing about them, she also would refuse to comment. The only thing she could say on this subject was: one of them had been a "rather corny affair," and "when I say corny I don't mean Katharina, I mean the visitor." If authorized by Katharina she would tell them all she knew about it; she thought it quite out of the question that Katharina's long drives had taken her to that person. Yes, this man did exist, and if she hesitated to say more about him it was because she did not want him to become a laughing-stock. In any case, Katharina's part in both cases—that of Götten and of the gentleman visitor—had been quite beyond reproach. Katharina had always been a hardworking, respectable girl, a bit timid, or rather intimidated, and as a child she had even been a devout and faithful churchgoer. But then her mother, who used to clean the church in Gemmelsbroich, had been reprimanded several times for irregular behavior, and once she had even been caught sharing a bottle of sacramental wine with the verger in the sacristy. This had been blown up into an "orgy" and a scandal, and Katharina had had to suffer in school at the hands of the pastor. Yes, Mrs. Blum, Katharina's mother, had been very unstable and at times an alcoholic, but one must picture that husband—Katharina's father—always grumbling, always ailing, who had returned from the war a total wreck, then the embittered mother and the brother, who, one was bound to say, had turned out badly. She also knew the story of the marriage that had gone so hopelessly wrong. In fact, she had advised Katharina against it from the very beginning, Brettloh being an—she apologized for the expression—ass-licker, typical of those who kowtow to all authority, both secular and religious; besides, he was a most disgusting show-off. She had regarded Katharina's early marriage as a flight from her terrible home environment and, as was plain to see, the moment Katharina escaped from that environment and her imprudent marriage, she developed into a wonderful person. Her job qualifications were unimpeachable. That was something to which she—Miss Woltersheim—could attest not only verbally but also, if need be, in writing since she was a member of the Trade Council's examining board. With the growing trend in private and public entertaining toward what was now being called "organized buffet style," the opportunities for a woman like Katharina Blum were opening out accordingly, since she was a highly suitable person, as well as highly trained in organization, pricing, and attractive presentation. Although now, of course, if she failed to get satisfaction from the News, Katharina's interest in her career would fade along with her interest in her apartment.

At this point in her statement, Miss Woltersheim was informed that it was not the job of the police or the public prosecutor's office "to pursue certain undoubtedly reprehensible forms of journalism by bringing criminal charges." Freedom of the press was not to be lightly tampered with, and she could rest assured that a private complaint would be handled with justice and a charge on grounds of illegal sources of information brought against a person or persons unknown. It was Korten, the young public prosecutor, who, in an impassioned plea for freedom of the press and the right to protect the identity of sources of information, stressed that a person who did not keep or fall into bad company could obviously never give the press cause for wild and potentially damaging reporting.

The whole affair—that was to say, the sudden appearance of Götten and of the shadowy figure of Karl, the man dressed as a sheikh—did, Korten must say, imply a strange casualness in social intercourse. This had not as yet been adequately explained to him, and he was counting on receiving plausible explanations during the interrogation of the two young ladies concerned. She, Miss Woltersheim, could not escape the reproach of having been less than fastidious in the choice of her guests. Miss Woltersheim refused to be taken to task in this way by a person considerably younger than herself, and pointed out that she had invited the two girls each to bring a friend, and that she must say it was not her custom to ask her guests for their friends' identification papers or a police certificate of good conduct; whereupon she was rebuked and told that in this instance age was not a factor whereas the status of the public prosecutor, Mr. Korten, was, and a very considerable one at that. She must realize that the matter now under investigation was a serious one, a grave, if not the gravest, case of crime by violence, in which Götten, as the evidence showed, was involved. She must leave it to the state's legal representative to decide which details and which admonishments were appropriate.

When asked once again whether Götten and the gentleman visitor could be one and the same person, Miss Woltersheim said no, there was absolutely no possibility of that. But then when she was asked whether she knew the "gentleman visitor" personally, whether she had ever seen him or ever met him, she had to reply in the negative, and since she had also been unaware of such an important personal detail as the mysterious automobile drives her testimony was termed unsatisfactory, and for the time being she was dismissed "on a sour note." Before leaving the room, obviously annoyed, she further declared that Karl, the man dressed as a sheikh, had seemed to her at least as suspicious as Götten. In any event, he had kept talking to himself while in the washroom and had then disappeared without saying good-bye.

29

Since it was Hertha Scheumel, a salesgirl, aged seventeen, who had brought Götten to the party, she was the next to be interrogated. She was obviously nervous, saying she had never had anything to do with the police before, but then proceeded to offer a relatively plausible explanation for knowing Götten. "I live," she stated, "with my girl friend Claudia Sterm, who works in a chocolate factory, in a one-room apartment with kitchen and shower. We both come from Kuir-Oftersbroich and are both distantly related to Miss Woltersheim as well as to Katharina Blum" (although Miss Scheumel wished to describe the remoteness of the relationship in more detail by mentioning grandparents who had been cousins of grandparents, a precise degree of relationship was not deemed necessary and the term "distant" was regarded as adequate). "We call Miss Woltersheim Auntie and think of Katharina as a cousin.

"That evening, Wednesday, February 20, 1974, we were both, Claudia and I, in a real bind. We had promised Auntie Else to bring our boyfriends to her dance as otherwise there wouldn't be enough men to go around. Well, it so happened that my boyfriend, who is doing his military service in the Army at the moment, or, to be more exact, with the Engineers, has suddenly—as usual—been assigned to barracks duty, and although I suggested he simply take off I couldn't persuade him, because he'd already done that a few times and was scared of getting into real trouble. As for Claudia's boyfriend, by early afternoon he was so drunk we had to put him to bed. So we decided to go to the Café Polkt and pick up a couple of nice fellows there, since we didn't want to lose face with Auntie. There's always something going on at the café during Carnival time. People meet there before and after the dances and the Carnival ceremonies, and you can always be sure of finding lots of young people there.

"By late Wednesday afternoon the atmosphere at the café was already pretty good. I was twice asked to dance by this young man, and by the way I have only just learned that his name is Ludwig Götten and that he's a wanted criminal, and during the second dance I asked him if he wouldn't like to go to a party with me. He seemed delighted and agreed at once. He said he was just passing through, had no place to stay and no idea how he was going to spend the evening, and he would like to come with me very much. At the very moment when I was, you might say, fixing up a date with this Götten, Claudia happened to be dancing next to me with a man dressed as a sheikh, and I suppose they must have overheard what we were saying because the sheikh, who I learned later was called Karl, at once asked Claudia, in a kind of humble way which was meant to be funny, whether we couldn't find some small corner for him at this party as well, he was lonesome too and had no plans for the evening.

"Anyway, we'd got what we were after, and soon after that we drove in Ludwig's—I mean Mr. Götten's—car to Auntie Else's apartment. It was a Porsche, not very comfortable for four, but then we didn't have far to go. If I was asked whether Katharina Blum knew we were going to the Café Polkt to pick up a couple of fellows, I'd answer Yes. I had called her that morning at the Blornas, where she works, and told her that Claudia and I would have to go alone if we couldn't find anybody. I also told her we were going to the Café Polkt. She didn't think that was a good idea, she said we were too gullible, too irresponsible. But then we all know Katharina's funny about such things. That's why I was so surprised when Katharina grabbed hold of Götten almost immediately and danced with him the whole evening, as if they'd known each other all their lives."

30

Bertha Scheumel's statement was confirmed almost word for word by her friend Claudia Sterm. There was only one point, an insignificant one, in which they differed. She said she had danced three times, not twice, with the sheikh, because Karl had asked her to dance earlier than Götten had asked Bertha. And Claudia Sterm also expressed surprise at how quickly Katharina, who was always considered so standoffish, had become friendly, you might almost say familiar, with Götten.

31

There were three further guests at the party to be interrogated: Konrad Beiters, aged fifty-six, textile agent and friend of Miss Woltersheim's, and Mr. Georg Plotten (aged forty-two) and his wife Hedwig (aged thirty-six), both municipal employees. All three agreed in their account of the evening, from the arrival of Katharina Blum, of Bertha Scheumel accompanied by Ludwig Götten, and of Claudia Sterm accompanied by Karl in his sheikh costume. Furthermore, it had been a very nice evening, with dancing, and general conversation in which Karl had turned out to be especially amusing. The only wrong note—if you could call it that, for no doubt those two hadn't felt it to be one—was, according to Georg Plotten, the "total monopoly of Katharina Blum by Ludwig Götten." It had lent a serious, almost solemn note to the evening, something that wasn't too well suited to Carnival parties. Mrs. Bedwig Plot ten stated that, after the departure of Katharina and Ludwig, when she had gone into the kitchen to get some more ice, she too had noticed Karl the sheikh talking to himself in the washroom. Moreover, this Karl had left shortly afterward, without saying good-bye.

32

Katharina Blum, brought back for questioning, confirmed her telephone conversation with Bertha Scheumel but persisted in her denial that it had concerned any arrangement for a meeting with Götten, for it was suggested to her—not by Beizmenne but by Korten, the younger of the two prosecutors—that she would do well to admit that Götten had called her up after her telephone conversation with Bertha Scheumel, and that she had been smart enough to send Götten to the Café Polkt and have him get into conversation with Bertha Scheumel so that he could meet her (Katharina) at Miss Woltersheim's without attracting attention. This had been easy enough to do since Miss Scheumel was a striking blonde, somewhat flashily dressed. Katharina Blum, by now almost totally apathetic, merely shook her head as she sat there still clutching the two issues of the News. She was then dismissed and, together with Miss Woltersheim and Konrad Beiters, left police headquarters.

33

In discussing the signed depositions and rechecking them for possible gaps, Korten raised the question of whether some serious effort should not be made to bring in this sheikh by the name of Karl and investigate his highly obscure role in the affair. He must say he was very surprised that no measures had been taken to trace this "Karl." After all, this Karl had obviously turned up simultaneously, if not together, with Götten at the Café Polkt and had likewise "crashed" the party, and to him—Korten—his role appeared mysterious if not suspicious.

At this point all those present burst out laughing; even the normally reserved Policewoman Pletzer permitted herself a smile. The stenographer, Mrs. Anna Lockster, laughed so raucously that she had to be called to order by Beizmenne. And finally, since Korten still had not understood, his colleague Hach enlightened him. Had Korten not realized, or noticed, that Commissioner Beizmenne had deliberately passed over or failed to mention the sheikh? Surely it was obvious that he was "one of our men" and that the alleged monologue in the washroom was nothing more than a method—clumsily executed, it was true—of instructing his colleagues by pocket transmitter to start shadowing Götten and Blum, for of course by this time Blum's address was known. "And no doubt you also realize, Mr. Korten, that during Carnival time sheikh costumes are the ideal disguise, since nowadays, for obvious reasons, sheikhs are more popular than cowboys." And Beizmenne added: "Of course, we realized right away that the Carnival would make it easier for the lawbreakers to drop out of sight and more difficult for us to remain hot on the trail, Götten having been tailed for the past thirty-six hours. Götten—who, by the way, was not disguised—had spent the night in a VW bus on the parking lot from which he later stole the Porsche, and he had breakfast in a café where he then shaved and changed in the washroom. We didn't lose sight of him for a single minute, we had about a dozen policemen disguised as sheikhs, cowboys, and Spaniards on his tail, all equipped with pocket transmitters and acting like revelers somewhat the worse for wear, ready to report instantly on any attempts at contact. The persons Götten contacted before entering the Café Polkt have all been traced and checked out:

a bartender at whose counter he had a beer;
two girls with whom he danced at a nightclub in the old quarter of the town;
a gas-station attendant near the Holzmarkt who filled up the stolen Porsche;
a man at the newsstand on Matthias-Strasse;
a sales clerk (male) in a tobacco store;
a bank teller at whose window he changed seven hundred US dollars which probably originated from a bank holdup.

"All these persons have been identified unequivocally as chance encounters rather than planned contacts, and none of the words exchanged with each individual person suggests a code. However, I will not be persuaded that Miss Blum was also a chance encounter. Her telephone conversation with Miss Scheumel, the punctuality with which she turned up at Miss Woltersheim's, and that damned intimacy with which the two of them danced right from the very first second—and the speed with which they made off. together—everything speaks against chance. But, above all, the fact that she apparently let him leave without saying good-bye and quite obviously showed him a way out of the apartment building that must have been overlooked by our strict surveillance. The apartment building—that is, the building within the apartment complex where she lives—was never out of our sight for one moment. Of course, we could not keep the entire area of almost one and a half square kilometers under complete surveillance. She must have known an escape route and shown it to him; besides, I am certain that she found a hideout for him—and possibly others too—and knows exactly where he is. The buildings of her employers have already been checked out, we have made inquiries in her own village, and Miss Woltersheim's apartment has again been thoroughly searched while she was here for questioning. Nothing. In my opinion the best thing would be to let her run around freely so she can make a mistake, and probably the trail will lead to his present quarters via that mysterious gentleman visitor, and I am certain that the trail to the escape route inside the apartment building leads via Mrs. Blorna, whom we now know also as 'Trude the Red' and who was one of the architects who designed the apartment complex."

34

This brings us to the end of the first backing-up process, we have moved from the Friday to the Saturday. Everything will be done to avoid further blockages and unnecessary buildups of tension. It will probably not be possible to avoid them entirely.

However, it may be illuminating to note that, after the final interrogation on Friday afternoon, Katharina Blum asked Else Woltersheim and Konrad Beiters to drive her first to her apartment and—please, please—to go up with her. She told them she was scared: during that Thursday night, shortly after her telephone conversation with Götten (any outsider should recognize her innocence from the fact that she spoke openly, although not while being questioned, about her telephone contacts with Götten!) something absolutely revolting had happened. Almost immediately after her call from Götten, in fact she had hardly replaced the receiver, the phone rang again, and in the "wild hope" that it was Götten again she had at once picked up the receiver, but instead of Götten on the line it had been a "horribly soft" male voice "whispering" a whole string of "nasty things" to her, wicked things, and the worst of it was that the fellow had said he lived in the same building and why, if she was so keen on intimacies, did she look for them so far away, he was willing and able to offer her every conceivable variety of intimacy. Yes, it was because of this phone call that she had gone to Else's that same night. She was scared, scared of the phone even, and, since Götten had her phone number although she didn't have Götten's, she was still hoping for a call while at the same time being scared of the phone. Well, we must not withhold the fact that there were more scares in store for Katharina Blum. To begin with: her mailbox, which so far had played a very insignificant role in her life and which she generally glanced into simply "because everyone does" but without success. On this Friday morning it was full to overflowing, and in a manner far from delighting Katharina. For, although Else W. and Beiters did their utmost to intercept her mail, she would not be deterred and, presumably in the hope of some sign of life from her dear Ludwig, looked through all the letters and circulars—totaling about twenty—evidently without finding anything from Ludwig, and stuffed the whole bundle into her handbag. Even the ride up in the elevator was an ordeal since two other occupants of the building were riding up too. One man (it must be said, improbable though it may sound) dressed as a sheikh, who squeezed himself into a corner in an agony of attempted dissociation but fortunately got out at the fourth floor; and a woman (what's true is true, crazy though it may sound) dressed as an Andalusian, and this person, protected by her mask, far from moving away from Katharina remained standing directly beside her, looking her up and down with brazen curiosity out of "impudent, hard brown eyes." She continued up beyond the eighth floor.

Warning: there is worse to come. When she had finally reached her apartment, clinging to Beiters and Miss W. as she walked in, the telephone rang, and here Miss W. was quicker than Katharina: shaking off Katharina she ran to pick up the receiver, they saw her horrified expression, saw her turn pale, heard her "You filthy bitch, you filthy cowardly bitch," and instead of replacing the receiver she craftily put it down beside the cradle.

In vain did Miss W. and Beiters try to part Katharina from her mail: she kept the bundle of letters and circulars firmly clutched in her hands, together with the two issues of the News that she had also taken from her bag, and insisted on opening it all. It was useless. She read everyone!

Not all of it was anonymous. One letter that was not anonymous—the most detailed—came from a firm calling itself "Mail Orders Intimate" and offering her every variety of sex article. For a person of Katharina's sensibility, this was pretty strong stuff, and even worse was that someone had written by hand in the margin: "These are the genuine articles!" In short—or, better still, in statistical terms—the other eighteen items of mail were:

> seven anonymous postcards, handwritten with
> "crude" sexual propositions that in one way or
> another all included the words "Communist bitch":

four more anonymous postcards containing insulting
political remarks but no sexual propositions.
These remarks ranged from "Red agitator" to
"Kremlin stooge";

five letters containing clippings from the News,
most of which (some three or four) had comments
written in red ink in the margins such as:
"Where Stalin failed, you'll fail too";

two letters containing religious exhortations, and on
the tracts enclosed with them was written:
"You must learn to pray again, you poor lost
child," and "Kneel down and confess, God has
not yet abandoned you."

And only now did Else W. discover a piece of paper that had been
pushed under the door and which fortunately she was able to hide
from Katharina: "Why don't you make use of my sex catalogue?
Do I have to force your happiness on you? Your neighbor, whom
you have so haughtily rejected. I am warning you." This had been
printed in script from which Else W. thought she could deduce a
college education if not medical training.

35

It is, surely, astonishing that neither Miss W. nor Konrad B. was
astonished when, with no thought of intervening in any way, they
watched Katharina walk to the little bar in her living room, take
out one bottle each of sherry, whiskey, and red wine and a half-
empty bottle of cherry syrup and, with no visible sign of emotion,
throw them against the immaculate walls, where they smashed and
spewed their contents.

She did the same in her little kitchen, using tomato ketchup,
salad dressing, vinegar, and Worcester sauce for the same purpose.
Must we add that she did the same in her bathroom with tubes and
jars of face cream, powder, and bath oil—and in her bedroom with
a bottle of eau de cologne?

Through it all she appeared so systematic, so impassive, so convinced and convincing, that Else W. and Konrad B. never lifted a finger.

36

Naturally there have been a good many theories aimed at pinpointing the exact moment in time at which Katharina first formed her intention to commit a murder or devised her plan for murder and decided to carry it out. Some people think that first article in Thursday's News did the trick; others regard Friday as the crucial day because that day the News was still stirring up trouble and destroying (subjectively, at least) her neighborhood and the apartment of which she was so fond; then came the anonymous caller, the anonymous mail—and to cap it all the News of Saturday, plus (here we are looking ahead!) the Sunday News. Surely such speculations are idle: she planned the murder and carried it out—and that's that! Without a doubt something in her "came to a head"—the statements of her former husband particularly upset her, and we can be certain that the contents of the Sunday News, if not actually the trigger, must have had a far from soothing effect on her.

37

Before our flashback may be regarded as complete and we can focus once again on Saturday, it remains necessary to describe Friday evening and Friday night at Miss Woltersheim's. Overall conclusion: surprisingly peaceful. True, attempts by Konrad Beiters to distract Katharina by putting on some dance records, even Latin American ones, and asking her to dance were not a success, nor was the attempt to part Katharina from the News and her anonymous mail; attempts to make out that the whole thing wasn't all that important and would soon pass also came to nothing. She'd been through worse, hadn't she? Her miserable childhood, her marriage with that wretch Brettloh, the alcoholism and, "to put it mildly, the depravity of your mother who, when all's said and done, is responsible for Kurt's leaving the straight and narrow." Wasn't Götten safe, at least for the time being, and his promise to come for her to be taken seriously? Wasn't it Carnival, and wasn't her financial position secure? Weren't there all those nice people like the Blornas and the Hiepertzes, and wasn't even that "conceited jackass"—there was still some reluctance to name the gentleman visitor by name—actually quite an amusing character and far from sinister?

Katharina would have none of this and reminded them of the "stupid ring and that silly fancy envelope" that had got them both into such a terrible jam and might even have brought suspicion on Ludwig. Could she ever have known that that jackass would spend all that money for the sake of his vanity? No indeed, she certainly couldn't call him amusing. No.

When they turned to practical matters—whether, for instance, she should look for a new apartment and whether it wasn't time to discuss where—Katharina became evasive, saying the only practical matter she had in mind was to make herself a Carnival costume, and she asked Else to lend her a big sheet since, in view of the vogue for sheikhs, she intended to "join the crowds" on Saturday or Sunday dressed as a Bedouin woman. So what's happened that is so bad? Scarcely a thing, if you look at it closely or, to be more precise: almost everything has been good, for isn't it a fact that Katharina has met "the One who was to come," hasn't she "spent a night of romance" with him? Granted, she has been questioned, or rather interrogated, and it is clear that Ludwig is no mere "butterfly hunter." Then there has been the usual filth in the News, a few filthy beasts have made anonymous phone calls, others have written anonymous letters. But doesn't life go on? Isn't Ludwig being well—in fact comfortably—provided for, as she and only she knows? Now we're fixing up a Carnival costume which will make Katharina look delightful, a white burnous; how pretty she'll look when she "joins the crowds" in it!

Finally even Nature demands her due, and one falls asleep, dozes off, wakes up again, dozes off again. How about a little drink? Why not? Peace and quiet reign: a young woman fallen asleep over her sewing while an older man and woman move cautiously around her "so as not to interfere with Nature." Nature is so little interfered with that Katharina is not even roused by the telephone when it rings around two-thirty in the morning. Why do the hands of sober Else Woltersheim start trembling as she lifts the receiver? Is she expecting anonymous intimacies such as she heard a few hours ago? Mind you, two-thirty in the morning is an alarming hour for anyone to call, but she grabs the receiver, which Beiters snatches from her, and when he says "Yes?" the receiver at the other end is replaced immediately. And it rings again, and again—the moment he picks it up, even before he says "Yes?"—the caller replaces the receiver. Naturally there are people who want to turn a person into a nervous wreck once they've got one's name and address from the News, and the best thing is not to replace the receiver.

And at that point it is decided to shield Katharina at least from the Saturday edition of the Newa; but Katharina has taken advantage of a few moments while Else W. is asleep and Konrad B. is shaving in the bathroom, and she has crept out onto the street, where in the early-morning light she has flung open the first Newsbox she comes to and committed a kind of sacrilege: she has abused the confidence of the News by taking a Newspaper without paying for it! At this juncture our flashback may be considered temporarily complete, this being the very hour at which the Blornas, this same Saturday, travel-worn, irritable, and depressed, leave the night train and pick up that same edition of the News, to be studied when they get home.

38

At the Blorna home it is a depressing Saturday morning, extremely depressing in fact, not only because of an almost sleepless night of being rattled and jolted about in the sleeper, not only because of the News, which, to quote Mrs. Blorna, pursues one like the plague wherever one goes, one isn't safe anywhere; depressing not only because of the reproachful telegrams sent by influential friends, business acquaintances, and *j* "Lüstra" (LÜding & STRÄubleder Investments) but also because of Hach, whom they call too early in the day, too early, that's all (and yet too late when they reflect that they would have done better to call him on Thursday). He could hardly be described as cordial, told them that Katharina's interrogation was over, couldn't say whether proceedings would be taken against her, at the moment she certainly needed support but so far not legal support. Had they forgotten it was Carnival and that even public prosecutors had the right to some free time and a bit of celebrating? Well, of course, they had known each other for twenty-four years, had been at university together, crammed together, sung together, even hiked together, and one is not going to let a few minutes of grumpiness upset one, especially since one is feeling so extremely depressed oneself, but then came the request—and from a public prosecutor!—to continue the discussion in person rather than over the long-distance phone. Yes, there was a certain amount of incriminating evidence against her, there was much that needed explaining, but no more now, maybe later that afternoon, when they could be together. Where? In town. They would walk up and down somewhere, that would be best. In the lobby of the museum. At four-thirty. No phone calls to Katharina's apartment, none to Miss Woltersheim, none to Mr. and Mrs. Hiepertz.

It was also depressing to find that the absence of Katharina's orderly hand made itself felt with such speed and clarity. How in the world did it happen that within half an hour—though all they had done was to make some coffee, get out some rye crisp, butter, and honey, and place their few pieces of baggage in the hall—chaos seemed already to have broken loose, and finally even Trude became irritable because he kept on asking her how she could possibly see any connection between Katharina's affair and Alois Sträubleder, let alone Lüding, and she didn't do a thing to help him, merely pointing, in her mock naive-ironic way, which at other times he liked but did not appreciate at all this morning, to the two issues of the News, and hadn't he been struck by one phrase in particular, and when he asked her what phrase she refused to tell him, remarking sarcastically that she wanted to test his perspicuity, and he read "this filth, this damn filth, that pursues a person wherever he goes," over and over again, not concentrating because the anger over his twisted statement and "Trude the Red" kept mounting in him afresh, until he finally capitulated and humbly asked Trude to help him out; he was so beside himself, he said, that his perspicuity failed him; besides, for years he had been only a corporation lawyer, had done scarcely any criminal work at all, to which she replied dryly, "Too bad," but then showed some mercy by saying, "You mean you didn't notice the phrase 'gentleman visitor,' or that I connected that phrase with the telegrams? Would anyone ever describe this Götting—no, Götten—just have a good look at his pictures again, would anyone ever describe him, no matter how he was dressed, as a 'gentleman visitor'? No, you must agree that someone like that would only be called a 'male visitor' in the language of amateur informers living in the building, and I'll turn myself into a prophet here and now and tell you that within one hour at the most we shall also be receiving a gentleman visitor, and another thing I'll prophesy is: trouble, confrontation—and possibly the end of an old friendship, trouble too with your Trude the Red and more than trouble with Katharina, who has two fatal characteristics: loyalty and pride, and she will never, never admit that she showed this boy an escape route, one which we—she and I—had looked over together. Take it easy, dear heart, take it easy: it'll never come out, but to tell the truth I'm the one responsible for this Götting, no Götten, vanishing from her apartment without being seen. I don't suppose you remember, but I had a diagram of the entire heating, ventilation, plumbing, and cable systems of 'Elegant Riverside Residences' hanging in my bedroom. It showed the heating ducts in red, the ventilation ducts in blue, the cables in green, and the plumbing in yellow. This diagram fascinated Katharina to such a degree—and you know what a person she is for order and planning, in fact she's positively brilliant at it—that she would stand in front of it for a long time and keep asking me about the relationships and significance of this 'abstract painting' as she called it, and I was just about to get hold of a copy and give it to her. I'm rather relieved I didn't, imagine if they'd found a copy of the diagram in her apartment—that would have been the best kind of support for the conspiracy theory, the idea of an arms depot, the link between 'Trude-the-Red-and-outlaws' and 'Katharina-and-gentleman-visitor.' Naturally a diagram like that would be an ideal guide for all kinds of intruders—burglars, lovers, whatever—who wanted to come and go without being seen. I even explained the height of the various passages to her: where you can walk up-right, where you have to duck, where you have to crawl, when pipes burst or cables break down. This is the only possible way our fine young gentleman, whose caresses she can now only dream about, can have slipped through the police, and if he's really a bank robber he'll have tumbled to the system at once. Maybe that's how the gentleman visitor went in and out too. These modern apartment blocks require totally different methods of surveillance from the old-fashioned apartment buildings. Sometime or other you must tip off the police and the public prosecutor's office. They watch the main entrances, and possibly the lobby and elevator, but there's also a service elevator leading directly to the basement—and there a person can crawl a few hundred yards, lift up a manhole cover somewhere, and vanish into thin air. Believe me, there's nothing to do now but pray, for the last thing Alois needs is News headlines in any shape or form. What he needs now is for the findings and the reports on them to be thoroughly doctored, and what he's just as scared of as headlines is the sourpuss expression of one Maud, his well and truly wedded wife, by whom, incidentally, he has four children. You mean to say you've never noticed how 'boyishly gay,' how 'high-spirited,' he was—and, I must say, he couldn't have been nicer the few times he danced with Katharina, and how he positively insisted on driving her home—and how boyishly disappointed he was when she got her own car? The very thing he needed, the very thing his heart desired—an exceptionally nice young person like Katharina, not 'fast' and yet—what do you men call it?—with a capacity for love, serious and yet young, and prettier than she ever realized. Hasn't she sometimes gladdened your manly heart a bit?"

Yes, of course she had: gladdened his manly heart, and he admitted it, and also admitted that he did more, much more, than just like her, and she, Trude, must know that everyone, not only men, sometimes had strange impulses just to take someone in their arms, and maybe more—but Katharina, no, there was something about her that could never, never have made him one of her gentlemen visitors, and if something had held him back, indeed made it impossible for him to become—or should he say, try to become—one it wasn't, and she knew how he meant this, it wasn't respect for her, Trude, or consideration for her, but respect for Katharina—that was it, respect, you might say reverence, more, fond reverence for her, hell, innocence—and more, more than innocence, something he couldn't find the right word for. It must be that strange, warm-hearted reserve of Katharina's and—although he was fifteen years her senior and God knew he had done pretty well in life—the way Katharina had set to work to plan and organize her ruined life—it was this that had held him back, if he had ever had any such ideas, because he had been afraid of destroying her or her life—she was so vulnerable, so damn vulnerable, and if it turned out that Alois actually had been her gentleman visitor he would—to put it plainly—"punch him in the jaw"; yes, they must help, help her, those tricks and interrogations and questionings were more than she could handle—and now it was too late, and somehow or other he must find Katharina before the day was out . . . but at this point he was interrupted in his revelatory musings by Trude remarking, in her inimitable wry manner: "The gentleman visitor has just driven up."

39

It must be established here and now that Blorna did not punch Straubleder in the jaw, although indeed it was he driving up in a flashy rented car. It is our wish not only that as little blood should flow here as possible, but also that the portrayal of physical violence, if it must be mentioned at all, should be kept to the minimum required by our reportorial obligations. This does not mean that the atmosphere at the Blornas became less depressing; on the contrary, it became more depressing than ever, for Trude B. could not resist greeting their old friend, as she went on stirring her coffee, with the words: "Hullo there, gentleman visitor." "I assume," said Blorna in embarrassment, "that Trude has once again hit the nail on the head." "Yes," said Straubleder, "I just wonder whether that's always so tactful."

Here it may be noted that the relationship between Mrs. Blorna and Alois Sträubleder had once become almost unbearably strained when he had tried, if not exactly to seduce her, certainly to make a pass at her and she in her dry way had given him to understand that, irresistible though he might be in his own eyes, he was not so in hers. In these circumstances it will be understood why Blorna escorted Sträubleder immediately to his study and asked his wife to leave them alone together and in the interval ("interval between what?" asked Mrs. Blorna) to make every possible effort to locate Katharina.

40

Why does one suddenly find one's own study so repulsive, everything upside down and dirty although there is not a speck of dust to be seen and everything is in its proper place? What makes the red leather armchairs, in which one has clinched many a good business deal and had many a confidential chat, in which one can be really relaxed and listen to music, suddenly seem so repulsive, even the bookshelves disgusting and the signed Chagall on the wall down-right suspect, as if it were a fake done by the artist himself? Ash-trays, lighters, whiskey decanter—what makes one dislike these harmless if expensive objects? What makes such a depressing day after an extremely depressing night so intolerable and the tension between old friends so powerful that sparks are ready to fly? Why does one dislike the walls, stippled in soft yellow and adorned with contemporary graphic art?

"It's like this," said Alois Sträubleder, "I really only came to tell you that I no longer need your help in this affair. You lost your nerve again, out there at the airport in the fog. An hour after you both lost your nerve or your patience the fog lifted, and you could still have been here by 6:30 in the evening. If you'd thought it over quietly, you could have called the airport in Munich and found out that flights were leaving on time again. But never mind about that. To be perfectly honest with you—even if there'd been no fog and the plane had left on time, you'd have got here too late because the crucial part of the questioning was over long before and there'd have been nothing left for you to prevent."

"I'm no match for the News anyway," said Blorna.

"The News," said Sträubleder, "is no threat, Lüding's seen to that, but there are other papers, and I don't mind any kind of head-line except this kind that associates me with outlaws. If an affair with a woman gets me into trouble, it's private trouble, not public. Even a picture of me with a woman as attractive as Katharina Blum wouldn't harm me, and by the way they're dropping the theory of the male visitor, and neither the ring nor the letter—well yes, I did give her a rather valuable ring, which they've found, and I did write her a few letters, of which all they've found is one envelope—neither of those things is going to present a problem. The bad part is that this Tötges uses a different name when he writes things for the weeklies which the News is not allowed to print, and that—well—Katharina has promised him an exclusive interview. I just found this out a few minutes ago, from Lüding, what's more he's glad Tötges is taking up the offer since, as I say, the News has been taken care of, but we've no influence on Tötges's other journalistic activities, he handles those through a go-between. You don't seem to be in the picture at all, do you?"

"I've no idea what's going on," said Blorna.

"An odd state of affairs for an attorney whose client I am, I must say; that comes from frittering away one's time in rattling trains instead of getting in touch with weather bureaus which could have told one that the fog would soon lift. So you haven't been in touch with her yet?"

"No, have you?"

"No, not directly. I only know that about an hour ago she called the News and promised Tötges an exclusive interview for tomorrow afternoon. He accepted. And there's something else that worries me more, much much more, it's tying my stomach in knots" (here Sträubleder's face showed something like emotion and his voice became strained), "starting tomorrow you can say what you like about me, and as much as you like, because it's true that I've abused your confidence and Trude's—but on the other hand we do live in a free country where it's permitted to lead a free love life, and you must believe me when I say I would do anything to help her, I would even gamble my reputation, for—go ahead, laugh—I love that woman, but: she's beyond helping—I can still use some help—she simply won't let herself be helped. . . ."

"And is there no way you can help her, protect her from the News, from those bastards?"

"Now listen, you mustn't take that business with the News so seriously, even if they have rather got their claws into you and Trude. For God's sake let's not quarrel now over the yellow press and the freedom of the press. I'll come to the point: I'd appreciate it if you could be present at the interview as my attorney and hers. You see, the really devastating part still hasn't come out either in the interrogations or in the press: six months ago I induced her to accept a key to our country place in Kohlforstenheim. They didn't find the key when they searched either the house or Katharina, but she has it, or at least she did have it, if she hasn't just thrown it away. It was just a sentimental impulse on my part, call it what you like, but I wanted her to have a key to the house because I refused to give up hope that she would come to me there one day. You must believe that I would help her, that I'd stand by her, that I'd even go to them and confess: Look, I'm the mysterious visitor—but I know only too well: while she'd let me down, she'd never let down that Ludwig of hers.''

There was something quite new, unexpected, in Sträubleder's expression, something that aroused, if not pity, at least curiosity in Blorna; it was a kind of humility, or was it jealousy?

"What's all this about jewelry and letters and now a key?"

"For God's sake, Hubert, don't you get it yet? It's something I can't tell either Lüding or Hach or the police—I'm convinced she's given the key to that fellow Ludwig and that that's where he's been hiding out the past two days. I'm scared, I tell you, about Katharina, about the police, and about that young idiot too who may be hiding out in my house in Kohlforstenheim. I'd like him to disappear before they find him, but at the same time I'd like them to catch him, to put an end to the whole business. Now do you get it? What's your advice?"

"You might call up there, in Kohlforstenheim, it seems to me."

"And do you really believe that if he's there he'll answer the phone?"

"All right, then you must call the police, there's no alternative. If only to prevent a disaster. Call them anonymously, if you must. If there's even the slightest possibility that Götten is at your place out there, you must notify the police immediately. Otherwise I will."

"So that my house and name get linked up in the headlines with that outlaw after all? I had a different idea. . . . I was thinking maybe you could drive out there, I mean to Kohlforstenheim, as my attorney, sort of, just to make sure the place is all right."

"At this moment in time? On Carnival Saturday, with the *News* already aware that I've abruptly broken off my vacation—and I'm supposed to have done that just to make sure everything's all right at your place in the country? The fridge still working, hm? The thermostat still set properly, no windows smashed, enough liquor in the bar and the sheets not damp? And for that an eminent corporation lawyer, owner of a luxury villa with a swimming pool and married to 'Trude the Red,' comes rushing back from his vacation? Do you really think that's such a smart idea, when we may be certain that the gentlemen from the News are watching my every move—and there I go driving, straight from the sleeper as it were, out to your country home to see if the crocuses will soon be peeking through or the snowdrops are already out? Do you really think that's such a great idea—quite apart from the fact that our friend Ludwig has already proved he's a pretty good shot?"

"Hell, I'm not sure whether your wisecracks are so appropriate right now. I ask you, as my attorney and my friend, to render me a service, and not even an especially personal one at that, really more a kind of citizen's duty—and you come back at me with snowdrops. Since yesterday this affair's been kept so secret that we haven't had so much as a grain of information out of them since this morning. All we know is what we read in the *News,* and we're lucky that Lüding has enough pull there. The public prosecutor's office and the police have even stopped calling the Ministry of the Interior, and Lüding has pull there too. It's a matter of life and death, Hubert."

Just then Trude entered without knocking, carrying the transistor radio and saying quietly: "No longer of death, only of life, thank God. They've caught the boy, he was stupid enough to shoot and so they shot at him, he's wounded but in no danger. In your garden, Alois, out in Kohlforstenheim, between the swimming pool and the pergola. They describe it as the super-luxury villa of one of Lüding's cronies. Incidentally, there's still such a thing as a true gentleman: the first thing our friend Lüdwig said was that Katharina had absolutely nothing to do with the whole business, it was a purely private love affair totally unrelated to the crimes with which he was charged but which he continued to deny. You'll probably have to have a few windows replaced, Alois—they banged around there quite a bit. Your name hasn't cropped up yet, but maybe you should call Maud, she must be upset and in need of consolation. By the way, they caught three of Götten's alleged accomplices at the same time, in other places. The whole thing is called a triumph for a certain Commissioner Beizmenne. And now get going, Alois my dear, and this time call on your wife for a change—maybe she could do with a gentleman visitor."

It is not hard to imagine that at this point Blorna's study came close to being the scene of a physical confrontation definitely not in keeping with the surroundings and furnishings of the room. Sträbleder allegedly-allegedly—flew at Trude's throat but was prevented by her husband, who pointed out to him that surely he did not intend to attack a lady. Sträubleder allegedly—allegedly—said that he wasn't sure whether the term "lady" applied to such a shrew, and there were some words that in certain circumstances, and especially in the wake of tragic events, should not be used sarcastically, and those words were loaded, and if he heard them once more, just once more, then—yes, what then—well, that would be the end. He had scarcely left the house and Blorna had had no chance to tell Trude that maybe she had gone a bit far when she cut in with: "Katharina's mother died last night. I did manage to locate her: she's in Kuir-Hochsackel."

41

Before embarking on our final diversion and rerouting maneuvers we must be permitted to make the following "technical" interjection. Too much is happening in this story. To an embarrassing, almost ungovernable degree, it is pregnant with action: to its disadvantage. Naturally it is to be deplored when a self-employed housekeeper shoots and kills a reporter, and a case of this kind undoubtedly has to be cleared up or at least an attempt must be made to do so. But what is to be done with successful attorneys who break off their hard-earned skiing vacations for the sake of a housekeeper? With industrialists (who are professors and politicos on the side) who in their callow sentimental way simply force keys to country homes (and themselves) on this housekeeper, in both cases unavailingly, as we know, and who want publicity, but only of a certain kind; with a whole raft of objects and people whom it is impossible to synchronize and who continually disturb the flow (i.e., the linear course of events), because they are, shall we say, immune? What is to be done with crime commissioners who continually, and successfully, demand "little plugs"? In a nutshell: it is all too full of holes, and yet, at what is for the narrator the crucial moment, not full enough, because, while it is possible to learn of this or that (from Hach, maybe, and a few male and female police officials), nothing, absolutely nothing of what they say holds water because it would never be confirmed by or even stated in a court of law. It is not conclusive evidence! It has not the slightest public value.

For example, this whole business of "little plugs." Of course, wiretapping yields information, but that very information—since the tapping is carried out by other than the investigating authorities—not only may not be used in public proceedings, it may not even be mentioned. Above all: what goes on in the "psyche" of the wiretapper? What passes through the mind of a blameless civil servant who is only doing his duty, who, we might say, is required to do his duty (albeit reluctantly) by the exigencies of earning a living if not of obedience to orders? What does he think when obliged to monitor a telephone conversation between that unknown apartment dweller, whom we will designate here the hawker of intimacies, and such an unusually nice, smart, virtually blameless person as Katharina Blum? Does he find himself in a state of moral or sexual excitement, or both? Does he become indignant, feel pity, or even derive some weird pleasure from a person nicknamed "the nun" being wounded in the depths of her soul by hoarse and menacing propositions?

With all this happening in the foreground, even more is going on in the background. What does a harmless wiretapper who is merely doing his job think when a certain Lüding, who has been mentioned here from time to time, calls up the editor in chief of the News and says something like: "S. right out, as of now, and B. in"? Naturally Lüding is not being tapped because *he* has to be kept under observation, but because of the threat that someone—blackmailer, politician, gangster, etc—may call him up. How is a blameless monitor to know that S. stands for Sträubleder and B. for Blorna, and that readers of the Sunday News will find nothing more about S. but a great deal about B.? And yet—who is to know or even suspect this?—Blorna is an attorney of whom Lüding has the highest opinion, one who time and again has proved his skill at both the national and international level. When elsewhere we speak of sources that "can never come together," all we are thinking of is the song about the prince and the princess whose candle is blown out by the false nun—and someone fell into rather deep water and drowned. And Mrs. Lüding tells her cook to call her husband's secretary and find out what kind of dessert Lüding would like on Sunday: crepes with poppy seed? Strawberries with ice cream and whipped cream, or with ice cream only or with whipped cream only? Whereupon the secretary, who would rather not disturb her boss but knows his tastes yet on the other hand may merely want to cause trouble, tells the cook with some asperity that she is convinced that this Sunday Mr. Lüding would prefer crème brûllée. The cook, who of course also knows Lüding's tastes, refuses to accept this, saying this is news to her and is the secretary sure she is not confusing her own tastes with those of Mr. Lüding, and would she kindly put her through so she can talk to Mr. Lüding personally about his dessert? Thereupon the secretary, who sometimes travels with Mr. Lüding to conferences and has lunch or dinner with him at some Palace or Inter Hotel or other, claims that when she is on a trip with him he invariably chooses crème brûlée. The cook: but this Sunday he wasn't going to be on a trip with her, the secretary, and mightn't Mr. Lüding's choice of dessert depend on the society he happened to be in? Etc. Etc. Finally there was a long argument about crêpes with poppy seed—and this entire conversation is recorded on tape at the taxpayer's expense! And the person playing back the tape, who of course has to be on the lookout for an anarchist code in which crêpes might stand for hand grenades or strawberries and ice cream for bombs—does he think: The problems some people have! or: I wouldn't mind having such problems, for his daughter might just have run away from home or his son have taken to hash, or the rent might have gone up again, and all this—these tape recordings—merely because someone once uttered a bomb threat against Lüding. And this is how some innocent civil servant or employee finally finds out what crêpes with poppy seed are—someone for whom even one crepe would do as a main meal.

Too much is happening in the foreground, and we know nothing about what is happening in the background. If only one could replay the tapes! To discover at last the degree of intimacy, if any, between Miss Else Woltersheim and Konrad Beiters. How much does "friend" mean in terms of the relationship between these two? Does she call him Sweetheart, or Darling, or does she just say Konrad or Conny? What kind of verbal intimacies, if any, do they exchange? Does he sing to her over the phone—since he is known to have a good baritone voice, if not of concert at least of choral quality? Lieder? Serenades? Pop tunes? Operatic arias? Or might there even be crude itemizations of past or future intimacies? One would like to know, for most people, being denied reliable telepathic communication, reach for the phone, which they feel is more reliable. Do the

authorities realize what they are asking of their employees in terms
of the psyche? Let us assume that a temporarily suspect person of a
vulgar nature, whose telephone is being officially tapped, calls up
his equally vulgar sex partner of the moment. Since we live in a free
country and may speak openly and frankly with one another, even
over the phone, what sort of things may buzz in the ears of some
moral, not to say moralistic, individual (regardless of sex) or come
fluttering out of the tape? Can this be justified? Is there any provi-
sion for psychiatric treatment? What does the Union of Public Services, Transportation, and Communications say to that? There is
concern for industrialists, anarchists, bank directors, bank robbers,
and bank employees, but who is concerned about our national
tape—security forces? Have the churches no comment to make on
this? Has the Bishops' Conference at Fulda or the Executive Committee of German Catholics no ideas on the subject? Why does the
Pope keep silent? Does no one realize all the things that assail innocent ears, ranging from crème brûlée to hardest porn? We see young
people being encouraged to enter the civil service—and to what are
they exposed? To moral outcasts of the telephone. Here at last we
have an area where church and trade union might cooperate. Surely
it should be possible to plan at least some kind of educational program for telephone monitors? History lessons on tape? That
shouldn't cost too much.

42

We now return contritely to the foreground, set to work on the in-
escapable channeling process—and must begin yet again with an
explanation! We promised to let no more blood flow, and we wish
to stress that, with the death of Mrs. Blum, Katharina's mother, this
promise has not been exactly broken. For this death, while not, of
course, a normal one, was not a bloody murder. Mrs. Blum's death
was brought on by violence, true, but by unintentional violence. In
any event—and this must be borne in mind—the person responsible
for her death had no intention of committing murder, manslaugh-
ter, or even mayhem. The person concerned—and for this there is
not only evidence but his own admission—was none other than

Tötges, the very man who himself came to such a bloody end as the result of deliberate violence.

As early as Thursday, Tötges had inquired after and obtained Mrs. Blum's address in Gemmelsbroich, but his attempts to get into the hospital to see her were unsuccessful. He was informed by the doorman, by Sister Edelgard, and by Dr. Heinen, that Mrs. Blum had just undergone a serious but successful cancer operation and was urgently in need of rest; that her recovery depended on not being exposed to any excitement whatever, and that an interview was out of the question. When reminded that, through her daughter's connection with Götten, Mrs. Blum was also a "public figure," the doctor countered with the remark that as far as he was concerned even public figures were first and foremost patients.

Now during this conversation Tötges had noticed that there were painters working in the building, and he later boasted to his colleagues that on Friday morning he succeeded, by using "the simplest trick in the book, the workman trick," that is, by getting hold of some overalls, a paint pot, and a paint brush, in getting in to see Mrs. Blum, for nothing was such a mine of information as a mother, even a sick one; he had, he said, confronted Mrs. Blum with the facts but wasn't quite sure whether she understood all he said, for the name Götten obviously didn't ring a bell with her and she had said: "Why did it have to end like this, why did it have to come to this?" out of which the News made: "It was bound to come to this, it was bound to end like this." Tötges accounted for the slight change in Mrs. Blum's statement by saying that as a reporter he was used to "helping simple people to express themselves more clearly."

43

It could not even be definitely established whether Tötges actually had got to see Mrs. Blum, or whether, in order to present the words quoted in the News as having been spoken by Katharina's mother in an interview, he had lied about or invented his visit as an example of his one-upmanship and efficiency as a reporter and to have something to boast about as well. Dr. Heinen, Sister Edelgard, a Spanish nurse called Huelva, a Portuguese cleaning woman called

Puelco—all consider it out of the question that "this fellow should actually have had the nerve to do such a thing" (Dr. Heinen). Now there is no doubt that the visit to Katharina's mother—admitted although possibly invented—was of crucial importance, and the question naturally arises as to whether i.e. hospital staff is simply denying what ought not to have happened, or whether Tötges, in order to authenticate the words of Katharina's mother, invented the visit. We must be scrupulously fair. There can be no doubt that it was after Katharina had arranged the interview with Tötges and after the Sunday News had published a further report by Tötges that she made herself the Bedouin costume in order to do some snooping in that very bar which the unfortunate Schönner had left "with some broad." So we must wait and see. One thing is certain, indeed confirmed, and that is that Dr. Heinen was surprised at the sudden death of his patient Maria Blum and that he could not "exclude the possibility of unforeseen influences, despite the lack of evidence." Innocent painters must not be saddled with the responsibility for this. The honor of the German craftsman must not be besmirched: neither Sister Edelgard nor the foreign ladies Huelva and Puelco can guarantee that all the painters—there were four of them, supplied by the firm of Merkens in Kuir—were in fact painters, and since all four were working in different parts of the building no one can be sure that someone in overalls and equipped with paint pot and brush did not sneak inside. The fact remains that Tötges claimed {the word "admitted" should not be used, since there is no actual evidence of his visit} to have seen Maria Blum and to have interviewed her, and Katharina knew of this claim. Furthermore, Mr. Merkens has admitted that of course not all of the four painters were present at the same time and that, *if* someone had wanted to sneak in, it would have been the simplest thing in the world. Dr. Heinen said later that he would bring a charge against the News for publishing the alleged remark of Katharina's mother and create a scandal for, if it was true, it was monstrous—but his threat remained as unexecuted as the "punch in the jaw" with which Blorna had threatened Sträubleder.

44

At about noon of that Saturday, February 23, 1974, the Blornas, Miss Woltersheim, Konrad Beiters, and Katharina finally all got together at the Café Kloog in Kuir, which was run by a nephew of the restaurant owner for whom Katharina had sometimes worked in the past, in the kitchen and as a waitress. Embraces were exchanged and tears were shed, even by Mrs. Blorna. Needless to say, the customers at the café were in Carnival mood, but the proprietor, Erwin Kloog, an old and admiring friend of Katharina's, put his own living room at the disposal of the little group. From here, Blorna telephoned at once to Hach, canceling the appointment for that afternoon in the museum lobby. He told Hach that Katharina's mother had died suddenly, probably as the result of a visit by Tötges from the News. Hach was more subdued than he had been that morning and asked Blorna to convey his personal sympathy to Katharina, who, he felt sure, bore him no grudge, and indeed why should she? Of course, he was at their disposal any time. Although he was very busy right now with the interrogation of Götten he would certainly find the time; incidentally, so far nothing had shown up in Götten's interrogation that could be damaging for Katharina. Götten had spoken of her with great affection and fairness. Permission for a visit, though, was not likely to be forthcoming since they were not related and the term "fiancée" would almost certainly prove too vague to pass muster.

It looks very much as though Katharina was not exactly in a state of collapse following the news of her mother's death; it almost seems as though she was relieved. Of course Katharina showed Dr. Heinen the edition of the News in which the Tötges interview was mentioned and her mother was quoted, but she certainly did not share Dr. Heinen's indignation about the interview: on the contrary, she felt these people were murderers and character-assassins, and while naturally she despised them it was obviously the duty of that type of newspaper person to deprive the innocent of their honor, reputation, and health. Dr. Heinen, mistakenly assuming her to be a Marxist (probably he too had read the insinuations of Brettloh, Katharina's divorced husband, in the News), was taken aback by her detachment and asked her whether she considered it—this modus operandi of the News—*to* be a problem of the social structure. Katharina did not know what he meant, and shook her head.

She then followed Sister Edelgard to the mortuary, which she entered together with Miss Woltersheim. Katharina drew back the sheet from her mother's face with her own hands, said "Yes," and kissed her on the forehead; when Sister Edelgard suggested Katharina say a short prayer, she shook her head and said "No." She replaced the sheet over her mother's face, thanked the nun, and only on leaving the mortuary did she start to cry, at first softly, then harder, then uncontrollably. Perhaps she was also thinking of her dead father whom, when she was a child of six, she had also seen for the last time in a hospital mortuary. Else Woltersheim remembered, or rather noted, that she had never seen Katharina cry before, not even as a child when she had been unhappy at school or because of her wretched environment. Very courteously, almost with a smile, Katharina insisted on thanking everyone, including the foreign ladies Huelva and Puelco, for all they had done for her mother. She left the hospital quite composed, nor did she forget to ask the hospital administration to send a telegram to the prison where her brother Kurt was confined so he might be informed.

That was how she remained the whole afternoon and throughout the evening: composed. Although again and again she took out the two issues of the News and confronted the Blornas, Else W., and Konrad B. with all the details and her interpretation of them, even her attitude toward the News seemed to have changed. In today's jargon: less emotional, more analytical. In this familiar and sympathetic circle of friends, in Erwin Kloog's living room, she also spoke openly of her relationship to Sträubleder: on one occasion he had brought her home after an evening at the Blornas and, although she had specifically and almost with revulsion told him not to, had accompanied her as far as her front door and even into her apartment by simply placing his foot in the door. And then of course he had tried to make advances, probably had felt insulted because she had not found him at all irresistible, and finally—it was already close to midnight—had left. From then on he had positively persecuted her, had kept coming back, sending flowers, writing letters, on a few occasions had even managed to get into her apartment, and it was on one of those that he had simply forced the ring on her. That was all. That was why she had not admitted to his visits or revealed his name, because she had felt it would be impossible to explain to her interrogators that there had been nothing, absolutely nothing, not even a single kiss, between them. Who was going to believe that she would resist a man like Sträubleder, who was not only very well off but downright famous in the political, economic, and academic world for his irresistible charm, almost like a movie star; and who was going to believe of a woman like herself, a domestic, that she would resist a movie star, and not for moral reasons either but for reasons of taste? He had simply not had the slightest attraction for her, and she regarded this whole business of male visitors as the most horrible interference in a sphere which she would not like to call intimate since that would give the wrong impression and she had not been even remotely intimate with Sträubleder—but because he had got her into a situation that she could not explain to anyone, let alone a team of investigators. In the end, however—and here she laughed—she had felt grateful to him in a way, for the key to his house had been a big help to Ludwig, or at least the address, for—here she laughed again—Ludwig would certainly have got in without a key, but of course the key made it easier, and she had known too that the villa would be vacant during Carnival, for only two days before Sträubleder had once again made the worst possible nuisance of himself, positively forcing himself upon her and suggesting they spend a Carnival weekend together at the house before he had to leave for the conference at Bad B. in which he had agreed to take part. Yes, Ludwig had told her the police were looking for him, but he had merely said he was an army deserter and about to leave the country, and—she laughed for the third time—she had enjoyed personally dispatching him into the heating duct and telling him where the emergency exit was that led above ground at the end of "Elegant Riverside Residences," at the corner of Hochkeppel-Strasse. No, she had not thought that she and Götten were being watched by the police, to her it had been a kind of cops-and-robbers affair, and it wasn't until next morning—Ludwig actually had left at six o'clock—that she had come to realize how serious the whole thing was. She registered relief that Götten had been arrested: now, she said, he wouldn't be able to do any more stupid things. She had been scared all the way through, there had been something downright weird about that Beizmenne.

45

At this juncture it must be noted that Saturday afternoon and evening passed quite pleasantly, so pleasantly that everyone—the Blornas, Else Woltersheim, and the strangely silent Konrad Beiters—felt almost reassured. Finally there was a general feeling—shared even by Katharina—that the "situation had relaxed." Götten arrested, Katharina's interrogation over, Katharina's mother released, albeit sooner than expected, from great suffering; funeral arrangements were already under way, all the necessary documents in Kuir promised for the Monday before Lent, an official having kindly declared his willingness to issue them that day although it was a holiday. And finally there was a certain consolation in the fact that the café proprietor Erwin Kloog, who would not hear of accepting payment for what had been consumed (i.e. coffee, liqueurs, potato salad, wieners, and cake), said as they left: "Chin up, Katie, not all of us here think badly of you." The consolation inherent in these words was perhaps only relative, for how much is "not all" worth? Still, the fact remained that it was "not all." They agreed to drive to the Blornas and spend the rest of the evening there. On arrival, Katharina was strictly forbidden to take a hand, even her orderly one: she was on vacation and was told to relax. It was Miss Woltersheim who made some sandwiches in the kitchen while Blorna and Beiters together saw to the fire. And Katharina actually did let herself be "spoiled for once." Everything was really very nice, and if it had not been for a death and the arrest of a very dear person they would certainly have had a little impromptu dance in the small hours, for in spite of everything it was Carnival. Blorna was unable to dissuade Katharina from the planned interview with Tötges. She remained calm and smiling, and later, after the interview—some "interview"!—Blorna felt his blood run cold at the recollection of the cool determination with which Katharina had insisted on the interview and how firmly she had declined his offer to be present. And yet, later, he was not quite sure whether Katharina had already decided on the murder that evening. It seemed to him much more likely that it had been triggered by the Sunday News. They bade each other a peaceful good night, again with embraces, this time without tears, after listening to both serious and popular music together and after both Katharina and Else Woltersheim had told the others something about life in Gemmelsbroich and Kuir. It was barely half-past ten when Katharina, Miss Woltersheim, and Beiters parted from the Blornas with assurances of deep regard and fellow-feeling, and the Blornas congratulated themselves on having returned in time—in time to help Katharina—after all. Over the ashes in the fireplace and a bottle of wine, they discussed fresh vacation plans and the character of their friend Sträubleder and his wife Maud. When Blorna asked his wife to try not to use the phrase "gentleman visitor" next time Sträubleder came, surely she must see how hypersensitive the term had become, Trude Blorna said: "It'll be a while before we see him again."

46

We can vouch for Katharina having spent the rest of the evening quietly. She tried on her Bedouin costume again, went over some of the seams, and decided to use a white handkerchief for a veil. They listened to the radio a while longer, ate some cookies, and then took themselves off to bed: Beiters going for the first time openly with Miss Woltersheim into her bedroom, and Katharina making herself comfortable on the sofa.

47

When Else Woltersheim and Konrad Beiters got up on Sunday morning, they found the breakfast table nicely prepared, the coffee decanted into the Thermos jug, and Katharina, who was already having her breakfast and clearly enjoying it, sitting at the living-room table reading the Sunday News. What follows is not so much comment as quotation. True, Katharina's "story" plus photo were no longer on the front page. This time the front page showed Ludwig Götten under the caption: "Intimate partner of Katharina Blum takes cover in industrialist's villa." The story itself was in greater detail than before and appeared on pages 7 to 9 with numerous pictures: Katharina as a First Communicant, her father as a returning soldier, the church in Gemmelsbroich, once again the Blorna villa; Katharina's mother at about forty, careworn, almost worn out, standing outside the cottage in Gemmelsbroich where they used to live, and finally a picture of the hospital where Katharina's mother had died Friday night. The text ran as follows:

A victim of her own daughter: so may we describe the mother of Katharina Blum, that shadowy figure who is still at large, Mrs.

Blum not having survived the shock of being informed of her daughter's activities. While it is strange enough that, as her mother lay dying, the daughter should have been dancing at a ball in the tender embrace of a robber and murderer, it surely borders on the utmost perversity that she should have shed not a single tear at the news of her mother's death. Is this woman in truth merely "ice-cold and calculating"? The wife of one of her former employers, a respected country doctor, describes her as follows: "She behaved like a real little floozy. I had to let her go for the sake of my teenage sons, our patients, and my husband's reputation." Is it possible that Katharina B. was involved in the embezzling activities of the notorious Fehnern? (The News published a complete report of that case at the time.) Was her father a malingerer? Why did her brother turn to crime? Still awaiting explanation are her rapid rise in the world and her substantial income.

It has now been definitely established that Katharina Blum provided Götten, the man with blood on his hands, with the means of escape; she shamelessly abused the affection, confidence, and spontaneous generosity of a highly respected professional man and industrialist. Information is now in the hands of the News proving almost conclusively that her activities consisted not in *receiving* male visitors but in making unsolicited visits of her own in order to "case" the villa. Blum's "mystery drives" are no longer so mysterious. Without a shred of scruple she gambled the reputation of an honorable man, the happiness of his family, and his political career (on which the News has published frequent reports), indifferent to the feelings of a loyal wife and four children. It would appear that Blum had been instructed by a Leftist group to destroy S.'s career.

Do the police and the public prosecutor's office really intend to believe the infamous Götten in his protestations of Blum's complete innocence in the affair? As so often in the past, once again the *News* raises the question: Can it be denied that our methods of interrogation are too mild? Are we to continue to treat with humanity those who commit inhuman acts?

Beneath the photos of Blorna, Mrs. Blorna, and the villa.

It was in this house that Katharina Blum worked from seven A.M. to four-thirty P.M., on her own and unobserved, enjoying the full confidence of Dr. and Mrs. Blorna. What was going on here while the unsuspecting Blornas pursued their professions? Or were they not so unsuspecting after all? Their relationship with Blum is described as very cordial, almost familiar. Neighbors told reporters that it could almost be described as friendship. We will pass over certain insinuations since they are not relevant. Or are they? What was the role played by Mrs. Gertrud Blorna, known to this day in the records of a respected technical college as "Trude the Red"? How did Götten manage to escape from the Blum apartment although the police were on his heels? Who was familiar, down to the last detail, with the blueprints of the apartment complex known as "Elegant Riverside Residences"? Mrs. Blorna, Bertha Sch., sales clerk, and Claudia St., factory worker, made identical comments to the News: "Those two, the way they danced together" (referring to Blum and the outlaw Götten) "—it was as if they'd known each other all their lives. That was no chance meeting, that was a reunion."

48

When Beizmenne was later criticized by his colleagues for having left Götten unmolested for almost forty-eight hours, although his presence at the Sträubleder villa had been known to the police since 11:30 P.M., Thursday, thus risking another escape on the part of Götten, Beizmenne laughed, saying that ever since midnight Thursday Götten had had no further chance of escaping: the house was in the woods but, by great good luck, was surrounded by shooting blinds, "as if by watchtowers"; the Minister for the Interior had been kept fully informed and had agreed to all the measures taken; a helicopter, which of course did not land within earshot, had put down a special detachment which was then deployed among the shooting blinds, and the following morning the local police force had been reinforced, very discreetly, by two dozen additional police officers. The main objective had been to observe Götten's attempts to make contact, and the success had justified the risk. Five contacts had been spotted, and of course it had first been necessary to pick up these five contacts and search their homes before arresting Götten. The police had waited to grab Götten until he had no further contacts to make and, out of either carelessness or bravado, had felt so safe that it had been possible to observe him from outside the villa.

Incidentally, there were certain important details for which he had to thank reporters from the News as well as the publishers of that paper and its affiliates that happened to have at their disposal more flexible and not always conventional methods of digging up information that had remained hidden from the investigating authorities. For example, Miss Woltersheim had turned out to be just as much of an unknown quantity as Mrs. Blorna. Woltersheim had been born in 1930, the illegitimate child of a factory worker. The mother was still alive, and where do you suppose? In East Germany, and by no means against her will but voluntarily; she had frequently been invited to return to her native Kuir, where she owned a small house and an acre of land—the first time in 1945, again in 1951, yet again in 1961 shortly before the Berlin Wall went up. But she had refused—three times and all three times categorically. Of even greater interest was Woltersheim's father, a man called Lumm, likewise a factory worker and in addition a member of the then German Communist Party, and in 1932 he had emigrated to the Soviet Union, where he is said to have disappeared without trace. He—Beizmenne—supposed that this kind of missing person was not among those listed by the German Army as "missing."

49

There is always the possibility that certain relatively clear pointers toward a relationship between various events and actions will be misinterpreted or lost as mere hints; one further pointer should, therefore, be permitted: the News, which, of course, through its reporter Tötges was responsible for the unquestionably premature death of Katharina's mother, depicted Katharina in the Sunday News as being to blame for her mother's death and, moreover, accused her—more or less openly—Of stealing Sträubleder's key to his country home! This point should be reemphasized, for one can never be sure; nor quite sure whether one has fully realized to what extent the News has slandered, lied, and distorted.

Let us take Blorna as an example of the extent to which the News was able to affect comparatively rational people. We need hardly say that in the residential area where the Blornas lived no one bought the Sunday News. Reading tastes were loftier there. This explains how Blorna, who thought it was all over and was somewhat nervously awaiting the outcome of Katharina's conversation with Tötges, knew nothing about the article in the Sunday News until he called Miss Woltersheim. Miss Woltersheim, in turn, had taken it for granted that Blorna had already read the Sunday News. Now it is to be hoped that Blorna has been established as deeply and sincerely concerned for Katharina but also as a very level-headed person. On Miss Woltersheim now reading the relevant passages from the Sunday News aloud to him over the telephone, he could not—as they say—believe his ears. He asked her to read that again, after which he had not much choice but to believe it, and—as they say—he hit the roof. He shouted, roared, and rushed into the kitchen for an empty bottle, found one, ran off with it to the garage where, fortunately, he was intercepted by his wife and prevented from rigging up a Molotov cocktail that he intended to throw into the editorial offices of the News, to be followed by a second one into Sträubleder's town house. One must picture the scene: a man of forty-two, a university graduate, the object for the past seven years of Lüding's admiration and Sträubleder's respect for his sober, clear-headed negotiating abilities—and this on an international level, i.e., in Brazil, Saudi Arabia, and Northern Ireland, in other words not one of your provincial types but a thoroughgoing man of the world: this is the man who wanted to rig up a Molotov cocktail!

Mrs. Blorna dismissed this instantly as spontaneous petit-bourgeois romantic anarchism, "charmed away" his impulse the way one "charms away" disease or pain from some part of the body, went to the telephone herself and had Miss Woltersheim read the relevant passages to her. It cannot be denied that she, even she, turned somewhat pale, and she did something that may have been worse than any Molotov cocktail: she reached for the phone, called Lüding (who happened to be enjoying his strawberries with whipped cream plus vanilla ice cream), and simply said to him: "You bastard, you miserable little bastard!" She did not give her name, but it is safe to assume that all who knew the Blornas knew

the voice of Mrs. Blorna, who was notorious for the asperity and
deadly aim of her remarks. This, in her husband's opinion, was in
turn going too far: he thought she was calling Sträubleder. Well, the
result was one row after another, between the Blornas, and between
the Blornas and other people, but since nobody was killed we must
be allowed to pass over them. We mention these trifling, even if deliberate, consequences of the Sunday News reporting merely to
point out how even well-educated, well-established people can be
so carried away by their indignation that they consider resorting to
violence of the crudest kind. It is known that at about this time—
around noon—Katharina, after spending an hour and a half,
unrecognized, at the reporters' hangout, presumably gathering information on Tötges, left the place known as the "Golden Duck"
and was waiting in her apartment for Tötges, who appeared some
fifteen minutes later. We assume there is no more to be said concerning the "interview." The outcome is known. (See page 9.)

50

In order to check the truth of the statement made by the Gemmelsbroich pastor—a statement that had surprised everyone involved—
that Katharina's father had been a Communist in disguise, Blorna
drove out to the village, where he spent a day. First of all: the pastor
confirmed his statement, saying that the News had quoted him correctly and word for word, no, he could offer no proof of his claim
nor did he want to, he even said he did not need to, he could still
rely on his sense of smell and he had simply smelled that Blum was
a Communist. When asked to define his sense of smell he refused,
nor was he very helpful when Blorna then asked him kindly to explain, if he could not define his sense of smell, what the smell of a
Communist was like, how a Communist smelled, and at this
point—it has to be said—the pastor became quite rude, asked
Blorna whether he was a Catholic and, when Blorna said yes, reminded him of his duty to be obedient, which Blorna did not understand. From then on, he ran into difficulties over his inquiries
concerning the Blums, who did not appear to have been especially
popular; he heard bad things about Katharina's deceased mother,
who had indeed finished one bottle of sacramental wine in the sac-

risty with the help of the verger (since dismissed); he heard bad things about Katharina's brother, who had been a regular nuisance, but the only words of Katharina's father to substantiate his Communism were a remark he made in 1949 to Scheumel, a farmer, in one of the seven village taverns, and this was supposed to have been: "There are worse things than Socialism." That was all he could glean. The only result for Blorna was that, at the conclusion of his inquiries in the village, he was himself described, if not precisely abused, as a Communist, and that came (something he found particularly painful) from a woman who until then had been quite helpful and had even displayed a certain sympathy toward him: the retired schoolteacher Elma Zubringer who, as he said good-bye, gave him a mocking smile, even a bit of a wink, saying: "Why don't you admit that you're one of them too—and your wife most of all?"

51

Unfortunately we cannot ignore one or two acts of violence that occurred while Blorna was preparing for the trial of Katharina. His greatest mistake was in acceding to Katharina's request to take over Götten's defense as well, and in repeatedly trying to obtain permission for the two to visit each other, insisting that they were engaged. It was, he maintained, in the course of that very evening, February 20, and of the ensuing night that the engagement had taken place. Etc. Etc. It is not hard to imagine the kind of thing the News wrote about him, about Götten and Katharina, about Mrs. Blorna. We do not intend to cite each instance here. Certain infringements of or departures from the level are to be undertaken only when necessary, and here they are not necessary because by this time the reader must know what to expect from the News. The rumor was being circulated that Blorna wanted a divorce, a rumor without a grain of truth to it but which nevertheless sowed the seeds of mistrust between husband and wife. It was claimed that he was in financial straits, which was bad because it was true. The fact was that he had somewhat overextended himself in assuming a kind of custodianship for Katharina's apartment, which was almost impossible to rent or sell because it was considered "bloodstained." Anyway, it dropped in value, yet Blorna had to continue the payments for amortization, interest, etc., in unreduced amounts. In fact there was already some indication that Haftex, the owners of "Elegant Riverside Residences," were considering suing Katharina Blum for damages, claiming that she had impaired the rental, commercial, and social value of their apartment complex. We see then: trouble, quite a lot of trouble. An application to the courts for permission to dismiss Mrs. Blorna from the architectural firm on grounds of breach of confidence (i.e., familiarizing Katharina with the substructure of the apartment complex) was turned down, but nobody is sure which way the appeal courts will decide. One more thing: the Blornas have already got rid of their second car, and recently there was a picture in the News of the Blorna limousine, which really is rather elegant, over the caption: "When will the 'red' attorney have to switch to the average man's car?"

52

Need we say that Blorna's association with Lüsträ has been affected if not dissolved? The only matters still under discussion now are the "winding up" of certain transactions. However, he was recently informed by Sträubleder over the telephone: "We're not going to let you and Trude starve," and what surprised Blorna in this was Sträubleder's inclusion of Trude. He still acts on behalf of Lüsträ and Haftex but no longer at the international or even the national level, only rarely at the regional and mostly at the local level. In other words, he has to grapple with petty defaulters and troublemakers who submit claims for the promised marble paneling when the walls have been faced with mere green slate; or types who, when they have been promised three coats of enamel on their bathroom doors, scrape off the paint with a knife and hire experts to confirm that there are only two coats. Then there are the dripping faucets and defective garbage disposals used as a pretext for withholding contractual payments–this is the kind of case now being dumped in his lap, whereas he used to be flying continually, if not continuously, between Buenos Aires and Persepolis to take part in plans for major projects. In the army this is known as a demotion, a process usually associated with some degree of humiliation. Result: no stomach ulcers yet, but Blorna's stomach is beginning to complain.

It was unfortunate that he made his own inquiries in Kohlforstenheim with a view to finding out from the local chief of police
whether the key had been on the inside or the outside of the door
at the time of Götten's arrest, or whether there had been any sign
of Götten having broken in. Why bother, now that the inquiries
have all been completed? This—there is no denying—is no way to
cure stomach ulcers, for all that Police Chief Hermanns was very
nice to him, and yet, far from accusing him of Communism, he did
strongly urge him not to interfere. There is one consolation for
Blorna: his wife is being nicer to him all the time, and although she
still has a sharp tongue she now reserves it for use against others
(although not against all others) instead of against him. So far the
only obstacle to her plan of selling the villa and buying Katharina's
apartment for themselves is the size of the apartment: it is too small,
for Blorna wants to give up his town office and wind up any outstanding business at home. Blorna, who used to be known as
liberal-minded and a bon vivant, a popular, jovial colleague who
gave wonderful parties, is beginning to take on the air of an ascetic
and to neglect his appearance, to which he had always attached
great importance; and because he is genuinely neglecting it, not just
as a fad, some of his colleagues are even saying that he is overlooking the most basic personal hygiene and no longer smells as he
should. Hence there is little reason to hope for a new career for him,
the fact being (nothing, nothing whatever, must be withheld) that
his body no longer smells as it used to, i.e., like that of a man who
every morning jumps into the shower and uses plenty of soap, de-
odorant, and toilet water. In short: a considerable change is taking
place in him. His friends—he still has a few, among them Hach,
with whom he happens to be professionally involved in the Götten
and Blum cases—are seriously concerned, especially since his ag-
gressions—e.g., vis-à-vis the News, which still remembers him from
time to time with short items—no longer explode but are quite obviously being swallowed. His friends' concern is such that they have
asked Trude Blorna to check discreetly whether Blorna is acquiring
any weapons or concocting explosives, for the murdered Tötges has
a successor who, under the name of Eginhard Templer, is carrying
on a kind of continuation of Tötges; this Templer managed to photograph Blorna just as the latter was entering a pawnshop; then, by
photographing through the window, he was able to offer readers of

the News a view of Blorna negotiating with the pawnbroker: under discussion was the loan value of a ring being scrutinized by the pawnbroker through a jeweler's loupe. Caption: "Have the 'red' sources really dried up, or is someone faking financial distress?"

53

Blorna's chief concern is to persuade Katharina to testify at the actual trial that she did not make the decision to take revenge on Tötges until the Sunday morning, and that her intention had been not to kill him but to scare him off. She was to say that, although on the Saturday, when she invited Tötges to an interview, she had meant to tell him what she thought of him in no uncertain terms and to point out what he had done to her life and her mother's life, she had not wanted to kill him even on the Sunday, even after reading the article in the Sunday News, He felt it was imperative to avoid the impression that Katharina had planned the murder for several days and had proceeded according to plan. Although she claims to have thought about murder on Thursday after reading the first article, he tried to make her realize that many people— including himself—occasionally do think about murder but that one must distinguish between thinking about murder and planning a murder.

Another thing worrying Blorna is that Katharina is still showing no signs of remorse, which means that she will not be able to show any in court, She is not at all depressed: on the contrary, she seems quite happy because she is living "under the same conditions as my dear Ludwig." She is considered a model prisoner, works in the kitchen but, if the opening of the trial is further delayed, is to be transferred to the commissary where, however (so one hears), she is most unenthusiastically awaited: there is dismay on the part of both administration and inmates at the reputation for integrity that precedes her, and the prospect of Katharina spending her entire prison term working within the commissary system (it is predicted that a sentence of fifteen years will be asked for and that she will get eight to ten) is spreading alarm through every prison in the country. Thus we see that integrity, combined with intelligent organizing ability, is not desired anywhere, not even in prisons, and not even by the administration.

54

As Hach informed Blorna in confidence, the murder charge against Götten is not likely to stand up and will therefore be dropped. The fact that he not only deserted from the army but also acted to the considerable detriment (both moral and material) of this hallowed institution is regarded as proven. His crime was not bank robbery but the total cleaning out of a safe that had contained the pay for two regiments as well as substantial cash reserves; also falsifying the accounts and theft of a weapon. Well, a sentence of eight to ten years is expected for him too. This means that when released he would be about thirty-four and Katharina about thirty-five, and she really does have plans for the future: she calculates that by the time she is released interest will have increased her capital substantially, and when the time comes she intends to open, "somewhere, not here of course," a "restaurant with outside catering service." Permission to consider herself Götten's fiancée will probably be decided at the highest, not merely a higher, level. The relevant applications have been submitted and are already on their long march from one department to another. Incidentally, the telephone contacts made by Götten from Sträubleder's country house were all to members of the army or their wives, including officers and officers' wives. A scandal of moderate dimensions is predicted.

55

While Katharina, restricted only in her freedom, is looking almost untroubled to the future, Else Woltersheim is on the way to a state of steadily increasing bitterness. She was extremely upset at the defamation of her mother and her deceased father, who is regarded as a victim of Stalinism. There are indications in Else Woltersheim of intensified antisocial tendencies which not even Konrad Beiters is able to alleviate. Since Else is now specializing more and more in cold buffets, i.e., in organizing, supplying, and supervising them, her aggressiveness is being increasingly directed at the guests, whether foreign or domestic journalists, industrialists, trade-union officials, bankers, or junior executives. "Sometimes," she told Blorna not long ago, "I have to force myself not to throw a bowl of potato salad over the tuxedo of some moron or a plate of smoked salmon down the cleavage of some stupid cow, just to see them shudder for once. Try and imagine the picture from our side: how they stand there with their mouths wide open and their tongues hanging out and how of course they all make a dash for the caviar canapés—and there are some who I know are millionaires, or the wives of millionaires, who even stuff their pockets and purses with cigarettes and matches and petits fours. Soon they'll be bringing along plastic containers to carry away the coffee—and all that, every bit of it, is being paid for one way or another out of our taxes. There are characters who go without breakfast or lunch so they can fall like vultures on a cold buffet—not that I mean to insult vultures."

56

So far we know of only one instance of an actual exchange of blows, one which unfortunately aroused a good deal of public attention. It was at the preview of the exhibition of the work of the painter Frederick Le Boche, whose patron Blorna is considered to be, that Blorna and Sträubleder came face to face again for the first time. As Sträubleder approached him with a broad grin, Blorna did not hold out his hand, but this did not prevent Sträubleder from grabbing it and whispering: "For God's sake, don't take it all so seriously! We're not going to let you and Trude go to the dogs— you're the one who's doing that." Well, if we are to be honest we have regretfully to report that at this moment Blorna did punch Sträubleder in the jaw. Without further ado, so that it may be forgotten without further ado: blood flowed, from Sträubleder's nose; according to private estimates, some four to seven drops but, what was worse: although Sträubleder backed away he did say: "I forgive you, I forgive you everything—considering your emotional state." And so it was that this remark apparently maddened Blorna, provoking something described by witnesses as a "scuffle," and, as is usually the case when the Sträubleders and Blornas of this world show themselves in public, a News photographer by the name of Kottensehl (successor to the murdered Schönner) was present, and we can hardly be shocked at the News (its nature being now known) for publishing the photograph of this scuffle under the heading: "Conservative politician assaulted by Leftist attorney." Not until the following morning, of course.

At the exhibition there was furthermore a confrontation between Maud Sträubleder and Trude Blorna. Maud Sträubleder said to Trude Blorna: "I do sympathize with you so, Trude dear," whereupon Trude B. said to Maud S.: "You can put your sympathy right back in the fridge where you keep all the rest of your feelings." Upon Maud again offering her forgiveness, indulgence, pity, indeed almost love, with the words: "Nothing, nothing, not even your destructive remarks, can lessen my sympathy," Trude B. replied in words that cannot be repeated here, only noted; ladylike is not the way to describe the words in which Trude B. hinted at Sträubleder's numerous advances to her and, among other things—thus violating the professional secrecy to which even the wife of an attorney is bound—alluded to the ring, the letters, and key which "your consistently rejected suitor left behind in a certain apartment." At this point the squabbling ladies "were parted by Frederick Le Boche," who with great presence of mind had seized upon the chance to catch Sträubleder's blood on a piece of blotting paper and had converted it into what he called "a specimen of instant art." This he entitled "End of a Long Friendship," signed, and gave not to Sträubleder but to Blorna, saying: "Here's something you can peddle to help you out of a hole." From this occurrence plus the preceding acts of violence it should be possible to deduce that Art still has a social function.

57

It is indeed deplorable that here, as we approach the conclusion, there should be so little harmony to report and but slight hope of any in the future. The outcome has been not integration but confrontation. Naturally the question must arise: Why? Here is a young woman, cheerfully, almost gaily, going off to a harmless little private dance, and four days later she becomes (since this is merely a report, not a judgment, we will confine ourselves to facts) a murderess, and this, if we examine the matter closely, because of newspaper reports. We see quarrels and tensions and finally scuffles arising between two men who have been friends for a very, very long time. Pointed remarks made by their wives. Rejected sympathy, in fact rejected love. Highly unpleasant developments. A genial, broad-minded man, who loves life, travel, luxury, neglects himself so seriously that he emits body odor! He has even been found to have bad breath. He puts his house up for sale, he goes to the pawnbroker. His wife is looking around "for another job" since she is convinced that her firm's second application for dismissal will go against her; she is even prepared—this talented woman is prepared—to work as little better than a sales clerk (with the title "Interior Decorating Consultant") for one of the large furniture outfits, but there she is told "that the circles in which we are accustomed to do business are precisely those, Madam, where you have made enemies."

In short: things do not look good. Hach, the public prosecutor, has already been whispering to friends something that he has not yet had the courage to tell Blorna: that Blorna may be turned down as defense counsel on grounds of his undue involvement. What will happen, how will it end? What will happen to Blorna if he can no longer visit Katharina and—it has to come out!—hold hands with her? There is no doubt about it: he loves her, she does not love him, and he hasn't a hope in the world, since everything, everything, belongs to her "dear Ludwig"! And we must add that this "holding hands" is a purely one-sided affair, for all it consists of is that, when Katharina passes files or notes or papers across to him, he places his hands on hers for longer—perhaps three, four, at most five tenths of a second longer—than is customary. How in the world are we to bring about harmony here. When not even his strong attachment to Katharina prompts him to, let us say, wash a bit more often? Not even the fact that he, he alone, discovered the origin of the murder weapon—where Beizmenne, Moeding, and their assistants had failed—was any comfort to him. Perhaps it is too much to say "discovered": what actually happened was that Konrad Beiters voluntarily admitted to having once been a Nazi and that this alone explained why so far no one had paid any attention to him. It was true, he had been Party leader in Kuir and at the time had been able to do something for Miss Woltersheim's mother, and, well, the pistol was an old service, one that he had kept hidden but stupidly enough occasionally shown to Else and Katharina; the three of them had once even gone out into the woods for some target practice; Katharina had turned out to be a good shot and had told him that as a girl she had worked as a waitress at Rifle Club meetings and had sometimes been allowed to fire a few rounds. Well, on the Saturday evening Katharina had asked him for the key to his apartment, saying she hoped he would understand, she just wanted to be alone for a while. Her own apartment was dead for her, dead—yet that Saturday night she had stayed with Else so she must have picked up the pistol from his apartment on the Sunday, it must have been after breakfast and after reading the Sunday News, when she had driven off in her Bedouin costume to that reporters' hangout.

58

But finally we do have something reasonably cheerful to report: Katharina told Blorna the whole story; she also told him how she had spent the six or seven hours between the murder and her appearance at Moeding's home. We are in the fortunate position of being able to quote. Fortunately, this account can be quoted verbatim, Katharina having written it all down and given Blorna permission to use it at the trial.

"The only reason I went to that reporters' bar was to have a look at him. I wanted to know what that kind of man looked like, what his movements were like, how he talked, drank, danced—that man who had destroyed my life. Yes, I did go first to Konrad's apartment to pick up the pistol, I even loaded it myself. I had asked him to show me how, that time we did some target practice in the woods.

"I waited in the bar for an hour and a half, maybe two hours, but he didn't show up. I had decided that, if he was too awful, I wouldn't even go to the interview, and it's true—if I had seen him before I wouldn't have gone. But he never came to the bar. To avoid being pestered, I asked the landlord—his name is Peter Kraffuhn, I know him from the extra jobs I take on, where he sometimes helps out as head waiter—I asked him to let me help serve behind the bar.

Of course Peter knew what the News had been saying about me, he had promised to give me the high sign if Tötges turned up. Seeing it was Carnival, I didn't mind being asked to dance a few times, but when Tötges failed to show up I must say I got very nervous, I didn't want to meet with him cold.

"So at noon I drove home, and I felt terrible in that stained and soiled apartment. I only had to wait a few minutes before the bell rang, just enough time to release the safety catch on the pistol and slip it into my handbag ready to pull out. And then the bell rang, and there he was outside the door when I opened it, and here I'd been thinking he had pressed it downstairs and I would have a few extra minutes, but he had already come up in the elevator, and there he was, standing right in front of me, and it was a shock. Well, I could see right away what a bastard he was, a real bastard. And good-looking, too. What people call good-looking. Anyway, you've seen his pictures. He said: 'Well, Blumikins, what'll we do now, you and me?' I didn't say a word, just stepped back into the living room, and he followed me in, saying: 'Why do you look at me like that, Blumikins, as if you're scared out of your wits? How about us having a bang for a start?' Well, by this time I had my hand in my purse, and as he went for my dress I thought: 'Bang, if that's what you want,' and I pulled out the pistol and shot him then and there. Twice, three times, four times—I don't remember exactly. The police report will tell you how many times. Now I don't think this was something new for me, a man going for my dress—when you've worked in other people's homes ever since you were fourteen, and even earlier, you're used to that. But this fellow—and then 'a bang'! and I thought: OK, bang away. Of course he hadn't counted on that, and for a split second he looked at me in amazement, like in the movies when someone gets shot out of a clear blue sky. Then he fell to the floor, and I think he was dead. I threw the pistol down beside him and fled, down in the elevator and back to the bar, and Peter was astonished, since I'd been gone hardly half an hour. I went on working at the bar but I didn't dance any more, and all the time I was thinking, 'It can't be true,' but I knew it was true. And now and again Peter would come up and say: 'He's not going to show today, that boy friend of yours,' and I would say: 'Doesn't look like it.' And behave as if I didn't care. Until four o'clock I poured schnapps and drew beer and opened champagne bottles and served snacks. Then I left, without saying goodbye to Peter. First I went into a church next door and sat there for maybe half an hour thinking about my mother and the wretched miserable life she had had, and about my father too, who was always grumbling, always always, and cursing the government and the church and the civil service, and officers and everything, but whenever he had anything to do with any of them he would crawl, almost whimper, as he groveled. And I thought about my husband, Brettloh, and about those rotten lies he told Tötges, and of course about my brother, who was forever after my money the minute I'd earned a few marks and managed to squeeze it out of me for some nonsense or other, like clothes or motorbikes or gambling, and of course about the pastor, who in school always used to call me 'our pink Katie,' and I didn't know what he meant, and the whole class would laugh because then I really would turn pink. Yes. And of course about Ludwig. Then I left the church and went to the nearest movie, and left the movie again, and went into another church, because on that Carnival Sunday it was the only place where a person could find a bit of peace. And of course I thought about the dead man back there in my apartment. Without remorse, without regret. He had wanted a bang, hadn't he, and I'd banged, hadn't I? And for a moment I thought it was the fellow who used to ring me up at night and who had pestered poor Else too. I thought: that's his voice all right, and I wanted to let him rattle on for a bit, to be quite sure, but what good would that have done me? And then I suddenly longed for some strong coffee and went to the Café Bekering, not to the restaurant but to the kitchen, because I knew Käthe Bekering, the owner's wife, from home-ec school. Käthe was very kind to me, although she was pretty busy. She gave me a cup of her own coffee, the kind Grandma used to make by pouring boiling water onto the ground coffee. But then she began talking about that stuff in the News, quite nicely yet somehow in a way that made me feel she believed at least a bit of it—and anyway how are people to know that it's all lies? I tried to explain to her, but she didn't understand, she just winked at me and said, 'So you really love this fellow?' and I said, 'Yes.' And then I thanked her for the coffee, and when I got outside I took a cab and drove to see Moeding, the police officer who had been so nice to me before."

Translated by Leila Vennewitz

PART THREE

AUTOBIOGRAPHICAL WRITINGS

Undine's Mighty Father

I am prepared to believe almost anything of the Rhine, but I have never been able to believe in its carefree summer mood; I have looked for this carefree mood but never found it. Perhaps it is a flaw in my vision or in my character that prevents me from discovering this aspect.

My Rhine is dark and brooding, it is too much a river of merchant cunning for me to be able to believe in its youthful summertime face.

I have traveled on its white ships, have walked over its bordering hills, cycled from Mainz to Cologne, from Rüdesheim to Deutz, from Cologne to Xanten, in fall, spring, and summer; in winter I have stayed at small riverside hotels, and my Rhine was never a summer Rhine.

My Rhine is the one I remember from earliest childhood: a dark, brooding river that I have always feared and loved. I was born three minutes' walk away from it. Before I could talk, when I could barely walk, I was already playing on its banks: we would wade knee-deep in the fallen leaves along the avenue, looking for the paper pinwheels we had entrusted to the east wind, the wind that, too fast for our childish legs, drove the pinwheels westward toward the old moats.

It was fall, the weather was stormy, heavy clouds and the acrid smoke from ships' funnels hung in the air; in the evenings the wind would subside, fog would lie over the Rhine valley, foghorns toot somberly, red and green signal lights at the mastheads float past as if on phantom ships, and we would lean over the bridge railings listening to the strained, high-pitched signal horns of the raftsmen as they traveled downriver.

Winter came: ice floes as big as football fields, white, covered with a thick layer of snow; on such clear days the Rhine was very quiet, the only passengers were the crows being carried by the ice floes toward Holland, calmly riding along on their huge, fantastically elegant taxis.

For many weeks the Rhine remained quiet: only a few narrow, gray channels between the big white floes. Seagulls sailed through the arches of the bridges, ice floes splintered against the piers, and in February or March we waited breathlessly for the great drifts coming down from the Upper Rhine. Ice masses evoking the Arctic came from upriver, and it was impossible to believe that this was a river on whose banks wine grew, good wine. Layer upon layer of cracking, splintering ice drifted past villages and towns, uprooting trees, crushing houses, less compacted, already less menacing, by the time it reached Cologne.

There is no doubt at all about there being two Rhines: the Upper, the wine drinker's Rhine, and the Lower, the schnapps drinker's Rhine—less well known and on whose behalf I would put in my plea: a Rhine that to this day has never really come to terms with its east bank. Where in bygone times smoke used to rise from the sacrificial fires of Teutonic tribes, now smoke rises from chimney stacks—from Cologne downriver to well north of Duisburg: red, yellow, and green flames, the ghostly silhouette of great industries, while the western, left bank, is more reminiscent of a pastoral riverbank: cows, willows, reeds, and the traces of the Romans' winter encampments. Here they stood, those Roman soldiers, staring at the unreconciled east bank; sacrificing to Venus, to Dionysus, celebrating the birth of Agrippina: a Rhenish girl was the daughter of Germanicus, the granddaughter of Caligula, the mother of Nero, the wife and murderess of Claudius, later murdered by her son, Nero. Rhenish blood in the veins of Nero! She was born in an area of barracks—even in those days, horsemen's barracks, sailors' barracks, legionaries' barracks—and, at the western end of Cologne, the villas of merchants, administrators, officers; bathhouses, swimming baths. Modern times have still not quite caught up with that luxury lying buried beneath the rubble of the centuries, thirty feet below our children's playgrounds.

This river, the old, green Rhine, has seen too many armies—Romans, Teutons, Huns, Cossacks, robber barons, victors and vanquished, and, representing history's most recent heralds, those who came from farthest away: the boys from Wisconsin, Cleveland, or Manila, who carried on the trade started by the Roman mercenaries in the year 0. This broad, green-gray, flowing Rhine has seen too much trade, too much history, for me to be able to believe in its youthful summer face. It is easier to believe in its brooding nature, its darkness; the grim ruins of the robber-baron castles on its hills are not the relics of a very joyful interregnum. Here Roman frippery was bartered in the year 0 for Teutonic feminine favors, and in the year 1947 Zeiss binoculars were bartered for coffee and cigarettes, those little white incense offerings to the transitory nature of life. Not even the Nibelungs, who lived where the wine grows, were a very joyful race; blood was their coin, one side of which was loyalty, the other treachery.

The wine drinker's Rhine ends roughly at Bonn, then passes through a sort of quarantine that reaches as far as Cologne, where the schnapps drinker's Rhine begins. To many this may mean that the Rhine stops here. My Rhine starts here, switches to tranquillity and brooding without forgetting what it had learned and witnessed farther up. It becomes more and more serious toward its mouth until it dies in the North Sea, its waters mingling with those of the open sea. The Rhine of the lovely Middle Rhine madonnas flows toward Rembrandt and is swallowed up by the mists of the North Sea.

My Rhine is the winter Rhine, the Rhine of the crows traveling northwest on their ice floes toward the Lowlands, a Breughel Rhine whose colors are green-gray, black, and white, much gray, and the brown façades of the buildings that wait for the approach of summer before sprucing up again; the quiet Rhine that is still sufficiently elemental to ward off the bustling of the worshipers of Mercury for at least a few weeks, maintaining its own sovereignty, abandoning its old bed to birds, fish, and ice floes. And I am still scared of the Rhine that in spring can become vicious, when household goods come drifting down the river, drowned cattle, uprooted trees, when posters saying "Warning!" in red are fixed to the trees along its banks, when the muddy tides rise, when the chains mooring the huge, floating boathouses threaten to snap—scared of the Rhine that murmurs so eerily and so gently through the dreams of children, a dark god bent on showing that it still demands sacrifices.

Heathen, pristine Nature, in no way beautiful, it widens out like a sea, thrusts itself into dwellings, rises greenly in cellars, surges out of canals, roars its way along under bridges: Undine's mighty father.

Translated by Leila Vennewitz

My Father's Cough

When my father reached the same age as I am now approaching, he (naturally?) seemed older to me than I feel. Birthdays were not celebrated in our family, that was considered a "Protestant aberration," so I cannot recall any celebration, only a few details of the mood prevailing that October 1930. (My father shared his year of birth, 1870, with Lenin, but that, I believe, was all)

It was a dismal year. Total financial collapse, not exactly a classic "failure," merely a "compromise with creditors," a procedure I didn't understand, but at any rate it sounded more dignified than "bankruptcy." It was somehow connected with the collapse of an artisans' bank whose manager, if I remember correctly, ended up behind bars. Abuse of confidence, forfeited guarantees, unwise speculations. Our house in the suburbs had to be sold, and not a penny remained of the sales price. Upset and confused, we moved into a large—too large—apartment on Ubier-Ring in Cologne, across from what was then the vocational school.

Bailiffs, bailiffs, affixing seal after seal. We pulled these off while they were still fresh, ignoring this preliminary step to seizure; later we became indifferent and left them in place, and eventually some pieces of furniture (the piano, for instance) bore whole accumulations of seals. We got along fine with the bailiffs. There was irony on both sides, rudeness on neither.

I can remember the appearance of that four-pfennig piece, something to do with political emergency regulations, and the tobacco tax. This four-pfennig piece was a large, attractively designed copper coin, but it may not have appeared until a year or so later, perhaps 1931–32. The Nazis marched triumphantly into the Reichstag. Brüning was chancellor. We read the Kolnische Volkszeitung. My older brothers and sisters swore by the RMV (Rhein-Mainische-Volkszeitung).

I said good-bye to outdoor games. Sadly. Out in the suburb of Raderberg we had still been able to play hockey on the streets (with old umbrella handles and empty condensed-milk cans); rounders often, soccer less often, in Vorgeberg Park. We used to decapitate roses in the park with our "tweakers," known elsewhere in Germany as slings. Our hoop-tossing consisted of flinging old bicycle-wheel rims down a gentle grassy slope; the one whose hoop rolled the farthest was the winner. Records were established, and we rolled our hoops all the way around the block: it wasn't "done" to use bought, wooden hoops. Ping-Pong on the terrace, the swing in the garden; target practice with air rifles on burned-out light bulbs, which in those days were still of the bayonet type. We never found anything military, let alone militaristic, about this target practice. Ten years of freedom and many free games, too numerous for me to list. (St. Martin's torches, building and flying paper kites, marbles.)

In the long corridor of the apartment on Ubier-Ring we continued our target practice, now with regulation targets and bolts that we called "plumets" (the dictionary tells me this comes from the Latin pluma: the bolts had little colored tufts attached to them). During target practice, of course, whoever wanted to go into the bathroom, the kitchen, or the bedroom, or happened to be in there, had to be warned. Overall mood: recklessness and fear, not mutually exclusive. Needless to say, not all our income was revealed to the bailiff. There was moonlighting, income from renting out woodworking machinery. Recently I read in Isaac Bashevis Singer's Enemies, a Love Story, "If one wanted to live, one had to break the law, because all laws condemned one to death." We wanted to live.

We lived on a modest scale, yet modesty did not become our guiding principle. We had more than enough worries and debts. The rent, food, clothing, books, heating, electricity. The only thing that kept us going was a temporary lightheartedness which, of course, we only achieved temporarily. Somehow, after all, money had also to be found for movies, for cigarettes, for the indispensable coffee: something we didn't always, but did sometimes, achieve. We discovered pawnshops.

It wasn't all as carefree as it may sound. The more modest the scale, the less did modesty become our guiding principle. I gratefully remember the devotion of my older brothers and sisters, who must have made life easier for me, the youngest, by letting me have a little something from time to time. What scared me most during that period was my father's cough. He was of slight build (between the ages of twenty and eighty-five his weight varied by only two or three pounds; only after the age of eighty-five did he start to lose weight). He was moderate in his habits but liked to smoke, never inhaled, and he refused to do without (or at least entirely without!) his "Lundi"—those thin, pungent cigarillos packed in round cans. He was sad in these circumstances, and also powerless against conditions, and I sometimes think that we children never paid enough attention to his sadness.

His cough drowned out even the roar of streetcar Number 16, and we could hear his cough from far away. But the place where I was most worried by his cough was crowded St. Severin's Church on Sundays. We never went to Mass en bloc, always individually, rarely did two or three of us youngsters sit together in one pew, so we waited, each in his own seat, full of nervous tension, for our father's cough, knowing it would start up, increase almost to the point of suffocation, and then, as my father left the church, subside. He would then probably stand outside and smoke a "Lundi" for his cough.

Now the same age as my father was then, I find that I (and I am not the only one) have apparently inherited his cough. There are some people in our household who, as I park outside amid heavy traffic, recognize me through the noise of all those cars by my cough. I hardly ever have to ring the bell or use my key: someone is opening the front door before I do either.

My cough must be on a wavelength that penetrates not only traffic noises and screeching brakes but even police sirens, yet I don't believe that my cough can be called "penetrating." It consists of variations on differing forms of hoarseness, usually denotes embarrassment, is seldom a sign of a cold; and there are some people who know that it is more than a cough—and less. A granddaughter, for example, who is a year old, apparently regards it as a form of speech or address; she imitates it, coughing dialogues develop between us of an ironically amused nature, dialogues in which we apparently both have something to communicate. I am reminded of Beuys, who once made a speech consisting only of harrumphings and little coughs—and a very clever speech it was, by the way.

Perhaps one should establish harrumphing schools, at least consider harrumphing as a school subject; anyway, rid it of its silly admonitory function—to stop someone from making that tactless remark, for instance. L'art pour l'art as applied to coughing and harrumphing.

It might also be worth considering whether clever heads shouldn't invent the harrumphing letter-to-the-editor.

Translated by Leila Vennewitz

What's to Become of the Boy? or, Something to Do with Books

1

On January 30, 1933, I was fifteen years and six weeks old, and almost exactly four years later, on February 6, 1937, when I was nineteen years and seven weeks old, I graduated from high school with a "Certificate of Maturity." This certificate contains two errors: my date of birth is incorrect, and my choice of career—"book trade"—was altered by the school principal, without consulting me, to "publishing," I have no idea why. These two errors, which I cherish, justify me in regarding all the other particulars, including my grades, with some skepticism.

I didn't discover either of these errors until two years later, when, as the 1939 university summer term was about to begin, I looked at the certificate before handing it in to the University of Cologne and discovered the incorrect birth date. It would never have occurred to me to have an error of that kind in such a solemn official document corrected: that error permits me to entertain a certain doubt as to whether I am really the person who is certified thereon as mature. Might the document refer to someone else? If so, to whom? This little game also allows me to consider the possibility that the entire document may be invalid.

There are a few further points that I must clarify. If it should be regarded as mandatory for German authors to have "suffered" under the school system, I must once again appear to have failed in my duty. Of course I suffered (do I hear a voice: "Who, old or young, does not suffer"?), but not in school. I maintain that I never let things get that far. I dealt with each problem as it arose, as I so often did in later life, aware of the implications. How, is something I shall explain later. I did find the transition from elementary to high school briefly painful, but I was ten at the time, so this is not relevant to the period I wish to describe. I was sometimes bored in school, annoyed, chiefly by our religion teacher (and he, of course by me: such comments are to be interpreted bilaterally), but did I "suffer"? No. Further clarification: my unconquerable (and still unconquered) aversion to the Nazis was not revolt: *they* revolted *me*, repelled me on every level of my existence: conscious *and* instinctive, aesthetic *and* political. To this day I have been unable to find any entertaining, let alone aesthetic, dimension to the Nazis and their era, a fact that makes me shudder when I see certain film and stage productions. I simply *could not* join the Hitler Youth, I did not join it, and that was that.

A further clarification (there is yet another to come!): justifiable mistrust of my memory. All this happened forty-eight to forty-four years ago, and I have no notes or jottings to resort to; they were burned or blown to bits in an attic of 17 Karolinger-Ring in Cologne. Moreover, I am no longer sure of how some of my personal experiences synchronize with historical events. For example, I would have bet almost anything that it was in the fall of 1934 that Göring, in his capacity as Prime Minister of Prussia, caused seven young Communists of Cologne to be beheaded with an ax. I would have lost that bet: it was the fall of 1933. And my memory doesn't betray me when I recall that one morning a schoolmate of mine, a member of the black-uniformed S.S., exhausted yet with the hectic light of the chase still in his eyes, told me they had spent the night scouring the villas of Godesberg for the former cabinet minister Treviranus. Thank God (as I, not he, thought) without success. But when, to make quite sure, I proceed to look it up, I find that Treviranus had already emigrated by 1933; in 1933, the minimum age for membership in the S.S. was eighteen, though we were only sixteen then; thus, this memory cannot be placed earlier than 1935 or 1936. In other words, either Treviranus must have reentered the German Reich illegally in 1935 or 1936, or the S.S. must have been fed wrong information. The story itself—that strange blend of exhaustion and eyes shining with the light of the chase—I can vouch for, but I cannot place it.

Final clarification or, if you prefer, warning: the title *What's to Become of the Boy?* should arouse neither false hopes nor false fears. Not every boy whose family and friends have reason to ask themselves and him this eternally apprehensive question does, after various delays and roundabout approaches, eventually become a writer; and I would like to stress that, at the time it was put, this question was both serious and warranted. In fact, I am not sure whether my mother, were she still alive, wouldn't still be asking the same question today: "What's to become of the boy?" Perhaps there are times when we should be asking it about elderly and successful politicians, church dignitaries, writers, et cetera.

2

So it is somewhat warily that I now enter upon the "realistic," the chronologically confused path, wary of my own and other people's autobiographical pronouncements. The mood and the situation I can vouch for, also the facts bound up with moods and situations; but, confronted with verifiable historical facts, I cannot vouch for the synchronization, as witness the above examples.

I simply don't remember whether in January 1933 I was still or no longer a member of a Marian youth fellowship; nor would it be accurate if I were to say that I had "gone to school" for four years under Nazi rule. For I did *not* go to school for four years; there were, if not countless, certainly uncounted days when—apart from vacations, holidays, sickness, which must in any case be deducted—I didn't go to school at all. I loved what I might call the "school of the streets" (I can't say "school of the bushes," since Cologne's old town has little, and never had much, in the way of bushes). Those streets between the Waidmarkt and the cathedral, the side streets off the Neumarkt and the Heumarkt, all the streets going right and left down to the cathedral from Hohe Strasse: how I loved roaming around in the town, sometimes not even taking my schoolbag along as an alibi but leaving it at home among the galoshes and long overcoats in the hall closet. Long before I knew Anouilh's play *Traveller without Luggage*, that was what I enjoyed being, and I still dream of being one. Hands in pockets, eyes open, street hawkers, pedlars, markets, churches, museums (yes, I loved

the museums, I was hungry for education, even if not very assidu-
ous in its pursuit), prostitutes (in Cologne there was hardly a street
without them)—dogs and cats, nuns and priests, monks—and the
Rhine, that great gray river, alive and lively, beside which I could
sit for hours at a time; I used to sit in movie theaters too, in the dusk
of the early performances that were frequented by a few idlers and
unemployed people. My mother knew a lot, suspected some things
but not all. According to family rumors—which, like all family rumors, must be taken with a grain of salt—during the last three years
of those four Nazi school years, I spent less than half the time in
school. Yes, those were my school days, but I didn't spend all my
days in school, so that in trying to describe those four years, I can
only make an "also" tale out of them, for the fact is that I "also"
went to school.

3

Forty-eight years going back, from 1981 to 1933, and four years
going forward, from 1933 to 1937: in this leapfrog procession
some things must fall by the wayside. The man of sixty-three smiles
down upon the boy of fifteen, but the boy of fifteen does not smile
up at the man of sixty-three, and it is here, in this unilateral perspective which is not matched by a corresponding perspective on the
part of the fifteen-year-old, that we must expect to find a source of
error.

On January 30, 1933, the fifteen-year-old is ill in bed with a severe case of flu, victim of an epidemic that I consider to have been
given insufficient consideration in analyses of Hitler's seizure of
power. It is a fact that public life was partially paralyzed, many
schools and government offices were closed, at least locally and re-
gionally. One of my classmates brought me the news as I lay sick in
bed. In those days we still had no radio, and homemade efforts to
build crystal sets hadn't yet begun. We didn't acquire the mini-
edition of the so-called people's radio until shortly before the out-
break of war, our reluctance almost outweighing the necessity.
After a second move within two years, we were now living at 32
Maternus-Strasse, facing the dismal rear wall of what was then the
engineering school. Nevertheless, we were not very far from the

Rhine, and from our corner bay window we could see the neo-Gothic, tri-gabled warehouse of the Rhenus Line, of which I painted innumerable water colors. Just around the corner was Römer Park, a little farther on, Hindenburg Park, where on fine days my mother could sit among the jobless or people who had been forced into early retirement.

I lay in bed and read—probably Jack London, whose works we borrowed in the book club edition from a friend, but it is also possible—oh raised eyebrows of the literary connoisseurs, how gladly I would smooth you down!—that I was *simultaneously* reading Trakl. The great tiled stove in our corner room had, for once, been lit, and from it, using a long paper spill, I took a light for my (forbidden) cigarette. My mother's comment on the appointment of Hitler: "That's war," or maybe it was: "Hitler, that means war."

The news of Hitler's appointment came as no surprise. After Hindenburg's "shameful betrayal" of Brüning (that's what my father called it), after von Papen and Schleicher, Hindenburg was obviously capable of anything. That strange (to this day still somewhat obscure) affair known at the time as the "Eastern agricultural support scandal," on which even our extremely reticent *Kölnische Volkszeitung* had reported, had deprived "the venerable old field marshal" of the last shred of what had been at best minimal credit—not politically, merely the shred of moral credit that people had been willing to attribute to his "Prussian integrity."

My mother hated Hitler from the very beginning (unfortunately she didn't live to see his death); she dubbed him *Rövekopp*, "turnip head," an allusion to the traditional St. Martin's torches roughly carved from sugar beets and leaving, wherever possible, something resembling a moustache. Hitler—he was beyond discussion, and his long-time delegate in Cologne, a certain Dr. Robert Ley (try to imagine a character like Ley later in control of the entire German work force!), had done little to render Hitler and his Nazis worthy of discussion: they were nothing more than the "howling void," without the human dimension that might have merited the term "rabble." The Nazis were "not even rabble." My mother's war theory was hotly denied: the fellow wouldn't even last long enough to be able to start a war. (As the world discovered to its consternation, he lasted long enough.)

I forget how long I had to stay in bed. The flu epidemic gave a modest boost to the liquor stores; cheap rum was in demand—in the form of grog, it was said to offer cure or prevention. We bought moderate quantities of it in a shop at the corner of Bonner-Strasse and Darmstädter-Strasse: the proprietor's name was, I believe, Volk, and he had a son with flaming red hair who went to our school. I forget whether the burning of the Reichstag building, the "excellent timing" of which was noted by many, occurred while I was still sick or during term time or even during vacation (at some point there must have also been the Carnival!). In any event, before the March election I was going back to school; and only after that election—one so easily forgets that the results just barely provided a majority for a coalition between Nazis and the German National Party—in April or May the first Hitler Youth shirts appeared in school, and one or two Storm Trooper uniforms in the higher grades.

There was also—I forget exactly when—a book-burning, an embarrassing, in fact a pathetic, exercise. The Nazi flag was hoisted, but I can't remember anyone making a speech, hurling anathemas at title after title, author after author, tossing books into the fire. The books must have been placed there, a little heap, in advance, and since that book-burning I know that books don't burn well. Someone must have forgotten to pour gasoline over them. I also find it hard to imagine that the modest library of our high school (which, although called the Kaiser Wilhelm State High School, was extremely Catholic) could have contained much "decadent" literature. The background of virtually the whole student body was lower middle class with few "excrescences" either upward or downward. It's possible that one or other of the teachers privately sacrificed his Remarque or his Tucholsky to feed the funeral pyre. Be that as it may, none of these authors was listed in the curriculum; and after the tangible, the visible and audible, barbarities occurring between January 30 and the Reichstag fire—increasingly so between Reichstag fire and March election—this act of *symbolic* barbarity was perhaps not all that impressive.

The nonsymbolic purges were visible and audible, were tangible: Social Democrats disappeared (Sollmann, Görlinger, and others), as did politicians of the Catholic Center Party and, needless to say, Communists, and it was no secret that the Storm Troopers were establishing concentration camps in the fortifications around Cologne's Militär-Ring: expressions such as "protective custody" and "shot while trying to escape" became familiar; even some of my father's friends were caught up in the process, men who later, on their return, maintained a stony silence. Paralysis spread, an atmosphere of fear prevailed, and the Nazi hordes, brutal and bloodthirsty, saw to it that the terror was not confined to rumors.

The streets left and right off Severin-Strasse, along which I walked to school (Alteburger-Strasse, Silvan-Strasse, Severin-Strasse, Perlen-Graben), constituted a far from "politically reliable" area. There were days, after the Reichstag fire and before the March election, when the area was entirely or partially cordoned off, the least reliable streets being those to the right of Severin-Strasse. Who was that woman screaming on Achter-Gässchen, who that man screaming on Landsberg-Strasse, who on Rosen-Strasse? Perhaps it is not in school but on our way to school that we learn lessons for life. It was obvious that along those streets, people were being beaten up, dragged out of their front doors. After the Reichstag fire and the March election it grew quieter, but it was still far from quiet. One must not forget that, after the November 1932 election, the Communist Party had become the second-strongest party in a city as Catholic as Cologne (Center Party 27.3 percent; Communists 24.5 percent; Nazis 20.5 percent; Social Democrats 17.5 percent), a state of affairs somewhat similar to that in Italy today. Despite its Catholic reputation and all the clerical machinations, Cologne was and still is a progressive city. Then in March 1933 the Nazis obtained 33.3 percent, the Center Party still as much as 25.6 percent, and the Communists and Social Democrats, despite terror and purges, 18.1 and 14.9 percent: the "unreliable area" was still far from being "normalized," there was plenty of work left for the Storm Troopers to do. (There would be a lot more to say about Cologne, but in my opinion, after the Cathedral Jubilee, Pope John Paul II's visit, and the Ludwig Museum, Cologne has had ample publicity. Moreover, the Rhine flows on.)

It must have been about this time that the father of one of my older sister's school friends, a quiet, reliable police officer with a Center Party background, took early retirement because he could no longer stand the sight of the "bloody towels" in his precinct:

those, too, were not symbolic signs; the "bloody towels" were related to the screams I had heard from Achter-Gässchen, from Rosen-Strasse and Landsberg-Strasse.

By now it will have become increasingly evident to the reader that, as far as school is concerned, this is no more than an "also" story, that, although it deals with my school days, it doesn't deal only with the days I spent in school. Although school was far from being a minor issue, it was not a primary issue during those four years.

A clean-up operation of a quite different kind brought considerable changes in my daily walk to school: the crackdown on the cigarette smugglers who stood at street corners or in doorways whispering offers of "Dutch merchandise." The cheapest legally acquired cigarette cost at least two and a half pfennigs, a feeble object, half as firmly packed as a Juno or an Eckstein, which cost three and a third pfennigs each. The Dutch product was pale gold, firm, a third plumper than an Eckstein, and was offered at one to one and a half pfennigs each. Naturally that was very enticing at a time when Brüning's penny-pinching policies were still having their effect, so my brother Alois would sometimes give me money to buy him illegal Dutch cigarettes. Between Rosen-Strasse and Perlen-Graben, the focal point being somewhere around Landsberg-Strasse, with scattered outposts extending as far as the Eulen-Garten (the smugglers' headquarters that were located close to our school on Heinrich-Strasse), I had to be both wary and alert, had to appear both confidence-inspiring and eager to buy. Apparently I succeeded, and that early training or schooling (which, as I say, cannot be acquired in school but only on the way to school), that education, if you prefer, turned out to be very useful to me in later years in many of the black markets of Europe. (I have dealt elsewhere with the fact that a dedicated feeling for legality does not form part of the Cologne attitude to life.)

So the Dutch merchandise would reach home safe and sound, and I would receive my cut in the form of fragrant cigarettes. On one occasion, I must admit, I was diddled: the neat little package with its Dutch revenue stamp contained, instead of twenty-five cigarettes, approximately twenty-five grams of . . . potato peelings! To this day I fail to understand *why* potato peelings, and not, say, sawdust or woodshavings. They had been carefully weighed, evenly distributed, packed in foil. (Contempt for wax seals, lead seals, bailiff's seals, revenue stamps—also a kind of seal—ingrained in me by my mother, turned out, after the war, to be my undoing when I broke the seal of an electricity meter and tampered with it—unfortunately in a detectable manner. Bailiff's seals were promptly removed as a matter of course.) I was enjoined by my brother in future to check the goods and was still puzzling over *how*, since everything had to be done so quickly, when suddenly the entire smuggling operation was smashed. Certain streets were virtually under siege, and I recall at least one armored vehicle. Police and customs agents—in the end without shooting—cleared out the whole smugglers' nest: there were rumors of millions of confiscated cigarettes and numerous arrests.

4

Yes, *school*, I know—I'll get back to that. I was still in the eighth grade, and my route to school became even quieter. For a time I must have been walking with my head down, since one day my father offered me a prize if I could name twenty-five stores between St. Severin's Church and Perlen-Graben. I lifted my head once again and won the prize: I also lifted my head to read *Der Stürmer*, the newspaper in its display case outside the former trade-union building on Severin-Strasse, not far from the corner that goes off to Perlen-Graben. What I read did not enhance my sympathies for the Nazis. (Today, alas, that area is a desert; war and the Nord-Süd freeway saw to that. Yet that little square outside the Church of St. John the Baptist used to be bustling with life.)

Not always with the prior but always with the subsequent approval of my mother, I went often to the school of the streets. (As reported elsewhere, my mother anyway used to run a kind of center for nonfamily truants under the coffee grinder that hung on the kitchen wall.) So, if I went to the school of the streets, it wasn't because my high school was particularly Nazist or Nazi-tainted. It was not, and I remember most of my teachers without any resentment at all. I don't even feel resentment toward our teacher of religion, although I argued with him—to the point of being kicked out of the classroom. The points of dispute were not the Nazis; on that score he was not vulnerable. On the contrary, I recall an excellent lecture he gave on the sentimental and commercial background to the Day of the German Mother. What aroused my ire was the overriding bourgeois element in his teaching. It was against this that I rebelled so inarticulately; he had no idea what I meant or how I meant it, he was more confused than angry.

The cause of my rebellion could be found in the totally indefinable social situation in which we found ourselves: had our financial plight lowered our social status or made us classless? To this day I don't know. We were neither true lower middle class nor conscious proletarians, and we had a strong streak of the Bohemian. "Bourgeois" had become a dirty word for us. The elements of those three classes, to none of which we truly belonged, had made what might be called "bourgeois" Christianity absolutely insufferable to us. Our teacher of religion probably never understood what I had in mind, and I probably didn't express it clearly enough. (Obviously the author has always irked, and been irked by, church and state. And, being a true son of Cologne, he has never taken secular and ecclesiastical authority very seriously, much less regarded them as important!)

Merely lowered socially or truly classless? The question remains unanswered. The other subjects, aside from religion? I can't remember anything special about them. Even in those days I was gradually starting to "orchestrate" school. And, since I did respect the intelligence of our teacher of religion, who, although bourgeois to the marrow, made no concessions to the Nazis, I began from time to time to attend school mass in the Franciscan Church of Ulrich-Gasse. It made for a change in my usual route along Rosen-Strasse. As for the church, I found it (no other word occurs to me) disgusting, with its corny statues and decorations and the stale smells emanating from the congregation. There is only one word for those smells: *fug*, trying to pass itself off as fervor. I went there quite pointedly, with only occasionally the aim of offering some slight consolation to our teacher of religion, since I certainly didn't hate him: it was just that sometimes we had violent arguments. He obviously suffered from high blood pressure, and some of the boys in the Hitler Youth couldn't resist taking advantage of him: not on their own—they could have done that before 1933—but by virtue of their uniforms and potential rank (there was all that braid!). He was helpless and unsuspecting, had no idea that their attitude was a mark of the "bourgeois" element's turning against him, that the boys who, until March 1933, had been good young Catholics now were sniffing the "new age" and intended to make the most of it. This harassment didn't last long, nor did it get worse; it soon died down, but our last lessons with him, barely three years later, were terrible, though for quite different reasons. No doubt he still considered me a Catholic, if not good.

But it was my own "Catholicity" that I was beginning to doubt, the more so after a further heavy blow: the signing of the Reich Concordat with the Vatican engineered by von Papen and Monsignor Kaas. After the seizure of power, the Reichstag fire, and the March election, it was, incredibly, the Vatican that accorded the Nazis their first major international recognition. Some members of our family—myself among them—seriously considered leaving the church, but that had become so fashionable among all those Germans who couldn't wait to join the Nazi Party after the March 1933 election that we didn't, since it might have been misconstrued as homage to the Nazis. That didn't exempt us from considerable crises, both existential and political, yet in the midst of that time of crisis, I took part in a procession, strutting proudly along as I carried a great flag (white with an enormous blue ⚓), accepting as an honor the occasional, not general, mockery of the spectators. I don't even remember in what procession or what group I was "performing"; all I can be sure of is the pride, the flag, and the recollection of one particular bunch of mockers on St. Apern-Strasse. It is quite possible that I was still a member of that Marian fellowship to which I had so enthusiastically belonged: those weekend outings, "leaving gray city walls behind," those amateur theatricals, puppet shows, hiking over hill and dale, the singing, pennants, campfires! I left the fellowship when it brought in a paramilitary drill that even included "wheeling" on almost a company scale. And during that time of crisis I agreed to help out the parish of St. Maternus by taking over the distribution of the *Junge Front*, the last weekly of Catholic youth until its brave demise. I was recruited for this job by Otto Vieth over streusel cake and ersatz coffee in the garden of St. Vincent's Hospital in Cologne-Nippes. The job was also a source of income: the ten pfennigs paid for each copy of the *Junge Front* didn't have to be turned in until the following week and helped us over many a straitened weekend.

At the time there was also a theory, almost officially sanctioned by the church, that one should join the Nazi organizations in order to "Christianize them from within"—whatever that may have meant, for to this day no one seems to know what "Christianization" consists of. A considerable number—among them our principal, I believe—acted on this theory, and after the war many of them, left in the lurch in the denazification process, had to pay for it.

Although I had long since ceased to be "organized," I still ostentatiously wore the ⚡ insignia on my lapel and more than once had to take abuse from an older student who, not surprisingly, had been a particularly enthusiastic member of the Catholic youth movement. That was the extent of what I had to put up with in school. I had no trouble with my classmates; they had known me and I them for five or six years; there were arguments but no attempts at conversion. Some disapproved of my occasional flippant remarks about Hitler and other Nazi bigwigs, but none of them, not even the S.S. member, would ever, I believe, have dreamed of denouncing me. I felt no resentment, not even toward the teachers. We still thought it possible that the Nazis wouldn't last; sometimes we'd even laugh in anticipation of further optimistic contortions of the "bourgeoisie" *when* . . . But *who* would then take over none of us tried to predict.

I kept up my friendships with several of my classmates even after graduation (although I avoided that S.S. fellow: in the three years preceding graduation I doubt if I exchanged more than two sentences with him). We pored over our homework together, and I tried to help some of them over that strange German math trauma, with the zeal of the convert: not long before, my brother Alfred had cured me of this trauma by systematically and patiently "probing back" to my basic knowledge, discovering gaps, closing them, and thus giving me a firm foundation. That had led us to such an enthusiasm for math that we spent weeks trying to discover a method of trisecting the angle, and sometimes we felt so close to the solution that we spoke only in whispers. The "furnished gentleman" living in the next room had a degree in engineering, which might have enabled him to appropriate our discovery.

Yes, I pored over textbooks with them, crammed for math and Latin (another of those traumatic subjects that fortunately never developed into a trauma for me). Sometimes we spent the evening in my father's office in the rear courtyard of the building at 28 Vondel-Strasse. Money being scarce and cigarettes and tobacco expensive, we would buy the very cheapest kind of cigars (five pfennigs each), cut them up with a razor blade, and roll them into cigarettes. (Today I am sure we were suffering from an economic delusion.) The tiny office building was seductively cozy, built entirely of wood, something between a log cabin and a shed. It contained fine, soldily built closets, with sliding doors of green glass, for the storage of metal fittings and drawings: little neo-Gothic turrets, miniature columns, flowers, figures of saints; designs for confessionals, pulpits, altars and communion benches, furniture; and there was also an old copying press from pre–World War I days, and a few remaining cartons of light bulbs for bayonet sockets, although we had shot hundreds of them to pieces in the garden on Kreuznacher-Strasse. Green desk lamps, a big table with a green linoleum top; slabs of glue, tools. When it came to gluing, the generational conflict between my father and my brother Alois was concentrated on the "barbaric, revolutionary" invention of cold glue, which my father didn't trust, while my brother demonstrated its reliability; but my father insisted on hot, boiled glue, the way it had to be prepared in the glue pot, with constant stirring, from the honey-colored slabs. There was no lack of other conflicts, but they have no place here.

5

Yes, also school, but first, in that horror-year of 1933 after Hitler's seizure of power, the Reichstag fire, terror, the March election, and the body blow of the Reich Concordat, something happened that caused even the middle classes of Cologne to tremble. In July—the Concordat had been completed but not yet signed—the trial took place in Cologne of seventeen members of the Red Front Fighters' League, for murder in two cases, attempted murder in one: the murders of Storm Troopers Winterburg and Spangenberg, who had just recently conveted from the Communist Party to the Nazis. But seventeen murders? Nobody believed that, nor was it ever established who had actually shot the two men. The trial began in July; in September, seven of the seventeen accused were condemned to death, and on November 3 they were beheaded with an ax. All pleas for mercy had been rejected. There was no pardon. Göring, Minister-President of Prussia, declared: "As a result of these incidents I have decided not to wait another day but to intervene with an iron fist. In future anyone who lays violent hands on a representative of the National Socialist movement or a representative of the State must realize that he will lose his life in short order."

The reason for my placing that event one year later, in the fall of 1934, may have something to do with June 30, 1934, that ultimate brutal step to the seizure of total power. That day has remained in my memory as a crucial signal—perhaps because the time up until June 30 seemed relatively quiet to me. Nowadays I often think of those seven young Communists in view of the miserably embarrassing palaver over recognition of the resistance group known as Edelweiss pirates.

One thing I do know, even if the date has shifted in my memory: on the day of the executions, shock hung over Cologne, fear and shock, the kind that before a thunderstorm makes birds flutter up into the sky and seek shelter. It became quiet, quieter; I no longer made flippant remarks about Hitler, except at home, and even there not in everyone's presence.

One of the executed men, the youngest, aged nineteen, wrote poems in his death cell. The place where they were written, the fate of the author, lift those lines far beyond what one might patronizingly call "touching," which is why, for fear of diminishing their deadly seriousness, I won't quote them. The poems, written by a Red Front fighter, reveal the "Italian" nature of Cologne Communism (as it then was). In one poem he gives thanks for the candles lighted for him in church, admitting that he was present at the deed and declaring that he did not commit murder; at the end of the poem he thanks his friend, a Red Front fighter, for having prayed with him at night—and asks that the Lord's Prayer be said at his grave.

For Göring, whose soldier-emperor fantasies seemed, in the observations of many of his contemporaries, comical if not almost endearing—for that robber, that murderer, that bloodthirsty fool, I and many other Cologne schoolkids were soon lining the streets. During those few hours in Cologne, he changed uniforms three if not four times. It surprises me that some waggish moviemaker has not yet discovered *this* character: that masklike face with its glittering morphine addict's eyes, that "mighty hunter before the Lord," that inflated Nimrod, known later as "Herr Meyer"—surely the perfect subject for a movie farce! As it was, his scenes with Dimitroff, the Bulgarian Communist, during the Reichstag fire trial did much to enhance our considerable political amusement. At the time when the executions were announced, however, the entire city trembled under that bloody fist—it's possible, of course, that I was crediting the whole city with my own horror.

6

School? Oh yes, that too. Soon I had reached that level of education known as "lower school-leaving certificate." For serious economic reasons my family considered taking me out of school and putting me to work as an apprentice. One possibility being considered was land surveying ("You'll always be out in the fresh air"—my aversion to fug being well known—"besides, it's a nice way of earning a living, what with math and all that, which you're so fond of"). Another suggestion: a commercial apprenticeship with a coffee wholesaler on (I forget whether Grosse or Kleine) Witsch-Gasse, where a friend of ours had some connections. Land surveyor: that really didn't sound too bad, and for a few hours I wavered, until I realized that it would mean a more or less bureaucratic occupation: that smelled of being forcibly organized. Yet, even today, when I drive through the countryside and see land surveyors at work with their instruments and measuring rods, I sometimes indulge in the fancy that I might have become one of them; the office of the coffee wholesaler on (Grosse or Kleine) Witsch-Gasse, when in later years I happened to pass by it, would provoke a strangely gentle nostalgia in me: that *would have been,* that *might have been:* although I was firmly resolved to become a writer, the detour via land surveying and the coffee business wouldn't have been any worse than other roundabout routes I subsequently took. (It is only now that I can appreciate, comprehend, how utterly horrified my family must have been when, between quitting my bookseller's apprenticeship and starting my stint in the Labor Service, between February and November 1938, when I was not yet twenty-one—and in the very midst of firmly entrenched Nazi terror—I actually set out to be a free-lance writer.)

The decision to take me out of school was dropped, as the result of my own strenuous objections and those of my older brothers and sisters. Employment of any kind inexorably meant being organized, and that was a condition I had always avoided and intended to go on avoiding. I enjoyed studying but wasn't that keen on school, started being bored for long periods of time, and might actually have dropped out if it hadn't been for the Nazis. But I knew, and was fully aware of the fact: school, *that* school at any rate, was the best hiding place I could find, and so, strictly speaking, I have the Nazis to thank for my graduation. Perhaps that is why I wasn't interested in the graduation ceremonies or in my certificate, submitting it unread when I later applied for a job as an apprentice.

From then on, after having acquired "my lower school-leaving certificate," I began to orchestrate the school for my own ends. Three more years to graduation, how many more years to war—perhaps less than three? And I was too much of a coward to risk becoming a conscientious objector. That much I knew: the mute, stony-faced men released from concentration camps, the idea of possible torture—no, I didn't have the guts. To escape the war, no matter where, was simply beyond the realm of the imagination. (Not long ago we were asked by Frank G., aged thirty-seven, born in the last year but one of the war, why we hadn't emigrated, and we found it hard to explain that such an idea was simply beyond the realm of our imagination: it was as if someone had asked why I hadn't ordered a taxi to the moon. Of course we knew that people had emigrated: Jewish friends—didn't I regularly read *Der Stürmer* in the display box on Severin-Strasse?—and even a man like Brüning, but *us?* Where to and in what capacity? We were, in a funny way, a Catholic family that happened to be against the Nazis; but all that is hindsight. At the time it was simply way beyond our thoughts. Later I did very briefly consider, and reject, a variation of emigration: desertion to a foreign army. You won't be *that* welcome over there, I thought, so I deserted in the other direction—to my home.)

That same year, 1934, all those who had believed that Hitler wouldn't last long were refuted: June 30 swept all those hopes away, a summer day rife with rumors, tensions, and a strange, indefinable admixture of euphoria. Surely that couldn't be true: that so many leading Nazis were criminals and even homosexuals? (That Röhm was one we knew, of course: the slogan "Wash your asses, Storm Troopers, Röhm's coming!" had been appearing on the walls of buildings before and even after 1933.) When all was said and done, the openness with which dirty linen was now being washed in public was truly amazing. Perhaps it was a sign of weakness. Within a few hours we realized the obvious: it was a sign of strength, and at long last we knew the meaning of a Party purge.

We still had no radio, and that day I was all over the place on my bike, for once (why "for once" will be explained—patience!) even in the center of town, at the Heumarkt, the Neumarkt, the cathedral, the railway station. Something was in the air, people were talking in whispers and undertones, full of hope—until at last Hitler spoke and the "special editions" appeared on the streets. I bought one and when I got home took the little bundle of Alva cigarette cards out of my desk drawer, the series showing all the prominent Nazis. I sorted out all those who had been shot: it was a tidy little pile. The faces that remain in my memory are those of Heines and Röhm.

That was—and we were aware of it—not merely the final seizure of power but also the ultimate test of power, the final unmasking of von Papen and Hindenburg. Klausener, Jung, and Schleicher were among the murdered, and apparently no one said a word, at least not audibly; no one said a word, nothing happened. It was the dawn of the eternity of Nazism. Did the middle classes, the Nationalists, know what was happening, the pass they had come to? I am afraid they still don't know: one of the most ludicrous days in German history, the day of Potsdam, March 21, 1933, when Hindenburg handed Germany over to a gentleman in a tailcoat, must have blinded them all.

That same year, right after June 30, according to a decree that had been made before June 30, the weekly National Youth Day was introduced; it didn't become law—that, I believe, didn't happen until 1939; it was merely *decreed*. Just try to imagine the situation: a state in which a character, a jerk, like Baldur von Schirach, was in control of the entire youth of the country! We knew, although meanwhile it appears to have been forgotten, that he was a poet: a German poet in control of German youth! From among his many poems there was one line we knew by heart, and we would hum and recite it *sotto voce:* "I was a leaf so free, searching for my tree." (Must I at this point come to the aid of praiseworthy lyric interpretation and explain who the leaf so free was and who the tree? I will if you like!) Sometime before 1933, when the University of Cologne was still on Claudius-Strasse, only a minute away from us, Schirach had been beaten up by "leftist students" after a poetry reading. So it was this jerk of a Schirach who had complete control over German youth, and German parents allowed him to hold sway over their sons and daughters.

Of the approximately two hundred boys at our school there were three who on National Youth Day were not exempted from classes to allow them to be "on duty." Being "on duty" probably meant participating in some sort of paramilitary sports: I don't know exactly, I never asked the other boys about it, not even those I did my homework with. We talked about movies and girls, not about politics, and when one of them tried to raise the subject I shut up. I was scared, whereas at home I could talk, even if one of them was present: surely no one would dare denounce our family. Today I sometimes think that some relatively high Nazi, who never revealed himself, must have "held his hand over our family."

So on Saturdays (Saturday being a regular school day) we three, Bollig, Koch, and myself, had to go to school and, under the supervision of a teacher, who obviously found it a bore and a nuisance (I suppose otherwise he would have had the day off), tidy up the school library. Every Saturday for three years we three tidied up that tiny little library housed in a room next to what used to be the caretaker's quarters. Not one title, not one author, not one book that I held in my hand has remained in my memory. No, I certainly didn't suffer, and I met with no difficulty whatever, not the sightest. I assume that after two Saturdays there was nothing left to tidy in what was from the start a tidy library; so we would smoke cigarettes (if we had any), drink school cocoa, go out for some ice cream, kill time. Usually the teacher in charge left us to our own devices from ten o'clock on and went home or to a café, putting Mirgeler the caretaker in charge, who in turn let us off by eleven o'clock at the latest.

Mirgeler was a kind, gentle person, one of the few disabled veterans who didn't talk about his war experiences. One could feel he was on our side, not explicitly—that would have been too dangerous and we didn't expect it of him. And of course one could always be sick on Saturday or get sick. With Mirgeler and several of the teachers, there was no need for explicitness, the expression on their faces was enough. For some of the teachers, as well as for Mirgeler, we were, at least after the occupation of the Rhineland in 1936, *morituri,* and that softened many a severe reprimand or punishment that would have been deserved in "normal times." If I were to say that, with the introduction of Schirach's National Youth Day, the pressure was increased, it would be an exaggeration. From time to time—not often, later not at all—we were summoned to the principal, one by one, and he would try to persuade us to join the Hitler Youth or, later, the Storm Troopers. He did not really press us, it was more of a plea, alluding, not very convincingly, to its being "for our own good." Obviously he was running into trouble, we three were lousing up the statistics. Quite clearly he didn't feel at ease on these occasions, and his pleas were in vain: we remained adamant all the time we were in school. I have always wondered why no personal friendships developed among us three. They didn't. Moreover, one or another of us was always absent those Saturdays, sometimes two of us or even all three. Eventually there was hardly so much as a pretense of checking up on that strange "library work."

The pleas in the principal's arguments were more dangerous than threats would have been, for—and I'm sorry to say he probably never discovered this—I rather liked him. He was gentler than he sometimes pretended or had to pretend to be, the type of person known as strict but fair, yet easily moved to tears: a good history teacher, and, besides Latin and math, history was one of my favorite and deliberately orchestrated courses. It is he whom I have to thank for my early insight into the nature of colonialism as exemplified by the Roman Empire; insight into the parasitic bribed-vote existence of the rabble of ancient Rome. He was probably what today I would call "blinded" by Hindenburg, a fatal attribute of many decent Germans: patriotic, not nationalistic, certainly not Nazist, but very much the veteran, fond of telling us about tight situations in trench warfare where as a young officer he had been wounded in the head; yet also Catholic, a Rhinelander with a gentle "von" to his name.

When the first former student of our school was killed in the Spanish Civil War, a member of the Condor Legion who was shot down—possibly over Guernica—he organized a memorial service and, with tears in his eyes, made a moving speech. I didn't feel comfortable at this service, didn't want to share his emotion although I had known the dead man, who had been a classmate of my brother's. Today I interpret that vague feeling of discomfort as follows: school prepared us not for life but for death. Year after year, German high school graduates were being prepared for death. Was dying for the Fatherland the supreme merit? To put it flippantly: at that service one might have gained the impression that our principal was sad at *not* having been killed at Langemarck. I know that sounds harsh, but I am not being unfair to a dead man: in the final analysis, the fatal role played by those highly educated, unquestionably decent German high school teachers led to Stalingrad and made Auschwitz possible: that Hindenburg blindness. I can't swear to the degree of truth contained in the following supposition: it has been said that the principal was told by high, if not the highest, clerics to join the Nazi Party, "in order to salvage what could be salvaged." (As we have since discovered, there was nothing to be salvaged; and I also know that it is easy enough to say that with hindsight.) We discussed the problem with our friends, found the idea not dishonorable but foolish. However, we didn't withdraw our friendship from those who were persuaded by the argument.

Incidentally, even our own family didn't withstand the pressure: when the *Kölnische Volkszeitung* and the *Rhein-Mainische Zeitung* ceased publication, we too subscribed to the *Westdeutsche Beobachter* and got mad at the ingenious articles by the Catholic author Heinz Steguweit. ("A swastika, a lovely sight, before which kneels Heinz Steguweit.") Following the insistent "advice" of our block warden, we too acquired a swastika flag after 1936, albeit a small one: on days when displaying the flag was compulsory, sentiments could *also* be deduced from the size of the flags.

By that time my father, insofar as he received any orders at all, had almost ceased working for churches and monasteries; almost all his orders were now government ones. And when those orders became even scarcer, he was urged to have at least one member of his family join a Nazi organization. A kind of family council was called, and my brother Alois became the victim of its decision, since, after some miserable receivership proceedings, he was officially the owner of the business. He was elected by the family to join the Storm Troopers. (To the end of his days he bore a grudge against us for this, and he was right: we should at least have drawn lots.) Of all the members of our family, he was the worst suited for that mimicry: the person least suited for a uniform I have ever known, and he *suffered,* he really suffered from those mob parades and route marches. I don't know how often he actually took part in those route marches—certainly not more than three times. Nor do I remember how often I went to see his platoon leader, a very recently converted former Communist who lived in a tiny attic above Tappert's drugstore at the corner of Bonner-Strasse and Roland-Strasse. There, on behalf of my brother, I would bribe that character—whom I remember as being depraved but not unfriendly—with a pack of ten R6 cigarettes, available in those days in nice-looking, flat, red packs, positively luxurious, to list my permanently absent brother as present. He did so, and among our flippant variations of the Rosary decades we included the words: "Thou who hast joined the Storm Troopers for our sakes." And the "Full is Her right hand of gifts" was changed to: "Full is thy right hand of R6's."

7

Yes, school. I had no problems, either educational or political; no one bothered me anymore. It was taken for granted that I must have passing grades; we couldn't afford for me to fail a year, yet the idea was tempting: it would have extended the duration of my hiding place by a year provided that . . . it must not be forgotten that we were moving toward war, it was a matter not of *après nous* but *avant nous le déluge.* I was determined not to learn for dying, which for many if not all German high school graduates had been preached as the highest goal in life. So in life I was learning for school, and in school—as will be shown—a few things for living. I concentrated entirely on the subjects I liked: Greek, Latin, math, history, studying for these subjects even when I didn't go to school. I enjoyed translating a Latin text for my own pleasure, with no direct benefit. In later years I sometimes stayed home to continue working by myself on Sophocles' *Antigone,* because the slow rate of progress in school made me impatient. In the other subjects I did enough not to slip below a C and, if it happened to suit me, turned up for tests.

If I pushed things too far, the principal would phone my mother and ask whether I was really that sick. I had an almost unshakable, permanent alibi, known in those days as chronic sinus infection, which actually did bother me for years, causing headache and nausea whenever I attempted to bend down. Today I sometimes think that condition was Nazi-induced (let doctors and psychologists mull that one over: I am sure there are such things as politically- or system-induced illnesses). There was one advantage to that condition: it released me from gym, which I hated. Yes, I admit it: I disliked gym, it always smelled of male sweat, of strenuous efforts, so the illness, even when I suffered no attacks for months on end, suited me down to the ground. (Oh those heat lamps, those hot camomile douches!) What I did miss, though, was track and field, and games—and my beloved streets of Cologne. On one or two occasions during my roamings, one of those Nazi hordes happened to come marching around the corner, and everyone ran to the curb to raise their right arms while I just barely managed to duck into a doorway. The horror lay deep (it still does!), and even the remotest possibility of such a horde suddenly turning up soured me toward the streets of Cologne.

It was a kind of banishment, so from being a pedestrian I became a cyclist, taking refuge in distant suburbs in the "green belt," riding up and down along the Rhine between Niehl and Rodenkirchen, across to Deutz. I came to love cycling, and cycling became my sole regular sport. I had enjoyed field sports (as for gym, Oh, that ludicrous virile earnestness!)—soccer and other games (including rounders), track and field: all that came to an end after the introduction of National Youth Day. The two afternoon periods known

officially as "Games" came to an end; how often we had extended
them far beyond the set time, on summer afternoons on the Poll
Meadows, and had played many of those games outside of school
hours, rounders especially. Meanwhile it was *verboten* to pursue
"unorganized" sports. My brother Alois was once briefly taken into
custody when he went off with a few boys from the parish to play
soccer on the Poll Meadows: it wasn't anything ominous, merely a
sign, and meant, as he was firmly told, as a warning.

So cycling became my only sport. I explored unfamiliar suburbs,
rode up or down beside the Rhine to quiet places along the banks,
and I read (yes, Hölderlin too). With repair kit, pump, and a car-
bide lamp, I was independent—almost, with only a few books on
the carrier and a bit of tobacco in my pocket, almost a "traveller
without luggage." And I could also go for a swim: totalitarianism
was not yet quite complete.

8

Yes, school too. At times I even obtained quite good grades in German literature. Not that I've retained much from my reading of it:
there are only a few authors I can still call to mind, one of them by
the name of Adolf Hitler, author of *Mein Kampf,* compulsory reading. Our teacher, Mr. Schmitz, a man of penetrating, witty, dry
irony (for some authors a little *too* dry!), used the hallowed texts of
Adolf Hitler the writer to demonstrate the importance of concise
expression, known also as brevity. This meant we had to take four
or five pages from *Mein Kampf* and reduce them to two, if possible
one and a half: "condense" that unspeakable, badly convoluted
German (there also exists some very nicely convoluted German!).
Think what that meant: "condensing" the Führer's texts! Taking
that kind of German apart and tightening it up appealed to me. So
I read *Mein Kampf* minutely, which, again, didn't increase my respect for the Nazis by one iota. Just the same, I can thank Adolf
Hitler the writer for a few badly needed B's in German literature;
perhaps also—something else I learned in school for my life—for
some qualification to be a publisher's reader and a liking for brevity. To this day I am surprised that no one noted the lack of respect
implied in the process of "condensing" the Führer's texts, and it

was many years before I realized this myself, realized all the implications of such an assignment. And it was a great many years later, when my former teacher Karl Schmitz, plagued by terrible headaches, would sometimes come to see us on Schiller-Strasse, after 1945, for a cup of black market coffee, that I could show him my respect and gratitude.

Another author, but one I cannot thank for good grades, was a certain Hanns Johst, whose play *Schlageter* we had not only to read but see performed: every school in Cologne was virtually herded through the theater, and, if I remember rightly, there were even morning performances. My impression: a very weak play. The hero, who was executed by the French in the occupied Rhineland in 1923 for sabotage, impressed me neither as a Catholic nor as a saboteur; on the other hand, he wasn't weak enough to impress me as an anti-hero.

For some of my good grades in German literature (which were rare enough), I have Jeremias Gotthelf to thank. No longer under Schmitz, we made a thorough study of those nineteenth-century rustic novels *Uli the Plowboy* and *Uli the Tenant Farmer* and wrote essays on them. No doubt about it, Vreneli the maid appealed to me more than Uli did. I filled pages and pages with Vreneli's generosity of spirit as compared to Uli's timid pettiness, thinking what men often think: that girl was too good for him! And I elaborated (may God and Gotthelf forgive me!) on the differences between the two being "milieu-conditioned."

I presume that Gotthelf found his way into the curriculum because some Nazi "blood and soil" strategist believed that through him we would be brought closer to peasant emotions, thoughts, and behavior. Our study of Gotthelf culminated in a final essay entitled "City and Land, Hand in Hand" (a popular Nazi slogan). In this essay I made an impassioned plea for the city, boldly (and erroneously, as I have long since realized) declaring Vreneli to have been an urban type. (It would be worth while making a study someday of the stupid mistakes and superficial ideological assumptions that allow certain books to be "permitted" or to "slip through" under dictatorships, as, for instance, Evelyn Waugh, whom we promptly took to be a woman, or Bloy and Bernanos, whose anti-clericalism was thoroughly misinterpreted.)

9

Yes, school too. Times got colder, tougher, even financially, and we were moving toward the war. Much remained: the loyalty of my parents and my brothers and sisters, of friends, even those who had long since joined Nazi organizations. There remained the irreplaceable, almost sacred bicycle, that swift vehicle of mobility, an escape-vehicle light of build, worthy of many a paean and, as I found out by 1945, the only reliable and the most valuable mechanical means of locomotion. Think of everything an automobile requires! How clumsy it actually is, dependent on a thousand minor factors, to say nothing of fuel, of roads: on a bicycle a person can go anywhere. And let us not forget: the Vietnam war was won on bicycles against tanks and planes. Repair kit, pump, lamp—easy to carry, almost no luggage at all. And how about all the things you can, if you have to, hang onto a bike or load onto it?

The sinus condition remained too, right through my stint with the glorious Labor Service and the equally glorious Army; but the moment I became a prisoner of war, in that strange state of simultaneous liberation and imprisonment, and in the years after the war and up to this very day: gone without a trace! Was it really Nazi-induced? It may well have been, for I was *also* allergic to the Nazis.

While still living on Maternus-Strasse, we used to walk across the grim-looking South Bridge, along the Rhine past Poll, through Poll, between wheat fields fragrant with summer, on dusty field paths, the water tower as a landmark ahead of us, toward the fortifications where my brother Alfred was doing his "voluntary" labor service. (Completion of this "voluntary" labor service happened to be "merely" a requirement for entering university.) Those dim, dank casemates built in the 1880's, from which—contrary to expectations since my brother wasn't yet eligible to leave camp—we asked for him to be summoned! He would emerge looking to me like a convict, thoroughly cowed. As a high school graduate he was automatically an "intellectual" and, as such, had to take a lot of abuse and do the heaviest work. At the camp entrance stood two—always the same two—young yet already worn-out whores, pathetic creatures who for a pittance would lie down in the bushes with anyone who managed to bribe or persuade the sentry. That conglomeration

244 · Heinrich Böll

of underground, damp, dismal Wilhelminian fortifications, the
smell, the depressing atmosphere, the two whores who weren't even
minimally "dolled up" (they were the only ones available for miles
around)—all of that was anything but uplifting. We would take
along a few cigarettes, chat dejectedly for a while, conscious of the
barbarity of visits in or outside any barracks. (Oh, Lili Marleen,
don't you know we never stood "by the lantern?" Who would ever
choose to stand with a girl, let alone *his* girl, by the lantern outside
"the heavy door?" In the darkest corner along the wall, that's
where we stood—and it wasn't sweet either: out of your arms back
into that stale, sweaty male atmosphere!) Depressed, we would
wend our way home, along the railway embankment, the dust of
summer on our lips, the smell of the wheat fields—I had it in my
heart, my brain, my consciousness, that *foretaste,* which, only a few
years later, turned out to be correct: I knew that I would be caught
up in it, that I lacked the strength and the courage to elude the two
uniforms in store for me.

We walked home, summer evening, water tower, railway embankment, wheat fields, the Rhine. Had they already started building the barracks in Poll-Porz that year? That rumor led to many an
interrogation and arrest of those who were already claiming something that soon turned out to be true: barracks were being built
there, although the Rhineland was still a demilitarized zone. Were
the foundations already being laid at that time for the Cologne–
Rodenkirchen autobahn bridge, that strategic opening toward the
West?

Once again, and again: school, *too,* yes. With the two real Nazis
among the teachers (both the loudmouth, roughneck type), we had
nothing to do, so I had no problems with my teachers, though they
may have had some with me. Whenever a student tried to offset his
miserable Greek or Latin with his uniform (which didn't happen
very often), Mr. Bauer, whom I had as a teacher from the fourth to
the twelfth grades, would catch my eye. There was no need for
words between us; he was a democrat, a humanist, not even remotely obsessed with war. He pointed out how relevant to our own
time was the element of parody in Greek comedy; sometimes he
would talk about smoking cigars and drinking sherry; he overlooked impudence; and later he read Juvenal with us. Juvenal and
Tacitus were his Latin favorites. (I saw Bauer one last time, in the

late fall of 1944, from a moving hospital train: he was in a wheelchair on the station platform in Ahrweiler or Remagen.)

Problems with teachers? No. Even my problem with our teacher of religion subsided. I didn't even have one with our gym teacher: although I was "exempt from gym" (hence, in the eyes of a gym teacher, almost asocial), he would sometimes invite me to his home or ask me to take part illicitly in a rounders match against another school. I wasn't a bad batter—it ran in the family, my two older brothers being practically rounders stars, and we had played a lot on the meadows of the Vorgebirg Park. So there I would be, illicitly hitting the ball beside Aachen Pond or in Blücher Park in a game against one of the Cologne high schools.

One thing I must make clear: I never thought of myself as being better than my classmates, or even "untainted," merely—oh, tiny "merely"!—alien, everything going on outside of me seemed alien and became more and more alien. Only my bike and my truancy saved me from shutting myself away in my room, yet now I was spending more time there, translating Latin or Greek texts for my own pleasure, and, long before I reached eighteen, I must have been well on the way to turning from an outsider into an eccentric. My bike wasn't my only salvation; there were also a few girls.

However, my progress was far from reassuring. My family, our friends, were justifiably worried, and more and more often the question was asked: "What's to become of the boy?" My brothers and sisters all either had a profession or were clearly on the road to one: schoolteacher, bookkeeper, cabinetmaker, theology student. Theology? Not so farfetched, and it would have offered an escape, but within minutes I had decided and declared that theology was not for me. As a study it had its attractions, but in those days theology and the priesthood were synonymous, and to that there was an obstacle that I would like to define as discreetly as possible: the beauties and other charms—profound and less profound—of the female sex were no secret to me, and I was of no mind to renounce them. Celibacy—what a horrifying word that was! To start out by contemplating double moral standards was beyond all consideration, and in those days such a thing as laicization (but then why become a priest if you are already speculating about laicization?) was as unimaginable as a trip to the moon. And finally: *vestigia terrebant*. The traces were frightening. I knew of cases of entanglements with family and friends, of those who had "tripped," "stumbled," "slipped," "fallen"; and many a one essaying a trip to the moon had landed flat on his face.

My father had done a lot of work for churches and monasteries, and his knowledge of that world, which he did not withhold from us, was more than adequate; probably it explained why he had strictly forbidden us to act as altar boys (an activity, by the way, that had never even remotely appealed to me). And then, of course, there was—an option that was vigorously discussed, there being plenty of theology students around—the path of "sublimation," but I hadn't the slightest desire to sublimate *that*.

10

The view is occasionlly expressed that, after January 30, 1933, the day of Hitler's seizure of power, some kind of economic miracle took place. However, as far as our family is concerned, I cannot affirm this. The fact of my brother's having joined the Storm Troopers availed us nothing (variation of the Rosary line: "Thou who has joined the Storm Troopers for our sakes in vain"). We were worse off than before 1933, and that can't have been due entirely to "political unreliability." My father had many well-disposed, old friends in government positions. Nevertheless, our most time-consuming and laborious occupation continued to be: opening up new credit for groceries or paying off old accounts so we could buy on credit again, and then the never-ending burden of: the rent.

To this day I don't know what we lived on. How? To say we lived "from hand to mouth" would be euphemistic. There is no doubt— and I suggest the political economists cudgel their brains before they shake their heads—that we lived *beyond* and *below* our means. One thing is verifiable: we survived, so those years were a kind of survival training. If there were any films, data, or bookkeeping relative to that time, I would gladly study them in order to discover *how*, but there are no records: there were merely repeated family councils where lists were drawn up, budgets decided upon, and pocket money—according to age and sex ("But the girls need stockings!")—was entered in my father's little black notebooks. All that might be called quite "literary." But as for being an economic miracle, far from it. There were frequent quotations from Dickens, especially Mr. Micawber in *David Copperfield,* who, as we know, was a mathematical wizard, a financial genius—although unrecognized—able to calculate to the last penny precisely how one rose to affluence, descended to poverty—and who was forever landing in the debtors' prison. My father was in no sense a Mr. Micawber: he was serious and conscientious, desperate too, with a certain inclination to "escape into the never-never," preferring to live beyond rather than below his means.

And so in 1936 we moved again—for the third time in six years. It was the last time my parents moved house, the bombs took care of the rest; it was an "escape into the never-never," into a somewhat more expensive area, to Karolinger-Ring, into an apartment that had been built thirty years earlier as "high-style accommodation." Having had two "furnished gentlemen" on Ubier-Ring and one on Maternus-Strasse, we now permitted ourselves the luxury (might as well go down in style!) of having none at all. In view of our financial situation, which was anything but improved, that move was certainly not logical, but it was consistent. We had the mad, perhaps even criminal, desire to *live* and to survive. Somehow we managed.

School? Yes. Studying was still important to me, even if I did my best to avoid school. I pored over math books and Latin texts, and there was one subject in which my desire to learn, indeed my craving for knowledge, was not satisfied in school: geography. I loved atlases, at times collected them, tried to find out *how* and *on what* people lived *where*. I suppose that's called economic geography. I hunted through encyclopedias and—somehow—got hold of reading material. In my father's library (which, on the whole, I despised), I found a multivolume anthropological work by a missionary that I devoured in my search for accounts of expeditions—all this on the side, of course.

Also on the side I became "secretary" to Chaplain Paul Heinen of St. Maternus Church. I set up a filing system for him, took care of some of his correspondence, and from time to time he would give me a coin or two from his pittance of a salary. It wasn't much more than a "game" and an escape: the deluge was not yet behind us, it still lay ahead. At some point in 1936 I saw Heinen for the last time, ran into him on Severin-Strasse. I was surprised at his haste, the way he could barely wait to say good-bye. A few days later I learned that on that very day he had been on his way out of the country, to emigrate via Holland to America. I believe he must have been too friendly with (then still Chaplain) Rossaint. I never heard any details.

11

Material survival took priority over political survival. There were grim days, weeks, and months; there were many pleasures and friends. There were the cheap, magnificent concerts in Gürzenich Hall, surprisingly bold lectures at the Catholic Academic League initiated by the priest Robert Grosche. There were movies, and at night, after dark, when you no longer had to worry about the Nazi hordes, you could go for a carefree walk, perhaps even with a girl. Cologne was still a livable city. And within a short time there appeared on the scene that special girl, called Annemarie. But that would take me too far beyond the time I am describing, and if I were to go beyond that period—back long before 1933, if possible as far back as 1750, and forward beyond 1937, perhaps up to 1981—if I were to go beyond that period, it would lead to an enormous family tome: interesting perhaps, as interesting as any family history, but no more interesting than that. So I will limit myself to the period in question, as far as possible to its *externals*, revealing only those internal goings-on that form part of, or arise from, the externals. Not even a hint, therefore, of the tensions, conflicts, problems, and semi-tragedies; and if I have a stab at those four years and some gaiety should show up here and there, it's nothing but the truth. However, that gaiety was often of the desperate kind seen in some medieval paintings, where the laughter of the redeemed is sometimes akin to the expression on the faces of the damned.

So somehow we managed, and after each move not only our relatives and friends but also the bailiff and the beggars were quick to discover our new address: my mother never sent anyone away, and she had an unruffled way of neither regarding bailiffs as enemies nor treating them as such. As a result, we received much good advice from them, and the pawnshop remained a familiar place to us.

I can't say it was a good time. We were both depressed and reckless, not the slightest bit sensible. At the very moment when we could least afford it, we would go out to a restaurant for a meal. We would invite "furnished gentlemen," as long as we had any, for a game of cards, slyly intending to win twenty pfennigs for a pack of Alvas or Ecksteins, until we found to our amusement that they had similar plans, so we would pool our resources and enjoy a smoke together.

Every opportunity to make money was seized on; the worst catastrophe of all was an attempt we made to earn some, perhaps even acquire wealth, by addressing envelopes. We did own a typewriter, the one I later used to type my first short stories, influenced by Dostoievski, later by Bloy. (But I also wrote a novel, by hand, somewhat to the surprise of my future wife because the "hero" had two women.) The enterprise ended in disaster. Our employer, who was unemployed, also hoped to get rich with homemade birch rods for St. Nicholas to use on naughty boys. Not only did he expect us to type the addresses: we also had to pick them out of a telephone directory and supply the stationery. Question: who needs birch rods for St. Nicholas? Bakeries, pastry shops, grocery stores—a laborious job. Eventually it turned out that our employer was even worse off than we were—I don't know whether he ever unloaded any birch rods, and we never asked for more than the agreed wage, which came nowhere near covering our expenses.

And of course we helped in the workshop, if any help happened to be needed. With a wobbly two-wheeled handcart (which also did duty during our moves), we conveyed great stacks of new or repaired furniture to government offices. (Memories of Revenue Offices South, Old Town, and North! And the Regional Finance Administration on Wörth-Strasse, past which we sometimes stroll today on our way to the Rhine.) At night in the cashier's office of Revenue Office South (originally a Carthusian monastery secularized in 1806), we renovated the floor, which was said to date from Napoleonic times. We hoped to find coins, old ones if possible, overlooking the fact that Carthusian monks of the eighteenth century weren't likely to have walked around with purses in their habits, and that latter-day visitors to the Revenue Office kept a tight grip on their pennies.

I was somewhat more successful in giving private lessons. The demand was small, the supply enormous: there was a plethora of unemployed teachers, B.A.'s, M.A.'s, and students, as well as sufficient *not* unemployed elementary and high school teachers anxious for some extra income. Immense supply, tiny demand, and that, of course, pushed down the prices (Oh, free market economy!). I found my first pupil through an advertisement, a nice boy whom I coached in Latin and math for fifty pfennigs an hour. I was more scared of his tests in school than he was; the result of those tests was the mark of success for which his parents were watching and waiting. I applied the method my brother had used with me: opening up gaps, closing gaps, and lo, he improved. An attempt at tutoring in French failed miserably, due to that boy's mother's excellent knowledge of French; she was quick to discover *my* gaps, graciously paid me off, and sent me home.

Before I dilate on the value of fifty pfennigs, let me merely point out that eight years later the hourly wage of an unskilled nursery-garden employee wasn't much higher—rather lower, in fact—than fifty pfennigs, and that weekly unemployment assistance for a family of three, including rental allowance, amounted to less than seventeen marks. At the time I am speaking of, my sister Mechthild, an unemployed junior high school teacher, always loyal to the family, was working as a governess in an aristocratic family in Westphalia for thirty marks a month, of which she sent home twenty-five. So a weekly extra income for a totally "unskilled" person (who was later able to increase his rate to seventy-five pfennigs an hour) of four or five marks was, considering it was pure pocket money, not to be sneezed at. It even permitted me to open an account with a modern secondhand bookstore, where I was allowed to pay in installments. I have no intention here of playing off hard times against good times, a ridiculous pastime for veterans, in my opinion.

Fifty pfennigs meant two or three secondhand books—a Balzac for ten pfennigs and a Dostoievski for twenty are what I still remember from the book bin of a secondhand bookstore on Herzog-Strasse next door to the Skala movie theater. Fifty pfennigs meant a ticket to the cheapest seats in the movies plus three cigarettes; it meant a piano recital on a student ticket (Oh, Monique Haas!), two cups of coffee plus three cigarettes, but also—and I sometimes treated my mother and my sister Gertrud—four fresh rolls and three or four slices of boiled ham, since, the Lord be both praised and reproached, we always had an appetite. My sister Gertrud would often reciprocate. And well-informed sources assured me that the minimum price for bought love in the back rooms of certain cafés in certain districts—provided by amateurs, I might add—had dropped to fifty pfennigs; of course only in "politically unreliable" areas—in a Germany that had just "awakened"!

12

I have come to the conclusion (at this late date!) that it really was living far, far beyond our means to let all the children in the family finish high school and then go on to university. Both my parents had only gone to elementary school: in their parents' eyes, secondary school was only for sons, and university was only considered if one of them wanted to study theology. (As a result, a boy with a passion and great talent for law became a not very happy priest, and a potential theologian became an atheistic high school teacher.) No doubt my parents had suffered more severely from this and other limitations than they admitted, and they wanted to see us children free, "unfolding freely."

The only reliable source of income was from time to time the "furnished gentlemen," but they didn't even cover the rent, and of the three small apartment buildings my father had built to take care of his old age (at the time he was already approaching seventy), only one remained, an old tenement house, 28 Vondel-Strasse, which also contained his workshop and office. But that building was rarely in our own hands, and then only for a short time; hardly ever was it *not* in receivership. There were the inexorable municipal taxes, the mortgage interest, the insurance premiums—there was always someone bringing down an iron fist upon us. What glorious times those were when the building happened to be free and my sister Gertrud went around collecting rents! Glorious but very brief times, for soon that fist would come crashing down again. Times didn't improve until later, after the period I am describing, when my brothers and sisters were earning a bit of money.

Clever people will say—and rightly so—what clever people were always saying at the time, that we were *not sensible*. That's right, we weren't, for we were even crazy enough to buy books and to read them: almost everything published by Jacob Hegener, as well as Mauriac, Bernanos, and Bloy, plus Chesterton and Dickens and Dostoievski, even old Weininger and Claudel and Bergengruen (as long as he was available), even *Hammer Blows* by Lersch and, as I mentioned before, Evelyn Waugh and Timmermanns, Ernest Hello, Reinhold Schneider, Gertrud von Le Fort and, of course, Theodor Haecker. No, it wasn't at all sensible, and sensible people borrowed the books from us, enjoyed dropping in at our place for discussions, and then sometimes a fractional Nazi, a quarter, a half, or even a whole Nazi, would come in for some abuse.

Those were lively sessions, yet at the same time a paralyzing pessimism lay over everything. We also played cards all night long, for money, although we knew that none of us would keep our winnings, and gaming debts piled up and were canceled, yet we went on playing as if in earnest. And I suppose it wasn't sensible either for a brother and sister of mine to work for my father—my brother in the workshop and my sister in the office—in a business where there was so little to do. Yet it was necessary for them to be there so as to keep the income derived from renting out the excellent machinery by the hour from getting into the hands of the bailiff. Things remained that tight until war broke out. (In wartime—and here I am going beyond 1937—money always flows easily, of course, and soon there was plenty to repair in Cologne. Wars also solve unemployment problems, a fact that is sometimes forgotten or suppressed when people talk about Hitler's "economic miracle." And wars also regulate the prices of cigarettes, which ultimately rose from one or one and a half pfennigs for the pale Dutch ones to eight hundred pfennigs for a single American cigarette.)

13

Yes, school too—I assure you, I'll soon get back to that. After all, I was still a pupil, a pupil of life so to speak, subject to despondency and recklessness, yet bound and determined not to become a pupil of death—if that could possibly be avoided. So, once again: somehow we managed. What was *vitally* important (I will forgo a few dozen anecdotes), and also a good schooling, was that our financial difficulties made us not humble but arrogant, not undemanding but demanding, and in some non-sensible way they made us sensible. No, we weren't expecting the pot of gold, but we did always expect more than we were entitled to or more than others considered we were entitled to ("others" being, for instance, the mathematical acrobats who worked out a subsistence minimum for us), and in the family we used to say: "Oliver Twist is asking for more." We developed an arrogance that assumed hysterical proportions, we made derogatory or blasphemous remarks about public institutions and personalities, and we needed no alcohol: words were enough.

After an evening of smearing and smirching, of more and more feverish, even frenetic, laughter at the expense of church, state, institutions, and personalities, my brother Alois, in a kind of hiatus of exhaustion, said something that then became a household phrase: "Now let's be Christians again!" And another expression for naïve, credulous, idealistic Nazis that we all hung onto was: "A blissful idiot." Those occasions were not only not comfortable, they were never harmonious; they were marked by a permanently dissonant loyalty. The three different elements blended in varying proportions in the individual members of the family, resulting in friction and tensions. Many a time, more than words flew through the air—bits and pieces, sometimes even quite sharp objects. Within each of us and among all of us, the elements clashed. Within each of us and among all of us, there was a class struggle. And then there were also periods influenced by alcohol, when we happened to have some money; on those occasions the products of the Hermanns distillery near the Severin Gate castle set the tone.

Yes, school. I didn't want the time I was spending there to be wasted, and my graduation certificate might survive—with me!—both the war and the Nazis, although it didn't look like it. The Nazis had become an eternity, the war was to become one, and war plus Nazis were a double eternity—yet I wanted to try to live beyond those four eternities (besides, for ten years my graduation certificate brought me the advantage of the flexible and useful occupational category of "student." But we aren't there yet).

Aside from school, Nazis, economic crises, there were other problems; for example, the ageless one of . . . *amore.* I tried—with what success I don't know—to keep all that a secret from the family, who were tearing their hair out anyway at the thought of my future—Oh my God, girls too? Or women even? There were many blows to come: after the introduction of conscription, the final blow was the occupation of the Rhineland, which we perceived as just that, an occupation. It may not have meant much, but, after all, the Rhineland had up to then, 1936, remained a demilitarized zone, and the last British occupation forces had taken their ceremonial departure only six years earlier. For my father, who, after Brüning's dismissal, had almost given up hope, the occupation of the Rhineland was the last straw, and now he too no longer doubted the imminence of war. Nazis disguised as Prussians, Prussians disguised as Nazis, in the Rhineland! We—I, at any rate—would have preferred to see the French—in spite of Schlageter!—or the British march in from the other side.

At this time my father would sometimes act out for our benefit again how, as a reservist en route to Verdun, he had caused himself to be arrived off the train in Trier with a simulated attack of appendicitis—and it had worked: although he had to undergo an operation, he was never sent to the front. Final and very impressive memory of Maternus-Strasse: an illegal meeting of the leaders of a Catholic young men's association; the deep, ineradicable impression made on me by Franz Steber: serious, determined, with no illusions—and he paid dearly for that determination. Shortly afterward, he was arrested, and during five years of imprisonment by the Gestapo, his serious eye trouble advanced to almost total blindness.

Less serious, but serious enough: shortly after our move, which was followed not much later by my passing into the twelfth grade, I picked up an acute inner ear infection while on an extended weekend outing (by bike and with a girl) into the Bergische Land on a sleety Shrove Tuesday. This infection kept me in bed far beyond Easter. When I was allowed to get up again, my love had evaporated (yes, a pity, but it had simply evaporated), and I was moved up to the twelfth, with the serious warning that I would have to work hard.

I did, I caught up with the class, became used to my new, quiet route to school: Karolinger-Ring, Sachsen-Ring, Ulrich-Gasse, Vor den Siebenbürgen, Schnur-Gasse (past the pawnshop), a few yards along Martinsfeld as far as Heinrich-Strasse, which I now entered from the other, very quiet end. The worry about "what's to become of the boy?" grew ever more serious, more justified. Heinen, before disappearing out of the country, had also participated in the discussion and suggested the career of librarian, but he had forgotten about the book-burnings, and wasn't the profession of librarian an endangered one? Was I supposed to spend my life lending out Hanns Johst or Hans Friedrich Blunck, or concerning myself with the collected articles of Heinz Steguweit? After I had rejected a librarian's career, someone in my family—I don't know who—came up with the idea that it should be "something to do with books." Too bad that, given the circumstances, the boy couldn't be persuaded to take an interest in theology.

14

That summer, shortly after the move, which entailed the usual chaos (new curtains for the big windows, allocation of rooms, frequent, and fruitless family budget councils), I went off on my bike, by myself on a sort of study trip via Mainz, Würzburg, through the Spessart and Steigerwald hills to Bamberg; and, since I wished to avoid the mixture of Hitler Youth and League of German Girls in the youth hostels, my father obtained a letter of introduction for me to the "Kolping houses" along the way. As an old member of the Kolping (a Catholic guild of journeymen-artisans), he had good connections with its headquarters in Cologne. This meant I had access to cheap bed-and-breakfast; I also became acquainted with the activities of the Kolping Brothers, and gratefully accepted coffee and bread, soup and milk, in canteens from the hands of South German nuns.

Mainz: that broad-hipped Romanesque cathedral of red sandstone was more to my liking than Cologne Cathedral; even in Cologne I had felt greater affinity with the gray Romanesque churches. My father was a good guide through churches and museums. And for me, coming as I did from an almost completely un-Baroque city, Würzburg was both alien and pleasing: a different world, "occupied" not only by churches and palaces but also by Leonhard Frank's *Robber Band*, which we boys had devoured. In Bamberg I was surprised by the coolness of the statue of my namesake to which I was really making a pilgrimage. The princely horseman, whose picture probably hung over the desk or bed of almost every young German, seemed cold to me, clever and competent—he inspired no affection in me. When I got home, I took down his picture from the wall and put it in a drawer. Devout Catholic though he was, he seemed to me—I couldn't help it—"somehow Protestant," and, after all, *Catholic* was what we wanted to be and to remain, in spite of all our derisive laughter and abuse. Taht was why the appearance, shortly before the end of 1936, of Léon Bloy's *Blood of the Poor* hit us like a bombshell, a long way indeed from the Dostoievski bombshell, yet in its effect, similar to it. Add to this the pyrotechnics of Chesterton—a strange mixture, I know, into which German literature, even the banned and officially disgraced literature, didn't enter. *Buddenbrooks* did, peripherally, but someone like Tucholsky not at all; Kästner yes. For the rest, though, everything smacked of "Berlin," and Berlin was not loved, was even less loved since the Nazis had taken it over. Unfair, I know (meanwhile I have learned a bit more).

15

For some time now an innovation for secondary schools had existed: training camps. The oldest students from two different schools would spend three weeks together in a youth hostel so as to become acquainted with each other, the countryside, and the local people, as well as attending lectures and taking part in marches and sports. I participated fully in the first one, in Zülpich, where we joined the parallel class of Aloysius College, Father Hubert Becher, that kindly, cultured Jesuit, had a mitigating influence. We marched through the vast sugarbeet fields of that "Merovingian land," visited Roman ruins, felt the spirit of Chlodwig. We went over an old textile factory in Euskirchen where bales and bales of army cloth were being produced. I passed up another camp in Oberwesel—I forget whether it was the last or the last but one—by more or less extorting an impressive medical certificate from our family doctor. Then there was another one in Ludweiler near Völklingen on the Saar at which I stayed for half the time, but there the loudmouthed Hitler Youth mentality was already so prevalent that I lost my nerve and simply went home. In Ludweiler the writer Johannes Kirch-weng read to us from his works. He didn't seem—to me at any rate—entirely at ease with the whole thing, and by "thing" I mean all that Nazi business and those claims to lost German territory. Jo-hannes Kirchweng, worker's son and Catholic priest, seemed a nice fellow, but tired and sad, probably didn't quite trust his recent fame and was already foreseeing its abuse. He read from an autobio-graphical novel in which he described the harsh conditions of his father's working world, that of a glassblower. He did not, as I have just discovered, reach a great age: at his death in 1951 he was fifty-one, so in 1935 or 1936 he must have been thirty-five or thirty-six. I remember him as a very old man, a nice fellow and tired (and that reminds me of Heinrich Lersch, whose novel *Hammer Blows* was also about his father and *his* craft, that of a boilermaker).

In the taverns of Ludweiler or Völklingen, workmen would tell us in whispers that, instead of being able to buy French Riz-La ciga-rette paper for five pfennigs, they now had to pay fifteen pfennigs for the German Gizeh paper; but of course, they said, they weren't Frenchmen, you know, they were Germans of course, you know. Völklingen, the Röchling steel works, the strikes and all that, and why didn't we take a look at the foundry? It certainly wasn't pleas-ant or edifying: it smelled of poverty, stale, of a stifling all-pervad-ing Catholicism. There was also—and not only because of the cigarette paper—a certain wistfulness expressed not openly but in whispers.

And in the evening at the youth hostel there was all that whoop-ing and hollering of the triumphant Hitler Youth, and their threats against us—me and my friend Caspar Markard—because when they sang the Horst Wessel Song we would start up with: "If all are now unfaithful, then faithful we'll remain." I lost my nerve (as often happened later), I suppose one might say I was "hypersensi-tive"—or was I more than just an outsider, was I already an eccen-tric? At any rate, I simply went home, again with a taste of things to come. Yes, we sang: "If all are now unfaithful," and I wrote not only love poems but patriotic ones too, and I read Stefan George, whom I never for a moment regarded as a Nazi. Caspar Markard had been expelled from Brühl High School on account of political remarks and activities that were dubbed "Communist," and our school had accepted him.

16

It must not be forgotten that we were moving toward war. I bought Barbusse and Remarque. Barbusse impresssed me more than Remarque. In school—that's how it seemed, or how it seems to me today—the last vestiges of strictness, of severity even, disappeared, the kind that had been prevalent from teacher to student. There were arguments, but they were between younger and older *adults;* they were serious ones, they had lost their schoolboy character.

Our math teacher, Mr. Müllenmeister (known as MM), who was considered unusually strict and bore the marks of World War I but never talked about it, proved to be the mildest of all: during the late summer and fall he hardly disguised his efforts to familiarize us with the geometry and algebra questions we might expect in our final exams. In the eleventh grade, almost a third of the class, five or six students, had been failed, perhaps because the school wished to present a trim, secure graduating class: thirteen of us remained, awaiting graduation. That last school summer, the last school fall, seem to have lasted forever. There was not only the cultural pilgrimage to the statue of Heinrich II in Bamberg, not only the usual preparations for our final exams during which, using dictionaries as a concordance, we tried to work out what Latin and Greek texts to expect: there were also the Olympic Games, with the enormous, utterly depressing propaganda success, both at home and abroad, of the Nazis. And in a "postlude" in the Cologne stadium we saw the totally un-Germanic Olympic winners Jesse Owens and Ralph Metcalfe, the latter making the sign of the cross before the start of the race. A champion who was a Catholic and a Negro!

That summer my friend Caspar Markard took me along to meet Robert Grosche, the priest who had retired from the city to live in the country at Vochem near Brühl, where he used to receive a small group of students for a sort of weekly seminar. Grosche, the classic Rhinelander, the classic, highly educated abbé, the Claudel translator and expert, one of Germany's first truly ecumenical priests, yet intensely Roman: his study, crammed with books and always filled with pipe smoke, was an island that fascinated and at the same time intimidated me. We discussed "salvation arising from the Jews," he lent us books to which he had drawn our attention. As a sideline

Grosche was also editor of the Cologne bookdealers' "literary guide." Those were unforgettable evenings. Grosche was very West European yet very German, with a surprising admixture of nationalism; very Catholic, witty, of high caliber, courageous. We were sure he was a "born" cardinal, born to be the future Bishop of Cologne. But no: when Cardinal Schulte died, he was followed by Frings. Maybe Grosche was too lofty for the Vatican, perhaps even too cultured, and whether he would have suited the Nazis, who, according to the Concordat, had a say in the matter, is uncertain.

Here I will permit myself a brief speculation beyond the year 1937: Grosche, rather than Frings, Cardinal and Archbishop of Cologne after 1945; Grosche, who certainly favored and would have favored the Christian Democrats, as the decisive figure beside Adenauer in German postwar Catholicism? Things would have turned out differently. Whether better is something I dare not say. Even in those days, on leaving that marvelous, comfortable Vochem study, full of books and tobacco smoke, to go home to Cologne by train or on my bike, I would feel a bit intimidated by so much cultured composure, by that hint of nationalism, and the unmistakable if gentle overripeness of the bourgeoisie. It was tremendous to be there, to be with him, but it was not what I was looking for.

Our own family were turning their backs more and more on the bourgeoisie, and Grosche's study, equipped in the classic manner with piles of books and journals, and all that saturated culture flowing toward us from the lectures given by the Catholic Academic League—all that was not only well meant but also helpful, and it was good; yet I knew, or rather, merely suspected, that I didn't belong there.

At home, things were far from always being "comfortable": that explosive mixture of petty-bourgeoisie vestiges, Bohemian traits, and proletarian pride, not truly belonging to any class, yet arrogant rather than humble, in other words almost "class conscious" again. And of course, of course, in spite of everything, Catholic, Catholic, Catholic. There was no room for that "confounded" serenity of existence *sub specie æternitatis*. We lived *sub specie ætatis*. And I don't know whether I am in trouble again with my synchronization in assuming that it was during that summer that we became addicted to Pervitin, unwittingly—at least my mother, my older sister, and I did; the rest of the family didn't. The brother of a friend, a doctor, told us about this "stuff" used in hospitals, where they put it into the coffee of obstinate malingerers to encourage them to leave voluntarily. Apparently the "stuff" worked, and we bought it. Today it is one of the most strictly controlled prescription stimulants, but in those days it could be bought over the counter in any pharmacy: thirty tablets for 1.86 marks. We took it, and it worked: it induced a tremendous euphoria, and we could use some euphoria; it had a drier, I might almost say "more spiritual," effect than alcohol. (I used it well into the war, obtaining prescriptions for it from a young woman with whom I was friendly, a doctor's assistant, after prescriptions became required. Thank God I ran out of supplies one day, and I kicked the habit. It was dangerous stuff, and one of our best friends succumbed to it.)

Again and again our electricity was cut off, a harsh penalty for a family of such voracious readers: candles were expensive and quickly burned down, and my mother received such dire warnings on account of her tamperings with meter seals that in the end she desisted. It was just at that time that I began to feel so alien to the cozy atmosphere at Grosche's, legitimate and gracious though it was.

17

Whatever happened, I didn't want to jeopardize my graduation, didn't want to risk too much. For economic reasons, among others, that would have been irresponsible, and, besides, I was simply fed up with school. It was time to put an end to it and enter the deluge that was facing us. Then, right into the midst of my preparations for my final exams, a minor bombshell was dropped: that year the Nazis reduced the secondary school period by one year to eight years; but we had already done nine years, which meant we practically had our graduation in our pockets. The worst that could have happened—failing our final exams—would have meant taking them again two or three months later with the class immediately below us. In that case, failure was unlikely, since it would have meant that the school had declared someone to be ready for the twelfth grade who would drop back to the tenth-grade level. Since the dreaded written tests had been eliminated, it was merely a matter of finding volunteers for the oral tests in the tough subjects of Latin, Greek, and math, so that no one who was weak in those areas would risk being tested in one of them. We came quite openly to an arrangement with our teachers, and at the advice, at the urging almost, of Mr. Bauer I took on Latin; in return he as good as promised not to test me on Juvenal, whom we were then studying.

I don't know whether Juvenal was in our curriculum, or whether Bauer had recognized how topical he was and had chosen him for that reason: in Juvenal, arbitrariness, despotism, depravity, corruption of political mores, the decline of the Republican idea, were described with ample clarity, including even a few "June 30's," staged by the Praetorians, and allusions to Tigellinus. Then, without looking for it, I came across in a secondhand book bin a Juvenal translation with a detailed commentary, published in 1838. The commentary was almost twice as long as the text and made thrilling historical reading, besides being amusing for its Romantic vocabulary. I couldn't afford that copious tome but bought it anyhow, and it is one of the few books I managed to bring safely through the war and did *not* sacrifice to the black market afterward. (In those days—a forbidden look forward to 1945—there was a class of profiteers who had everything except books, which they urgently needed to decorate their fine walls, and we unloaded everything that we knew would be republished: an autographed copy of *Buddenbrooks*, for example, brought me a tidy little sum!)

I hung onto my Juvenal. In the twelfth grade I didn't use it as an aid to translation, that would have been against my principles: I merely devoured the commentary, which read like a thriller. In Greek we read *Antigone*. That needed no commentary, not even a knowing wink; and, as I have said, the tiring monotony of translating in class (Oh, the bent, bored backs of those who were forced to go through a classical high school! Why, I wonder?) made me impatient, and I would sit down at home with the dictionary and read on ahead. Brief appearances in class of Gerhard Nebel as a substitute teacher brought a little fire and a refreshing gust of anarchy; for the first time I heard about the Jünger brothers. It was said—and probably correctly—that Nebel had been transferred for disciplinary reasons. He also taught gym and boxing, in neither of which I took part. He claimed, fairly openly, that the recent introduction of boxing was due to a secret, repressed anglophilia on the part of the Nazis. Within a few years the Nazis closed down the school for good—which speaks for the school.

We ostentatiously took part in the penitent pilgrimages of the men of Cologne that led from the Heumarkt to the Kalk Chapel and back—tolerated by the Nazis and watched by informers.

Here I must mention, as a little epitaph for one of Cologne's first air-raid victims, our friend Hans S., who owned a beaver collar. This collar was our last, our very last reserve when we couldn't scrape up any more money and had nothing more to pawn; it brought in two marks at the pawnshop, and that meant three movie tickets and two packs of cigarettes, or four movie tickets without cigarettes, or four concert tickets—and we went to the movies a lot: it was dark in there, and even the Nazis had to keep quiet and were not distinguishable.

18

Our schooldays seemed to be drawing to a peaceful close; the arrangements with our teachers had been made. In the choice of careers, which had to be declared for inclusion in our graduation certificates, it turned out that we were the first graduating class in living memory, if not since the school's existence, not to provide a theologian. Traditionally the school had been a reliable supplier for the theological seminaries in Bonn. The fact that we sent no one there could have had nothing to do with the Nazis, for the class following us was once again a supplier. And it happened to be in religion that our schooldays came to a nasty rather than a peaceful close.

Among the members of the Hitler Youth, the Storm Troopers, and the S.S., there were, of course, not only superficial opportunists but also true believers, believers both as Nazis and as Catholics, and there were conflicts that we discussed in class, such as obedience, the Day of the German Mother (which our teacher of religion buried in a theologically convincing manner), and, since he was neither stupid nor humorless nor in the slightest degree opportunistic, something in the nature of a "skeptical trust" had been formed: we knew where we stood with each other, and there were neither boorish gibes nor denunciations. But all this was destroyed in a single hour, when he felt himself obliged or—as I am more inclined to believe since he did it with such painful reluctance—was obliged by the curriculum to enlighten us on sexual matters. Maybe that "enlightenment" had been on the twelfth-grade curriculum since 1880; I can't imagine the Cologne high school graduates of 1880 being any less enlightened than we were. Be that as it may, he did it, he enlightened us: blushing with embarrassment, keeping his eyelids lowered, he spoke about the fact of there being two different sexes. He spoke with dignity, not ludicrously at all, and we were still disposed to conceded that he was carrying out this long overdue task with a painful sense of duty.

But then came the moment of disaster when, in connection with the sex organs and their functions, he spoke of "strawberries and whipped cream." The youngest among us was at least eighteen, the oldest twenty-two, and we had grown up in a city famous and notorious not only for its sanctity but also for its tradition of widespread and widely varied prostitution. Whereas during the less embarrassing parts of his talk, during the awkward, stammered explanations, we had just managed to suppress our laughter, now it burst forth: cynical, cruel, almost lethal. Even the most hardened among us— and there were some hardened ones, of course—felt this comparison to be both an insult and a slur on their experiences, no matter how "dirty" these may have been. Our revenge was appalling: five filthy jokes were each reduced to a key word plus a number; word and number were written on the blackboard; and in the few remaining religion classes someone would mention one of the five numbers, whereupon the whole class remembered the entire obscenity and burst out laughing. I admit to having shared not only in the laughter but also in the choice and condensing of the obscenities.

During this cruel game, our teacher—and in retrospect I have to admire him—never lost his sense of humor, wanted to share in the cause of our laughter, went to the blackboard and read out—Oh disaster!—key words and numbers, looked at us in puzzlement, asked why we were laughing. It was cruel: a totally innocent man was being crucified, but perhaps that kind of innocent person should not be charged with enlightening twelfth-graders. It should not have been permitted: that "strawberries and whipped cream" was an insult to anyone who had or knew a girl; culinary comparisons in this "area" cannot be anything but revolting. As a further revenge, some of us brought binoculars to class to observe the somewhat inadequately dressed ladies in the rear windows of the buildings along Perlen-Graben, as they leaned out their kitchen windows or hung washing on their laundry racks, facing the school yard—permanent objects of young male curiosity, and we would comment on their visible feminine charms and their petticoats. In those days bras were not yet so common.

If I have since found that *almost nothing* of our music and drawing lessons has remained with me, I have no wish to blame the teachers for this: it is sad and a pity, and I am still suffering from that "wasted time." Perhaps it was because the "social status" of those teachers as non-academics among academics—that deplorable German resentment—made them and us uncertain. I can't help it: *almost nothing* has remained.

In December I started sending off applications for an apprenticeship in a bookstore: handwritten, with a photo, of course, and a notarized copy of my pre-graduation report, which my sister Gertrud obtained for me. All that cost money and, moreover, destroyed one illusion: obviously I would at the very least be automatically absorbed into the Nazi Labor Front. I dreamed of some quiet bookstore, not too big, with an owner who at least wasn't a Nazi. It was not so easy to find an apprenticeship: there was no economic miracle in that particular field. But finally I did find a shop, quiet, not too big, and not even remotely Nazi: on the contrary, neither the boss nor any of the staff was of that stripe, and I made a good friend there!

When it came, the final exam was not much more than a formality; it started at eight in the morning, and by one or two o'clock everything was over, for all of us. We were taken in alphabetical order, so my turn came first; I was given a passage from Cicero, was told all the words I didn't know, and passed. Regulations required that I also be examined in biology (everyone was examined in biology), so I reeled off the Mendelian laws, drew the appropriate red, white, and pink circles on the blackboard. I was through by eight thirty. At lunchtime we met for a glass of beer in a tavern: it was all over. I didn't even bother to attend the graduation ceremony: my brother Alfred, who went there for a class reunion, accepted the certificate on my behalf and brought it home.

Sometimes I still wonder whether the manufacturers of school supplies noticed a boom in pink chalk: in how many thousands of schools—and not only during final exams—was Mendelian pink drawn on the blackboard by how many hundreds of thousands of students?

Translated by Leila Vennewitz

PART FOUR

POLITICAL WRITINGS, SPEECHES, INTERVIEWS

In Defense of
"Rubble Literature"

The first literary attempts of our generation since 1945 have
been described as excessively preoccupied with the bomb-
ravaged cities and towns of Germany and hence dismissed as
"rubble literature." We have not defended ourselves against this ap-
pellation because it was justified: it is a fact that the people we
wrote about lived in and under ruins, men and women, even children, all equally war-scarred. And they were sharp-eyed: they could
see. Moreover, their living conditions were far from peacetime
ones, neither their surroundings nor their own state nor anything
else about them could be described as idyllic, and we writers felt
close enough to them to identify with them: to identify with black-
market operators and black-market victims, with refugees and with
all those who for one reason or another had lost their homes—but
above all, of course, with our own generation, which for the most
part found itself in a strange and significant situation: a generation
that was "coming home," coming home from a war which scarcely
a soul still believed would ever end.

So we wrote about the war, about coming home, and about what
we had seen during the war and were faced with on our return:
about ruins. Hence the three clichés with which this budding literature was labeled: a literature of war, of homecoming, and of rubble.

These labels, as such, are warranted: there had been a war lasting
six years, we were coming home from this war, we found rubble
and we wrote about it. What was odd, suspicious even, was the reproachful, almost injured tone accompanying these labels: although
we were not, apparently, being held responsible for the war, for the
ruins on all sides, we were obviously giving offense by having seen

these things and continuing to see them. But we were not blind-folded, we did see these things: and a sharp eye is one of a writer's essential tools.

To offer our contemporaries an escape into some idyll would have been too cruel for words, the awakening too appalling—or ought we really all to have played blind man's buff?

When the French Revolution erupted, it hit the greater part of the French aristocracy like a sudden thunderstorm: they were in fact thunderstruck, they had had not the slightest inkling. For almost a century they had spent their time in idyllic seclusion: the ladies dressed up as shepherdesses, the men as shepherds, they had strutted about in a make-believe rusticity, trilling and frolicking away hours devoted to pastoral romances. Inwardly corrupted by depravity, outwardly they mimicked a rustic freshness and innocence: they were all playing blind man's buff. This fashion, whose cloying corruption today turns our stomach, was evoked and kept alive by a certain kind of literature: by pastoral novels and plays. The authors who perpetrated this had been valiantly playing blind man's buff.

But the people of France replied to these idyllic pastimes with a revolution, a revolution whose effects are still palpable after more than a hundred and fifty years, whose freedoms we are still enjoying without always being aware of their origin.

However, in the early nineteenth century there was a young man living in London with no pleasant life to look back on: his father had been declared bankrupt and thrown into a debtor's prison, and the young man himself had worked in a shoe-polish factory before he was able to resume his neglected education and become a reporter. Before long he was writing novels, and in these novels he wrote about what he saw: he had looked into prisons, into work-houses, into the English schools, and what he had seen was not particularly pleasant, but he wrote about these things, and strangely enough his books were read, and read by a great many people, and the young man enjoyed a success rarely accorded an author: the prisons underwent reform, the workhouses and schools became the objects of a thorough reappraisal: they changed.

To be sure, the name of this young man was Charles Dickens, and he had very sharp eyes, eyes that normally are not quite dry but not wet either, rather a little damp—and the Latin for dampness is *humor*. Charles Dickens had very sharp eyes and a sense of humor. And his vision was good enough to enable him to describe things that his eyes had not seen—he did not use a magnifying glass, nor did he resort to the trick of reversing a telescope, by which he could have seen accurately enough but very remotely, nor did he wear a blindfold; and although his sense of humor allowed him on occasion to play blind man's buff with his children, he did not live in a permanently blindfolded state. The latter seems to be what is demanded of today's authors; blind man's buff not as a game but as a way of life. But, as I have said, a sharp eye is one of a writer's essential tools, an eye sharp enough to allow him to see even those things that have not yet appeared within his field of vision.

Let us suppose the writer's eye is looking into a basement: a man is standing there at a table kneading dough, a man with flour on his face: the baker. The writer sees him standing there just as Homer might have seen him, just as the eyes of Balzac and Dickens could not have failed to see him—the man who bakes our bread, as old as the world, with a future stretching to the end of the world. Yet that man down there in the basement smokes cigarettes, goes to the movies; his son was killed in Russia, lies buried two thousand miles away just outside a village: but the grave has been leveled, there is no cross on it, tractors have replaced the plow that once turned over that soil. All this is part of the pale, silent man down there in the basement baking our bread—this sorrow is part of him, just as certain joys are part of him too.

And behind the dusty windows of a small factory the writer's eye sees a young working girl standing at a machine punching out buttons, buttons without which our clothes would not be garments but pieces of cloth hanging loosely on us, neither adorning us nor keeping us warm: this young working girl wears lipstick when she is not at work, she also goes to the movies, smokes cigarettes, goes walking with a young man who repairs cars or drives a bus. And it is part of this young girl that her mother lies buried somewhere beneath a pile of rubble: under a mound of dirty bricks and mortar, somewhere deep in the ground lies the mother of this girl and, like the grave of the baker's son, her grave has no cross. Very rarely—

once a year—the girl goes to the spot and lays some flowers on that dirty pile of rubble under which her mother lies buried.

These two, the baker and the girl, are part of our time, they are suspended in time, dates are wrapped around them like a net. To free them from this net would mean depriving them of life—but the writer needs life, and what else could sustain the life of these two people but "rubble literature"? The blind-man's-buff writer looks inward, constructs his own world. Early in this century a young man in a prison in southern Germany wrote a great fat book: the young man was not a writer, nor did he ever become one, but he wrote a great fat book that enjoyed the protection of being unreadable yet sold millions of copies: it competed with the Bible! It was the work of a man whose eyes had seen nothing, who harbored nothing but hate and torment, loathing and much else that was repulsive—this man wrote a book, and we need only open our eyes to see all around us the destruction attributable to this man, whose name was Adolf Hitler and who had eyes to see with: his images were warped, his style was intolerable—he saw the world not with a human eye but in the distortion created by his inner self.

He who hath eyes to see, let him see! The words "to see" have a meaning transcending the optical: he who hath eyes to see, for him things become transparent, lucid, and he should be able to see through them, and by means of language we may attempt to see through them, to see into them. The writer's eye should be human and incorruptible: there is really no need to wear a blindfold, there are rose-tinted glasses, and glasses tinted blue or black, that color reality according to need. The rosy view is handsomely rewarded, it is usually very popular, and the opportunities for corruption are manifold; even black can occasionally be popular, and when that happens black is handsomely rewarded too. But we want to see things the way they are, with a human eye that normally is not quite dry and not quite wet, but damp, for let us not forget that the Latin for dampness is *humor*—nor that our eyes can become dry or wet too, that there are some things which do not call for humor. Each day our eyes see many things: they see the baker baking our bread, they see the girl working in the factory—and our eyes remember the graveyards, and our eyes see the rubble: the cities are destroyed, the cities are graveyards, and all around them our eyes see buildings arising that remind us of stage settings, buildings where people do not live but are "bureaucratized," as insurance customers, as citizens of a state, of a city, as persons depositing money or borrowing money—the reasons are legion for a person to be "bureaucratized."

It is our task to remind the world that a human being exists for something more than to be bureaucratized—and that the destruction in our world is not merely external or so trivial that we can presume to heal it within a few years.

Throughout our Western culture the name of Homer is above suspicion: Homer is the progenitor of the European epic, yet Homer tells of the Trojan War, of the destruction of Troy, and of Ulysses' homecoming—a literature of war, rubble, and homecoming. We have no reason to be ashamed of these labels.

Translated by Leila Vennewitz

In Defense
of Washtubs

After the publication of one of my books, a critic gave me an approving pat on the shoulder and remarked that I had abandoned the milieu of the poor and that my books were now free of the smell of washtubs and devoid of social protest. This praise was bestowed upon me at a time when it was first coming to light that two thirds of the human race are starving, that in Brazil children are dying who have never known the taste of milk: in a world stinking of exploitation, a world in which poverty is no longer either a stage in the class struggle or some mystical habitat but has become merely a kind of leprosy which one must be at pains to avoid and which an author can be censured for choosing as his subject, without the reader having to bother whether a congruence of form and content has been established.

For myself, I scarcely feel affected by the reproach. Of more significance in my eyes is the muddled thinking expressed in such a choice of words, for if a "washtub" and its surroundings are not a worthy literary locale, where are the locales worthy of literature, where should literature establish itself, as the nice vague saying goes? Let those who wish to do so, establish themselves—with the aid of a building loan and recourse to all the tax dodges.

The specter dreaded by this muddled thinking bears an ugly name: lower middle class. What meaning can this term still have in an age when the deportment of kings is more lower middle class than our grandfathers' ever was, when field marshals knot their ties to suit the taste of the man in the street, when everyone, even the most rabid nonconformist, keeps a nervous eye on his public? Why get so indignant about washtubs when retired generals become publicity managers for laundries?

Strangely enough, I cannot recall ever having described or even mentioned a washtub in any of my short stories or novels. I almost feel obliged to mention one in a forthcoming book; perhaps I shall write a washtub novel, but in that case I would lay the scene in China or the Near East. This would mean, of course, that I could not make use of the details I know so well from my wife's tales.

For my wife can tell you that, in the little town her grandmother came from (it so happens that my own grandmother came from the same little town, so I too would be able to give a wonderfully incisive description of everything), wash day was a special feast day. In our grandmothers' time, wash day was still celebrated in that little town—called Düren—as a feast day. In an age of well-stocked linen closets, the laundry was done only once a month; mountains of laundry were washed, then the wet linen was taken by cart to the meadows beside the River Rur where it was spread out to bleach, while kegs of beer, hams, loaves of bread, and little tubs of butter were unloaded from the carts. The laundry maids were joined by the teenage loafers of that era; there was dancing, drinking, fun and games—and in the evening the bleached laundry, the empty kegs and baskets, were loaded back onto the carts, and everyone drove home. Wash day was a gay affair, and I regret having hitherto allowed these episodes to pass me by.

Of course my mother did the washing too (what a humiliating state of affairs!); she stood at the washtubs, usually on Monday mornings. All over the world, the latter part of Monday mornings saw shirts and sheets, handkerchiefs and unmentionables, fluttering on clotheslines, a sight which, far from depressing me, has consoled me, signaling as it does the tireless energy of the human race to rid itself of dirt; and the Rhine barges, as I recall them from my childhood and as they are to this day, invariably display a bunting of laundry as they ply up and down the river. I have nothing against wash day and nothing against washtubs; it is just that, in an age of washing machines, they are becoming increasingly rare, and perhaps the day will come when washtubs will be exhibited in folklore museums: Washtub, Lower Middle Class, Early 20th Century.

I could imagine a drama taking place beside a washtub; after all, so many dramas are set in mansions, dramas in which the dialogue consists of a four-hour exchange of banalities. It is with a light heart that I defend the washtub I have never described. In the days when I used to carry kindling and briquets to my mother at the washtubs and try vainly—just as in later years, as an army drudge,

I tried countless times, equally vainly—to light the fire under the washtubs, the wisdom I learned and the stories I was told were not the least important: the number of oxen slaughtered at the annual country fair; how on Saturday nights the money was taken home from the taverns by the apronful; how certain people took the morning express to Cologne—as people said—to read the *Kölnische Zeitung* there; and how one of my forefathers devoted himself to drink with consistency that—"I saw it with my own eyes"—he ended up trading his last shirt for a few glasses of beer.

As far as the milieu of the poor is concerned, I have been wondering for a long time what other milieus there are: the milieu of the upper classes, the milieu of the lower classes (poor but honest, as they say), the milieu of the great; the skill of modern advertising has spared me the trouble of defining the latter: the great of this world wear Rolex watches. What more is there to say? The lower classes? I am dimension-blind, the way some people are color-blind, I am milieu-blind, and I try not to prejudge, which is only too often confused with failure to judge. Greatness is a word that does not depend on place in society, just as pain and joy have no social relevance; interminable exchanges of banalities take place beside washtubs too, and among the great of this world there may actually be greatness; let us give them the benefit of the doubt. Some of Dostoevski's novels have horribly unpleasant titles—*Poor People* and *The Insulted and the Injured*—and if we look at the world in which a certain Rodion Raskolnikov moves, or even a prince by the name of Mishkin, we are indeed appalled; they should all have been presented with Rolex watches in order to feel genuinely great, and Dostoevski should have been told it was high time he sought better-class circle; he should be posthumously asked whether in his day, too, more than two thirds of the human race were starving.

There was a time when everything not aristocratic was deemed hopelessly unfit for literature; to regard a businessman as worthy of a poet's pen was considered revolutionary, and in fact, it was; then came those criminals who made even the worker fit for literature, fit for art; meanwhile we have art theories that declare everything which is *not* working-class to be unworthy of literature. Is our blessed society going to produce a countertheory to this? That would be interesting, enlightening, and worthy of extended analysis.

Translated by Leila Vennewitz

The Freedom of Art: Third Wuppertaler Speech, September 24, 1966

On the occasion of the opening of the Wuppertaler Schauspiel-haus, Böll held this famous speech addressing the relationship between art and the artist to society and the state. His critical comments here about the state, while possibly reflecting general disillusionment with the end of the CDU's seventeen year term in power and the beginning of the Grand Coalition, would be taken out of context and frequently used to reproach him and his patriotism during the 1970's and the Federal Republic's struggle with terrorism. The irony is that there are few essays by Böll that have been more emptied of contemporary political statement. Though certainly critically intended, his referencing Beckett would suggest a broader aim, the intention to treat "State," "Society" and "Church" as abstractions beyond the contemporary equivalents of Federal Republic, West German society and the Catholic (or Protestant) church. To help provide this resonance within the text, these concepts have been capitalized in the translation.

An empty stage upon whose boards nothing has yet been played, nothing yet depicted, is an appropriate place for making a few observations about the works that get presented in this space; that should be presented in this space; about Art. Let me pronounce this vaunted, hollow-sounding word once, perhaps a second time. And if when speaking thus I capitalize the letter "A"—referring not to *the* arts, for example, but to Art as such—then you'll understand what I mean. What Art needs first and foremost is material. It doesn't need freedom, it *is* freedom. One can take some freedom in presenting Art, but nothing in this world can *give* Art its freedom; no nation, no city, no society accomplish the pretense that it is giving or has given Art that which it has by its nature. A granted freedom is none at all for Art—only that which it has, which it is, or which it takes itself. When Art transgresses, crosses a line—regardless of in whose opinion—when Art goes *too* far, there's no mistaking it, people start taking pot-shots at it. But *how* far Art can go or should have gone—this no one can dictate in advance. In fact Art is obliged to go *too* far in order to find out *how* far it should go, in order to approach the limit of its own free range. And so in speaking of Art, here in this beautiful temple you have built to it, I too, almost against my will, must go a little too far: my topic demands it.

Art doesn't only deliver, doesn't only offer, it *is* the only known expression of freedom on Earth. Obviously Art can't pull freedom out of its pocket like a coin, exchange or break it into smaller freedoms, which thereby make freedom capable of purchase. Art's burden is that it only is, has, delivers, offers freedom, when the material it has first ordered and formed (or what is the same thing: brought into disorder and deformed) is recognized as such. Yes—ordered and formed, brought into disorder and deformed, but not organized and arranged, not classified and straightened. These latter are what Society attempts to do with Art—have it organize and "fall in" to parade-form to the drum beat of the market economy—to parcel out its freedom into many smaller freedoms. In the place of Society I could say State if we had one. At the moment I don't perceive the State. As someone who works with Art and has a certain sense for material and order/disorder, I observe this absence of the State with heightened curiosity. The complete and utter deformation of the State—a process extending into the most minute of details—is of course a fairly exciting process to behold. A person involved with Art may not need the State, but he knows this: that virtually everyone else does. And so this slow devolution by the State into emptiness and formlessness fills him with dismay because he fears that someone will come, shall come, will be sought to bring order: a political messiah who will be clever enough to grant *Art* all its freedoms. He also knows that this monstrous, almost fetishistic obsession with Art is born of a misguided yearning for order; an order which the State, caught in its devolution, is not able to offer; an order therefore sought from Art. At that locus where the State might or should have been I find only the decaying remnants of power; and these obviously precious rudiments of rot are fought over with rat-like ferocity. But let us say no more of the State until it is ready to reappear. Let us turn instead to that great incomprehensible and uncomprehending mass which has taken the place of the State and to which we all belong, namely Society. I might add that Samuel Beckett has expressed all facets of this demise, rot and putrefaction in a manner that I can not possibly improve upon. "Endgame" and "Happy Days" are the plays of the day. For this city of Wuppertal another piece that fits here is a play called "The Wupper": full of darkness, dark humor, doom and ruin; written for the city by its own great daughter [Else Lasker-Schüler], a play full of poesy and filth, full of hope as well—what it presents to our eyes in the public sphere is Nothing in a smartly packaged form; gifted for its expression of Nothingness, managing a smart yet rotten feel, to smell like decay even from a television screen. And when something that is no longer there, simply because it is no longer there, actually grows in its presence through this absence—Beingness enhanced by Nothingness, then I call this little play an event, a happening that decisively transgresses and for far too long—and yet, *no* potshots are taken. The patience of German society is limitless; apparently it finds itself still processing in that phase which can still best be described as "the eleventh hour." But the object of our discussion today—Art—is unable to replace State freedom and order. It is unable to prevent the rot, even when it chooses decay as its material—hence the crisis of literature, the cabaret, painting, sculpture. As already mentioned, the morbid interest of Society in Art arises perhaps from the desire to find itself. And it does find itself, it finds incomprehensibility and incomprehension. As these should, so should we be clear about this since we ourselves are comprised in the incomprehension: those who concern themselves with it—let us name it again—with Art—do not need the State; I do not need one, but you do, and it poses no substitute of the State for you. It is free, it orders material and it is a third thing—it is disconsolate.

Though helpful here, it would lead me too far a field to provide a comprehensive analysis of all the errors, all the misunderstandings all the trouble that has come to pass by confusing unconsoling with disconsolate. Art is never unconsoling but always disconsolate—this is just one of the countless synonyms for poesy; free, ordered, and disconsolate—a secret trinity which cannot be broken, impossible to remove only one or the other. The State, Church, Society so gladly do just that when they move to *impose* order: a free order, an ordered disconsolation, a disconsolate freedom. And the most terrible of all: in the disconsolation of poesy there is concealed a certain consolation. Again and again in vain Art thrusts with her trident into the ocean of transience hoping to tear free something—anything—that might last. And for our assemblage here today—however momentarily Stateless, amusing ourselves with these thoughts—let me quickly move to prevent a new misunderstanding: it is not important to Art's creator that *it* be lasting. What is important is that something—anything—might be lasting on this earth. For Art is part and parcel of this earth. Whether love—yes—love, pain, darkness, light might last—all of these being objects to which State and Church are completely indifferent. Once more, then, for the sake of reinforcement: A person involved with Art needs no State—he needs a certain degree of provincial administration, for which he will pay his taxes, needs streetlamp lighters, who light his homeward path when he comes home drunk, needs garbage removal, to liberate him from his waste. Hidden behind Art's lasting passion, lasting error, futility, permanent wrath and its eternal desire (for it is a beautiful thing to be free, ordered and disconsolate) is the hope that Art might free itself from the curse to provide order, the hope to perhaps become like the others, whom the artist will never understand, who will forever be strange, foreign to him, because they don't know what he knows in the fiber of his being—that nothing escapes death. The hidden desire is to be like the rest of Society. By way of deceptive detours in the intransitive sense, it is this otherness that can sometimes make him appear modest. A dangerous deception which Society often gladly gives in to, for it makes its own clichés, its own little portraits of what it perceives as the opposite of modesty. For those who are involved with Art there is not a shred of modesty (humility, perhaps, when faced with the ocean's infinity). This may create the appearance of disdain, indifference, otherness. A close look also reveals no vanity, which is only a difficultly recognized embarrassing expression of modesty, because it accepts Society's clichés and portrayals. Vanity belongs to the freedoms, to the chump change of clichés, which some like to tinker with—in that way that some tinker with freedoms. All of these are mere deceptions which Society gives in to and which are intended to bring him down a peg, to make him in their own likeness—unfree, unordered and consoled by cheap diversions disguised as freedoms. At times this might even succeed and turn into quite a pretty little game.

An example: though only with considerable difficulty and under considerable attack literature has always and will always break taboos. And literature has done this not because it "understands something of love," but because it seeks love, has always and forever sought it in vain, a thing no State and no Church has ever understood in the least. State and Church can tolerate only two possibilities: marriage and prostitution, and in most cases they hold love in suspicion when found outside these corrals (and justly so, by the way, for in love is something of what we speak here today; love is free, ordered and disconsolate, hence poesy—and poesy is like dynamite to all the regimes of this world). In seeking this impossibility, literature uncovered something which Society immediately classified with the coin of its wretched, freedom-tinkering clichés, calling it the "transgression of sexual taboos." But at that moment when Society believes to have understood what it can never understand, when it removes only freedom from the trinity, finds unending consolation but not a trace of order, at that moment what was at one time great, begun with considerable difficulty and under considerable attack turns in a second, third, and nth regression to filth and obscenity. Traversing this detour via an obligatory subversion (since Society only functions by obligation) it is transformed to a new variant of hypocrisy. Prometheus, as "forethinker," did not bring fire to mortals from heaven just to fire the grills of the fast-food joints. He brought it "that the Earth might burn, and he was a crafty titan's son." When the transgressing of taboos becomes a neat and trendy thing in the hands of the fast-food joints—increasingly tickles the fancy of the bourgeoisie, earns them money, then literature must retreat. But no—not return fire to heaven, not a blank slate, a clean canvas, not treat State and Society. Rather, as crafty as any forethinker, literature must seek and find its own way, find what is free, ordered and disconsolate, what is poetic about love, perhaps take a detour through chastity, must save itself from the cheap diversions. Criticism that does not comprehend this, fails to recognize a ruse, is stupid, cowardly and vain—which are all essentially synonyms. Of course while in retreat literature will be attacked by those who encouraged it when it first crossed the border. The road back finds the backslappers turned to border guards, Society's new hires. The goal having been attained, they expect peace and quiet. But the goal is *never* attained, literature will never give concord, never recognize functioning or functionalized freedoms as such. And just as with the so-called sexual freedoms, the same holds for religious freedom. Art, which must always transgress borders, knows no peace and grants no quarter. In this sense I can only wish for the City of Wuppertal that on this stage as well Art will go *too* far.

Translated by Martin Black

from The Dignity of the Individual Shall Be Inviolable

Written in August of 1972 as the foreword to the volume *How Left Can Journalists Be?*, this essay is a companion piece of sorts to Böll's essay for the January 10, 1972, edition of *Der Spiegel*, entitled "Will Ulrike Meinhof Gnade oder freies Geleit" ("Does Ulrike Meinhof Want Mercy or Safe Conduct?"). This earlier piece, which took the *Bild* newspaper of the Springer Concern to task for ascribing a bank robbery to the Baader-Meinhof Gang when no concrete evidence for such a conclusion existed, unleashed a fire-storm against and around Böll (cf. Introduction). While this first essay declared a 'national state of emergency; an emergency of public consciousness,' Böll uses the piece here to continue his assault on the Springer Press by pointing to specific instances in which the extra-legal cooperation between the press and the authorities actually flaunt the constitution and the associated civil liberties they are supposedly at pains to protect. As such, Böll moves the debate past specific grievances with *Bild* to the larger issue of the growing need for civilian engagement as a necessary component for maintaining the 'sparkling new' West German constitution and the relatively young participatory democracy.

In the text here, Wagenbach is a left-leaning publishing house; *Quick*, a Springer weekly publication; Werner Hoppe was a member of the Baader-Meinhof Gang who was arrested in July 1971; Klaus von Bismarck was a founding member, and an administrator, of the WDR; Ernest Borneman was a psychologist, sexologist and a committed socialist; and the CDU/CSU chancellor candidate who ran against Willy Brandt in 1972 was Rainer Barzel. In its October 16, 1972, edition Time Magazine compared Barzel to Senator Joe McCarthy

and reported that he "founded an anti-Communist organization called "Save Freedom," whose primary activity was a
"red book" that accused 453 West German intellectuals and
artists of Communist ties."

The Basic Law of the Federal Republic of Germany is probably
the best of all possible constitutions that a state could give itself in the 20th century. Paragraph 1 of Article 1 of the Basic Law
(quotations are from the 10th printing of the dtv edition, March 1,
1970) states: "The dignity of the individual shall be inviolable. To
respect and protect it shall be the duty of all state authority." To
confront this Article with the typical news reporting style of the
Springer Press begs the following question: where has the state authority been hiding? Or more to the point: what has become of it,
if it can also so swiftly send 50 police officers through the front
door of the Wagenbach publishing house for the purpose of confis-
cating its *Schoolchildren's Calendar*? Another question we might
ask ourselves is whether the crocodile tears shed on account of the
misfortune inflicted upon that rag of a denunciation incubator,
Quick, aren't just a little over done. By contrast no camera team of
the SFB (Sender Freies Berlin) thought to object when the police visited the Wagenbach publishing house. And yet of course we are all
equal before the law.

It might not be fair to overtask the *Bild*-reader with details of
our democracy: for example, that not only suspects, but even criminals have a right to their dignity, that someone else must protect
that dignity for them should they themselves scorn or mock it. I
hope someday that a doctoral candidate will undertake as a study
the sexual psychopathology of the Springer Concern's "politico-
porno-crime" genre of news presentation. I know no other way to
describe the reporting style used on the Baader-Meinhof Gang. The
high point of this respect for the individual dignity of *Bild*-readers
was struck by the *Bild* edition featuring the arrest of Baader, Meins
and Raspe in Frankfurt. I assume that the full frontal photo of
Baader, who was laid out naked on the stretcher in all his masculine
glory, was meant as the Sunday afternoon pin-up for the dignity of
the German *Bild*-hausfrau. And someday perhaps a well-meaning
contemporary will hesitantly risk asking if he might be allowed to
know how it is that photos that could only be police photos (Gud-

run Ensslin in the police helicopter) find their way into the press, or since when it is allowed to publish an X-ray photo—surely this belongs to the sacred private sphere—without the permission of the person who has been represented to us by her organs, even if this person is known to contemporary history as Ulrike Meinhof.

All of these things are of course mere trifles, of little import in a society governed by the rule of law, in a society with the best of all possible constitutions. But before we sweep this too under the carpet, let us just ask ourselves this: who is it who has undermined our faith in the state and in state authority? "The dignity of the individual shall be inviolable. To respect and protect it shall be the duty of all state authority." Wouldn't it be a shock if just once, just for a change, the conservatives, the libertarians, the right, even the reactionaries—if they were the ones to protest? This would be tactically brilliant, not only from a moral standpoint and the defense of the rule of law, but also politically, perhaps even worthy of a special session of the Bundestag's Committee on Justice. What a blow to the left, to the pseudo-left! A protest, for example, against the sentence given Werner Hoppe. It is a complete mockery to sentence him to just ten years, to have reduced it like some sort of price discount from seventeen years. This judgment is the precursor to a second wave of intimidation to which the Federal Republic of Germany is currently being subjected. And it won't be the terrorists, the suspects, the criminals or the fellow travelers who are intimidated. We would probably never succeed in intimidating them in this fashion—in fact the case is more likely to confirm their theory of class justice more than anything else. No—this case will serve instead to intimidate the entire critical intelligentsia of the country, the very same country which possesses what is probably the best of all possible constitutions.

Like the fear of leprosy, the fear of contagion, a phenomenon related to anancasm [a form of compulsion] spreads across the land. A distancing mechanism bordering on imbecility. I understand that in some broadcasting studios, it is now considered too risky to use the word "capitalism." Another case: the word "proletarian" had to be cut from the title of an otherwise perfectly scientific broadcast. Why did Klaus von Bismarck feel the need to distance himself from the Borneman interview? Does he feel the need to distance himself from the occasionally unbearable morning music of the WDR, despite the fact that he neither composed nor played it himself? Since when must a person pronouncedly distance himself from a thing with which he has never been identified? From now on will every citizen who publishes be required to mindfully recite his 'distancing litany' every morning? Will I need to distance myself from the Flick Concern, or for that matter from my wife, to whom I am married, and yet not exactly identical? And who other than the Springer Press has been able to effect, with provisional success, this second wave of intimidation? Given the chance to read the Borneman interview critically and in relative peace, most readers will find a passage or two to take issue with, but does agreement mean that the reader has become Borneman? And since when is it no longer permitted for a psychologist to argue like a psychologist? Must the consequence be that he must be threatened with deportation, that radio and television avoid him like a leper?

Approximately six months ago Minister Dr. Posser wrote: "*Bild* Reigns Supreme: A Nightmare." Allow me to ask the counter question: doesn't *Bild* reign supreme, or at least co-govern, and don't images [in *Bild*] reign supreme if Article 1 of the Basic Law is mocked, disregarded and violated on a daily basis? Who, then, is responsible for destroying the trust in the state and in state authority? Is it once again those notoriously simpleminded humanitarians? Or is Article 1 of the Basic Law perhaps itself humanitarian nonsense? Eleven million citizens of this country lap up the politico-porno-cynicism of *Bild* on a daily basis. Helmut Schmidt supposedly once said that for a Bundestag representative to turn against Springer would be to commit political suicide. If we remove the burden of this quote from Helmut Schmidt and ascribe it to *any* politician, this new Bundestags-Hamlet might accurately frame it thus: death to the Basic Law, or death to me, that is the question at hand.

It is virtually incomprehensible that citizens of this country no longer have a memory for any other kind of violence than that of bombs and machine guns. Doesn't a *Bild* headline exercise violence? What type? What gets implanted in the heads, in the consciousness, in the potential for aggression of these eleven million addicts who are subjected to the politically most dangerous of all addictions, the *Bild*-addiction? And what sort of violence has been exercised by the some four billion DM which were spent on newspaper ads during 1971 alone? Not the least of course. I realize it has become the fashion simply to consider the Springer Press unassailable. I choose not to afford myself this intellectual luxury. The first successful wave of intimidation that waxed at the beginning and waned with the end of the 50s is still too clearly impressed on my memory: it was a full-blown hounding of intellectuals and communists in which the current federal chancellor candidate of the CDU/CSU played a deplorable and embarrassing role with his "Save Freedom" committee. This second intimidation campaign of the early 70s is more ominous than the first, because its aim is less visible, less tangible than the first. In the 50s the goal was to remilitarize. What is the goal today?

It occurs to me that the entire Halali Group, which is comprised of far more than just the Springer Concern, ought to erect a monument to the Baader-Meinhof Gang because the RAF has provided Halali with a more ideal pretext for rolling out their intimidation tactics than they themselves could have ever fabricated. The question is whether this tendency toward submissiveness, conformity and unity will last over time.

The Basic Law of the Federal Republic of Germany has 146 articles. Allow me to quote from just one more of these: from Paragraph 2 of Article 14: "Property imposes obligations. Its use should also serve the public weal." Did anyone get a chuckle out of this, especially someone who had just happened to read to what extent the Flick estate has been made to serve the public weal? Who might laugh at such a thing? Those whose property has simply obligated them to more property, and whose more-property has simply obligated them to still-more and perhaps even ever-more-property. The Springer Press has been allowed to mock and eradicate the moral seriousness of the Basic Law. May the reading of this book lead to the following deductions: that a relationship exists between the circulation of a newspaper and its income from ads; that newspaper publishers possess *almost* absolute power—and by this we don't mean one or another in Great Britain or the United States, where an unbroken tradition of capitalism exists as well as an unbroken tradition of the political strike (or at least in Great Britain which is lauded as having the oldest Western European democracy. Ironically, while noting this fact the smug observer will shake his head about the strikes without it occurring to him that the one might just have something to do with the other). The newspaper publishers in Germany are in a very different situation than are their Anglo-Saxon colleagues. Most of the former were granted licenses by the occupying powers. They received a license, a printing press and paper. And from the ground of these fairly modest privileges, powerful fiefdoms have arisen, arching skyward. Should it be permitted in this context to use the phrase "framework of control," and if the phrase is graciously permitted, then we might allow ourselves the following modest question: who rules how, where and with what, or who is ruled by whom, how, where and with what?

In closing I would like to revisit the two quotes from the Basic Law. Paragraph 1, Article 1: "The dignity of the individual shall be inviolable. To respect and protect it shall be the duty of all state authority."

Paragraph 2 of Article 14: "Property imposes obligations. Its use should also serve the public weal." I can only hope that quotes from the Basic Law don't yet sound like a mockery.

Translated by Martin Black

Nobel Prize Acceptance Speech, December 10, 1972, in Stockholm

Mr. President, Mrs. Palme, Ladies and Gentlemen:
During a visit to the Federal Republic of Germany, his Majesty the King of Sweden cast a learned glance into the shifting striations and sediment from whence we Germans come and upon which ground we live. The terrain is neither virginal, nor innocent; it has rarely seen peace. The much-coveted land on the Rhine, inhabited by a covetous folk, has had more than its share of rulers, and seen an equally disproportionate number of wars: colonial wars, national, regional and local wars, wars of religion, world wars. This soil has witnessed pogroms, evictions, expulsions; a continuous flow of the banished arriving from without, while others were being banished from within. And that German was spoken on this ground was obvious; enough so that there was little need to broadcast it within or without. That task was performed by others—those for whom the soft "d" did not suffice, who sought a harder "t," preferring "Teutsche" to "Deutsche."

Violence, destruction, pain and misunderstandings litter the path leading from this past, from these layers of past transience into a transient present. And these created fragmentations, refuse and rubble; dislocations to the east and west. But never what one might expect from this mad tumble of history: a sense of tranquility—a sense of belonging, of an "us"—the one half too western, the other not western enough; the one too worldly, the other not worldly enough. And to this day there remains a sense of mistrust among the demonstratively "Teutschen" as if the combination of western and German were still just an hallucination of a nation lately taken ill. And yet one thing remains certain—if this country ever had anything resembling a heart, it lies on this spot where the Rhine flows. The path leading to the Federal Republic of Germany has been a long one indeed.

As a boy in school I too heard the robust saying that the war was "father of all things." Yet at the same time I was also told, both in school and at church, that the peacemakers, the meek, the powerless would inherit the Promised Land. I suppose we will take this murderous contradiction with us to our graves: that the one promised heaven *and* earth, the other only heaven. And that in a country in which even the church has coveted, demanded, exercised an absolute form of dominion right down to the present day.

The path to this podium was a long one for me, the same one taken home from the war by many millions, possessing little more than empty hands in empty pockets; I was different from the others only in my passion to write and continue to write. It is writing that has brought me here today. Please understand when I find the fact that I am standing here somewhat beyond comprehension. When I think back to the young man who, after years of exile, years of being torn this way and that, returned to a banished homeland; not only having escaped death, but the wish for death; liberated, surviving. Born in 1917, "Peace" was just a word to me, neither an object of memory, nor a condition; the word "Republic"—a native enough term, was but a shattered memory. I owe a debt to a great number of people—foreign authors who became my liberators, liberating both the estranging and the strange from captivity. These estranging elements, for want of sheer materiality, cast themselves of their own accord back into their own specificity. The rest was a matter of commanding the language throughout this "return" to the material, to this handful of dust which appeared to lie at my doorstep and yet proved elusive and eluding. Thanks are also due both for the encouragement from German friends and German critics, and for the many attempts at discouragement; for after all: many things may be accomplished without war, but very little, it would seem, without resistance.

These twenty-seven years have been a long march, not just for the author, but for the citizen as well, through a wood thick with accusatory, pointed fingers, fingers which spring from the confounded dimension of our specific German difference, a peculiar space where lost wars are somehow transformed to victories. Not a few of these pointed fingers were cocked and loaded, their detonation part and parcel.

It is not without some consternation that I think to my German predecessors who have stood where I stand tonight, and whom, from the perspective of this damning dimension of German difference, can no longer be viewed as German. Nelly Sachs, saved by Selma Lagerhoef, narrowly escaped with her life. Thomas Mann, hounded and exiled. Hermann Hesse, choosing emigration early, had long forsworn his German passport when honored here. Five years before my birth, sixty years ago, the last German Prizewinner for Literature to die in Germany—Gerhard Hauptmann—stood on this spot. He spent the last years of his life in a version of his country to which, despite considerable misunderstandings, he did not belong.

As for myself I am neither given to this singularity nor without it; I am a German. My sole ID is that of the language in which I write, a passport for I which I need file neither application nor extension. As such, as a German, I am delighted by this great honor. I wish to thank the Swedish Academy and the country of Sweden for this honor, which has has not only been granted me, but also the language in which I write, and the country in which I call myself a citizen.

"This Type of Cheap Propaganda Is Extremely Dangerous"

An Interview with Gert Heidenreich (Bavarian Radio), September 28, 1977.

This interview was given by Böll approximately three weeks after the Red Army Faction (RAF) kidnapping of Hanns Martin Schleyer in Cologne, the businessman and former Nazi party member, in which two police officers and Schleyer's bodyguard were killed. The point of the kidnapping was to win the release of the "first generation" of RAF members, at the time being held in Stammheim Prison, including Andreas Baader, Gudrun Ensslin, Jan-Carl Raspe and Irmgard Möller. It is hard to find a time of more tension in the political life of the Federal Republic. In the weeks that followed the interview failure by the German police to locate Schleyer and the refusal by the government to release the prisoners led to further violence: the hijacking of a Lufthansa jet by the RAF, the murder of Schleyer and the apparent coordinated suicides by Baader, Ensslin and Raspe. The occasion for Böll to give the interview was the campaign of defamation and insinuation that the conservative media, in particular the Springer Press, was directing toward Böll, his family and fellow intellectuals and artists. Böll's insights on the subsequent effects on democracy and civil liberties in the Federal Republic as a result of the collusion between conservative politicians and the media are as strikingly relevant today as they were in 1977.

GERT HEIDENREICH: Herr Böll, following the murders in Cologne we are seeing, especially from the side of the CSU, public usage of the phrase "intellectual plane of terrorism." According to a report in the *Süddeutsche Zeitung*, someone has actually drawn up an unpublished list of sympathizers whom he intends to deal with, and the CSU-Representative Dietrich Spranger has immediately responded by naming several names. According to him, the following individuals were instigators for the murders: the theologian Gollwitzer, Professor Brückner, former chancellor Willy Brandt, your fellow writer Günter Grass and you as well.

HEINRICH BÖLL: Up until now I have followed this ritual from a considerable distance, and would like to briefly summarize for you my view of the ritual: these defamations are started on the serious side of the Springer Press apparatus by noted, but trustworthy denouncers. The stories are then taken up by the more frivolous Springer Press organs, where an additional set of both named and unnamed professional denouncers further disseminate the story. Next—I am only providing you with my own observations of the choreography—politicians sense that they can enhance their own profiles with names and events, and before you know it you have such things as Herr Schmitt-Vockenhausen's open letter to me—an incommunicative method for addressing someone. It is impossible to address me via *Bild* and *Welt* and Springer. And on it goes: Herr Albrecht joined the fray, then the *Deutsche Tagespost*, the *Bayernkurier* and it now looks to me like a procession of ministers to High Mass, also known as the CSU Party Convention, where Herr Strauß didn't exactly call for lynch justice or vigilantism but flirted with them in his way. Oddly enough I've been watching this ritual from a distance for three weeks now, but only discerned yesterday (Sept 27, 1977) the effect created when a denunciation and propaganda campaign becomes concrete: on the basis of an anonymous phone call, something anyone with 20 pfennig in their pocket can accomplish, my son was publicly denounced, and he has been neither politically active nor publicly taken sides through any of this. But the result was that 40 officials from the Schleyer-Special Commando Force broke into his apartment while he was away. Having up until now observed the ritual with objective calm, I am now analyzing the effects more closely. Especially the effects upon my family! Even if I am the darkest of villains, I cannot accept that the law would function along familial lines. I have to ask myself: if someone in Munich were to phone the police with an anonymous tip that Herr Strauß' son had a cache of weapons in his home, whether 40 Bavarian police officers would go marching into the apartment of Herr Strauß' son. That is the question. And we are currently taking counsel to consider how we might respond, legally or otherwise.

G.H.: When certain individuals allow themselves to be pulled into a general defamation campaign directed toward liberal and leftist artists and intellectuals, then I have to ask myself whether the terrorists, with the assistance of these accusations, have been able to achieve their goal after all, namely to force the Federal Republic into a situation in which discriminating reason no longer drives the political process, but rather the hell fires of raging emotion.

H.B.: Of course. If it was the wish of the terrorists to create an atmosphere of confrontation and provocation then they have adopted the best means to achieving their goal. We—those of us who have been targeted here: Gollwitzer, Brandt, Grass, myself and others—we have always been available for public comment and debate—and the goal here is obviously to prevent that. And I have to concede: after yesterday's police action which occurred in the presence of my daughter-in-law and grandson, I can no longer observe these events with detachment.

I assume the foreign press will cover the story, and that the image of Germany abroad will just get rosier . . . rosier and rosier . . .

G.H.: One question recently raised in this connection by the French press: if you take a man such as Willy Brandt, a Nobel Peace Prize laureate—and regardless of his political position—when a man such as this is cast in his own country as an "instigator" of terror, in other words a root cause of criminal violence, then you have to wonder what sort of an effect that will have outside Germany, especially where we are attempting to diminish this image of the "ugly German."

H.B.: If it continues like this, and if public opinion in all of its various articulations does not turn against these events, I fear we will completely isolate ourselves. The Federal Republic will find itself culturally, politically and intellectually completed isolated. And I mean in respect to Western Europe. One other thing I'd like to say on this aspect of foreign affairs: the handful of Germans living abroad—the few—who in fact work in opposition to this image of the ugly German—they find themselves being cast as ugly traitors *within* Germany. It is so utterly perverse, this entire set of circumstances so utterly insane, you have to wonder if we're at all normal.

G.H.: What I find the most frightening is the global nature of their rhetoric: casting you generally as everything from "falsifiers of the world order" and "poisoners of the language" to "intellectual authors with pen and microphone operating from the pulpit or the lectern."

H.B.: Yes—it reminds me rather vividly of the end of the 1920's.

G.H.: That type of talk ultimately leads to book burnings, and with them our individual freedoms. Do you see any parallels or do you fear that we are moving in that direction?

H.B.: I don't think so. The free market alone would prevent it. And it's anyway not going to happen like this. Instead I am gradually beginning to wonder whether it's even necessary to—to put it bluntly—do away with democracy. People are intimidated to such an extent—the media have become so cautious—that laws would hardly need to be changed. The whole thing occurs on a "fantastic" plane . . . Even the liberal newspapers are becoming extremely conformist and cautious—they hardly need to lift a finger.

G.H.: It almost looks to me as if you've been caught up in the middle of your own narrative—the one you created in your *Katharina Blum* novella.

H.B.: Yes. And although it's not quite that bad and won't have the same consequences as I describe in the fiction, I have to tell you honestly and plainly: we've had it—we are slowly getting sick and tired of this circus!

G.H.: What chance do you see for a suitable reaction?

H.B.: Well the only chance I see is that public opinion shrugs off its shyness, its fears, its intimidation. It is very easy to intimidate a minority of twenty, thirty—in this case five or six—who have been called out by name. That won't succeed. But the effect on the overall atmosphere! We are looking at these things far too rationally—this is really a case of framing, manufacturing the national mood—and the Springer Press functions in this case like a disseminator of the plague, a disseminator of leprosy. It turns us into lepers, untouchables.

G.H.: Why is it that this campaign of naming names comes up now? Why is it that CSU representative Günther Müller has just called for having the "perpetrators" locked up? Is there something to this that an entire group of intellectuals and artists have underestimated the potency of the terrorists? Or is this simply opportunism on the part of the right to deal with a bunch of leftists who have always been a thorn in their eye?

H.B.: I see it completely differently. I think that the demagogic manner in which they have publicly treated a complex set of problems has contributed to the escalation. As you know, almost all of the trials involving the terrorists have been conducted under considerable constraints which can be attributed to the fact that far too much had already wound up in the media. And among those of us who have now been named, not one of us has in any way encouraged the use of violence or terror. So the claims are rather far-fetched.

G.H.: Okay, but Strauß has been using the phrase "intellectual authors"—he has to have something concrete in mind. Probably not directly a call to violence, perhaps instead the tendency to minimize the threat.

H.B.: Now: the intellectual authorship of violence . . . *one* cause of violence is the Old Testament itself—read it again carefully. A second cause, which is a part of our elementary education, the *bellum gallicum* [Gallic Wars, Caesar]—not exactly a peace demonstration—we don't have time for a recitation of all of Western literature . . . of course you would have to prohibit, suppress it all. I haven't a clue what would remain. The entire canon of Western literature is full of the intellectual authorship of violence. If you read the calls to the crusades, which in fact bear a closer resemblance to what Herr Strauß and Müller are currently saying, they're not exactly a call to peace . . .

We can of course give some thought as to whether literature, whether philosophy are the cause of terror, but we would have to go back a long way, not just to Marx etc.

G.H.: If we have any chance of extracting ourselves from the current situation without seeing an unbridled wave of foment directed against intellectuals, it would have to involve drawing engaged, rational discourse in this country back into the center of news coverage and reporting. Do you see any chance of this— aside from legal action, the possibility of fighting back by engaging directly and actively in this way?

H.B.: Legal action is of course just a private side of the matter. I look at it this way: I believe that large parts of the CDU and also of the CDU leadership might be made accountable for the very real dangers posed by this propaganda campaign. And I have recently interpreted the CSU Convention in Munich as clearly signaling the attempt to bring rational discourse under the sway of irrationality. And if this happens, if this type of smear campaign becomes popular, if it wins votes, then so much for reason; I don't give rational discourse much of a chance. It is now a matter for the media in all its variations—the newspapers, radio, television—to go on a sort of counter attack and not to brook further intimidation.

G.H.: And your own medium? Writing?

H.B.: Yes, I will continue to write.

G.H.: Do you intend to take direct issue?

H.B.: No. No, I'm not really interested, at least as far as my own person is concerned. I know how the game is played—I've been observing this ritual for the last ten years. But when it involves my family, when aspersions are cast along familial lines, then of course I need to consider a different course of action. That has a completely different set of dimensions. Anyone in this country who wants to become active or engaged has to be prepared for hostility and persecution, has to be prepared for slander and defamation—that's the way things will be, if we let Herr Springer muddle on like this. But at this level when the family is drawn in—and this has happened to me now several times—I could list out for you at least three or four cases in which relatives of mine have had their civil liberties trampled on in the basest of ways— then I'm not really sure what can be done, unless the public finally grasps that this type of cheap propaganda is extremely dangerous.

Translated by Martin Black

Manuscript of the Speech to the October 10, 1981 Bonn Peace Demonstration

The NATO "dual-track" decision of 1979, which lead to the deployment of a new generation of medium-range nuclear (Pershing 2) missiles across Western Europe, unleashed powerful public protest in West Germany, reviving the Peace Movement of the 1960's. While the center-left coalition of Helmut Schmidt's SPD and Genscher's FDP ultimately foundered over the issue, replaced in 1983 by a CDU/CSU/FDP alliance led by Helmut Kohl, popular protest continued to build across these years and, advised and guided by intellectuals such as Böll, Grass and others, led in late 1983 to a "campaign" of nonviolent civil disobedience including a blockade of a US military base in Mutlangen. Within months of this "hot autumn," the Reagan Administration began considerable efforts to reengage in friendship with the German populace. It is not accidental that Böll refers here obliquely to Vietnam, that he expresses concern about possible efforts by "disruptive elements" to discredit the movement by provoking violence, nor that he addresses possible reception of these events in the East German press: mindful of how the demonstrations might be twisted in the media, he is exercising here his own masterful media packaging.

When Chancellor Schmidt stated—and I am inclined to believe him—that he and Mr. Genscher have managed to pressure the US Administration to the negotiating table, then maybe, just maybe, the Peace Movement—especially the Protestant Church Council in Hamburg—and all the many initiatives—maybe, just maybe, played a role in these pressuring tactics. And it might just be that this very rally, and the many that will follow, will play a role—a political role. As such this rally is by no means directed against the federal government. To-date none of the new missiles have yet been stationed here; to-date no neutron bombs yet acquiesced to. The political influence of this demonstration—and that is after all our goal—depends in no small part on our conduct here today. So let me ask any here today who happen to have a stone or worse in their pocket or camping gear: throw it away—leave it to the good people of the Bonn sanitation department, who even without that have more than enough to do on our account.

One other request: let us not pretend that we are the only ones for peace. Even the politicians—the very ones for whom we make this show—to "demonstrate" means, after all, "to show," in the sense of "to show the way" or even "to remonstrate"—even they want peace. Hence, we are not demonstrating against a planned war, rather against the strategic provisioning for a possible war. And while the term "Zero Option" still falls from the lips of our highest officials, let us still demonstrate for this Zero Option.

It is the right, perhaps even the duty of the American government to represent its interests, and to do so energetically, occasionally even brutally. But the question is this: whether these interests are in agreement with those of Europe, particularly Germany, and I mean Germany, not the Federal Republic and the GDR. We are here to contest the agreement of interests in the case of this new generation of missiles. That's called a conflict of interest—nothing more—a completely normal phenomenon in international politics. But: we want to know from our government *where* this conflict begins, where the line will be drawn between their options and those of the US Government—nothing more. The geographical situation of Germany—one glance at the map is all you need—makes it clear that we have reason enough to be concerned. In the event of a possible war it is completely conceivable that the two Germanys would be reunified not *on* the battlefield but *as* the battlefield, and the archaic German term for the same (Schlachtfeld) become literal ("field of slaughter") in horrific fashion.

Let us not forget the sacrifices of the United States, those killed or wounded in wars since 1945, regardless of whether we have condoned the goals of those wars. There is one major distinction between the citizens of the North American continent and us: Europe lived, suffered, absorbed the war on its own soil—yes, soil—from Moscow to Cardiff, from Catania to Narvik. It was a conventional war and I believe we all had our fill, regardless of what side we fought on, what mistakes we fell victim to. Fifty-five million dead in a conventional war! And whatever one drew from Hitler's "Schutz der Heimat" ("protect the homeland") excuse for war at the time, the number of civilian deaths came to total approximately that of soldiers. In this conventional war.

To the preposterous charge against us that we are anti-American: the Reagan administration's defense policy is contested in the USA as well. At the moment there is a great deal of perplexity, if not distraction, in the US House, the US Senate and their committees—debate over the numbers, fighting over weapon systems and their usefulness, and even a little fear and anxiety on account of the gigantic, the astronomical sums of money, the zeros for which are themselves uncountable. So in the USA as well there is not consensus. The same goes for economic policy there, which is of course closely connected to the armaments policy. And there is little question that every American would grant us at least as much say-so as they have the citizens of Utah and Nevada, who have successfully defended themselves against an insane bunkering of their landscape (a Carter Administration plan).

Where the American armaments policy is currently *not* contested is right here at home: among the opposition in the German Bundestag. There are plenty of points on which we all may differ, but the blind, almost manic obsession with which the opposition grasps at every new weapon, each new system to hit the market—this is a sickness, a case for psychoanalysis. And in that entire grand old Union Party, not one voice raises itself, not one little squawk. It is *this* I find deeply unsettling, deeply worrying. Among their coalition partners at least there is some flapping on the party wings. But the Union is silent—silent—silent—not one voice. And this is not about choosing the hamburger over the turkey club—this is about our future, the role being assigned us! If the general population of the Federal Republic only knew, were enlightened, to the weapons contagion already upon us—and to this new weapons plague that might yet descend—you can be sure that the electoral results of this not war-driven, but virtually weapons-driven party would be considerably diminished. So let us at least be happy that the CDU/CSU does not sit in the American Senate or Congress, not to mention a few of the political editors of some of our newspapers, who would be more American than the Americans, and the über-clever commentators, who can be even more embarrassing. In the face of this obsequiousness and submissiveness by the Union, they make it embarrassing to be German. To our great fortune it is Americans sitting in those seats, a people whose nation was born of a revolution, an uprising, and it is precisely the Americans who will better understand us than these German pedal pushers. While the Americans may well welcome these CSU politicians today as a political expedient, at heart, like so many model students, they will come to despise them. America is a land of great diversity. From America we have learned that large demonstrations can be successful in democracies. Our bearing is not, and we are not, anti-American.

Our federal government can have it otherwise: they can have a lame and apathetic citizenry that has forgotten the past, gives little thought to the future, and, ruddering only from one breakfast to the next, humbled and obedient, keeps its head down in the face of the onset of the new armaments plague—they can have a comfortable citizenry. I believe they should prefer an uncomfortable, a disgruntled one. All parties should make it their business to understand that today's manifestation here, and those that will follow elsewhere, are not the assemblies of some moralizing fringe. And they should also know that our thoughts and actions are completely independent of praise or rebuke by the press and other organs in the socialist countries. I am as indifferent to any praise received from those quarters as I am the rebuke—the latter of which I have often enough received. Let us be plainly independent of such discreditable reflexes. Of course I would consider it a positive step—I would be delighted—if the Soviet Union would withdraw its missiles; they threaten us, on this we all agree, and it would be a positive step if this argument—that of the missiles—could be resolved in advance of the treaty negotiations. Even without the missiles both sides—here and there—would retain their overkill capacity, and I especially direct these words to the communist demonstrators here today.

In conclusion let me repeat: let us not pretend that we are the only ones for peace. And a final word to the stones or worse which might possibly be lurking in pockets or camping gear: let this call for peace end peacefully. The Interior Minister of the State of North-Rhine Westphalia equipped his police officers—against whom we are not demonstrating—not in riot-gear, but standard uniforms. They are also here to protect us, they are not our opponents, and certainly not our enemy. A parting word to the *agents provocateurs* who might possibly be among us today. Politicians have called upon us to provide for a peaceful execution of today's demonstration. This is terribly naïve: we have no secret police, no executive authority—we can only make this naïve request: leave us in peace. And with that, I will do the same with these final words: if we had the chance to compensate *you* for any lost wages or service hours that might result, we would do so.

Translated by Martin Black

Subordinated by the Cameras

Written on the occasion of Ronald Reagan and Helmut Kohl's visit to a military cemetery in Bitburg to honor Germany's war losses on the 40th anniversary of the German capitulation, May 8, 1945, and delivered as a radio speech just weeks before Böll's death in July, 1985. An international furor had arisen when it was discovered that some of the war dead at Bitburg had been members of the Waffen-SS, the elite, military arm of the Reich's police conglomerate. But official ceremonies in Bitburg and neighboring Nesselwang went forward, with military representatives (in particular the American General Ridgeway and German General Steinhoff) and politicians (German President Richard von Weizsäcker, and Bundestag Representatives Dr. Alfred Dregger, CDU Fulda, and Dr. Alois Mertes, CDU, Bitburg) occupying the stage at various times. The piece begins with references to von Weizsäcker's "no reconciliation without remembrance" speech. The Rommel mentioned here is the grandson of German General Erwin Rommel. Klaus Barbie is the infamous French Nazi collaborator also known as the "butcher of Lyon."

The week of national embarrassments found a dignified conclusion after all in President von Weizsäcker's speech in Parliament on the eighth of May. In it, he sought to put the national house back in order, unfailingly mentioning all parties victimized by the Nazi State, and time and again linking cause—the 30th of January, 1933—and effect by war's end; and this from a man whose father had been tried and sentenced as a war criminal.

His speech of May 8, 1985, should be featured in school books as the best possible introduction and consensus on how to how to come to terms with the history of the Nazi Reich. Further: the speech managed to sweep away the occasionally unbearable kitsch that had been thrust upon us in the course of the week. In the middle of this kitsch a truly sensational announcement was lost in the fanfare: the Israeli Government expressed its gratitude to the Soviet Army for the liberation of the concentration camps. One can only hope that the applause which von Weizsäcker's speech received in Parliament was an expression not only of decorum, a tribute paid a presiding official in the presence of foreign guests. A further blessing afforded by the speech: absolution from the embarrassing parts played by Dregger and Mertes. We West Germans must certainly know by now the debt we owe the victims of the war—all the victims, not just those of our own. Von Weizsäker's speech, omitting none of the atrocities, should give all war veterans pause to reflect. Let us hope that the applause was accorded for what he said and how he said it.

There is also cause for reflection upon the graves. And the perception that the statement: "no collective guilt" does not mean "collective innocence." Reconciliation over graves of soldiers? The Federal Republic has been a member of NATO for thirty years. Hasn't that been reconciliation enough? All the more embarrassing then, if not degrading, the dumb show cooked up for Generals Ridgeway and Steinhoff. I can't begin to guess how many hands of how many generals—British, French and American, but also Dutch, and Norwegian—Steinhoff shook during his years of service as a high-ranking NATO officer. Was it really necessary for the two to *repeat* what is for them a matter of course? Personally, I found their role as altar boys an embarrassing spectacle. Not undignified, but degrading.

Repetition is of course one of the signature characteristics of television news production: President and Chancellor shake hands on the chancellery stairs, but since each network wants an *exclusive* of the handshake—perhaps one of the network crews was too late to capture the first—the whole charade, though always the same empty gesture, has to be repeated. For CBS. For NBC. For ABS, ZDF, the ARD—what do I know. And they willingly do it; if necessary, they repeat the handshake again and again. And why? Because when it comes to television news production, the politicians are subordinated by the cameras.

Politics as ersatz entertainment, or additional entertainment— one can only hope that viewers are not drawn in. Reconciliation over graves of soldiers? Neither Reagan nor Kohl have any idea of what actually happens on an actual field of battle. Kohl might remember the bombing of Ludwigshafen, Reagan never saw any military action, except in films. The two generals who had to officiate knew that only rarely, if ever, is a soldier's dying a heroic act. This is also well known to the older veterans assembled in Nesselwang to provide the summit additional gravitas and the photo journalists their livelihood. The survivors delude themselves, and perpetuate delusion, in using the phrase "fallen," "killed in action." Fallen— that sounds as if, in the middle of an attack, they had all been killed by a shot to the head and fallen on the spot. Medics, doctors, nurses, and soldiers know better. If we had a tape, many thousands of hours of tape, that would register the crying, swearing, moaning, the praying and the last words of the dying soldiers, the cries for wives, girlfriends, mothers—it would be louder than all the rock and pop bands of this world—and one would have to listen very long and very carefully, probably for many years, in order to hear the words fatherland, leader, nation, just once as the last word of a dying man. The smug pride with which the veterans exchanged their stories, and the pride of those who turned a Nesselwang hotel into a mock fortification—all these things would be shown for what they are—empty theatrics—by such a recording. Or imagine yet another tape—one containing the screams of those who were tortured, those murdered on an industrial scale, with machine-like precision according to plan. Every death is the death of an individual, guilt or innocence is not to be found engraved on the tombstones. Even the US President's well-meaning acquittal of the buried SS soldiers on the basis of their age—this, too, must not deceive us. A 17- or 18-year-old who has been indoctrinated and equipped, *empowered*, with the authority and prestige of uniform and weapon is potentially more terrifying than a 30- or 40-year-old, who perhaps because of his membership in the SS has grown tired of spreading death and destruction. Gravestone inscriptions say nothing of guilt or innocence. How much more fitting a tribute to these silent dead if survivors visiting grave sites observed a similar silence. Another deception is hidden in the phrase "The Unknown Soldier," which is used internationally. Whenever wreaths are laid down accompanied by somber music, the thought is going through my mind: instead of "unknown," it should be "unrecognizable" *(statt unbekannt, unkenntlich).* That is: he was no longer identifiable; he had neither photos nor letters on him, no orders, no dog-tags. *Unkenntlich.* Police detectives and coroners know well what that means, an unidentifiable corpse whose identity can often only be established, if at all, after months of arduous work. "Un-known," of course, sounds better than "unrecognizable through acts of war" *(durch Kriegseinwirkung unkenntlich geworden).*

Quite possibly there is no soldier's graveyard that doesn't con-tain at least one or two members of the Waffen-SS. The gravestones themselves don't always give the military unit of the dead; that sort of thing is found in registers carefully protected in weather proof metal canisters. Bitburg is a symbol for everywhere, and it would be senseless if Bitburg should suffer international disrepute as a re-sult of these events. Dachau, too, was everywhere: *places* are inno-cent. The right to interment, the return to the earth from whence we come, is a human right. Even capital criminals and murderers receive a burial.

In recent times it has only been the deceased from Stammheim who have been denied the right to burial, and it was actually Rom-mel, Lord Mayor of Stuttgart, who insisted that they too be granted this last rite. One name there is still that is yet to be found on the headstone of any SS man: the name of Klaus Barbie. He passes his days in Lyon and probably has a little something up his sleeve to snicker about.

Translated by Martin Black and Volkmar Sander

Publisher's Acknowledgments

"What's to Become of the Boy?," "In the Darkness," "My Uncle Fred," "The Postcard," "Murke's Collected Silences," "When the War Broke Out," "When the War Was Over," "The Staech Affair," "Till Death Do Us Part," "My Father's Cough," "Rendezvous With Margaret or: Happy Ending," copyright © 1966 by Heinrich Böll. Reprinted here by permission of Kiepenhauer & Witsch via the Joan Daves Agency of New York, and by permission of Leila Vennewitz. Reprinted in the United States, its dependencies, the Philippines, and Canada with the permission of Northwestern University Press.

"Undine's Mighty Father" from *The Stories of Heinrich Böll*, translated by Leila Vennewitz, copyright © 1986 by Leila Vennewitz and the Estate of Heinrich Böll. Used by permission of Alfred A. Knopf, a division of Random House, Inc., and by permission of the translator and Kiepenhauer & Witsch.